Hardluck Ironclad

Hardluck Ironclad

———◇———

THE SINKING AND SALVAGE
OF THE CAIRO

Revised Edition

Edwin C. Bearss

LOUISIANA STATE UNIVERSITY PRESS

BATON ROUGE

Published by Louisiana State University Press
Copyright © 1966, 1980 by Louisiana State University Press
All rights reserved
Manufactured in the United States of America

Louisiana Paperback Edition, 1980

LIBRARY OF CONGRESS CATALOGING-IN-PUBLICATION DATA
Bearss, Edwin C.
    Hardluck ironclad.

    Bibliography : p.
    Includes index.
    1. Cairo (Gunboat) I. Title
VA65.C28B4   1980   359.3'2'5   79-25985
    ISBN 978-0-8071-0684-6 (pbk. : alk. paper)

The paper in this book meets the guidelines for permanence
and durability of the Committee on Production Guidelines for
Book Longevity of the Council on Library Resources. ∞

To Mother

Contents

Illustrations

Preface

This is the story, as complete as I have been able to make it, of the *Cairo,* one of the United States' first ironclad gunboats—a vessel which seemed to be dogged by an unbroken streak of hard luck from its Civil War building and sinking through twentieth-century salvage efforts. Because the *Cairo* was one of seven sister boats and because, more often than not, she operated in concert with other vessels of the Western Flotilla, this, to some degree, is the story of the flotilla as well.

There are a number of other stories which could be written about the *Cairo*—a story of the raw courage of the divers who entered her dangerous interior and worked in the black water of the Yazoo River by touch. This will have to be written by someone else. Another book could be written about the many people involved in her salvage. Strangely, two of the most important of these have met tragic deaths —Dr. Walter Johnston drowned in the Yazoo in 1964, and Joe Bullock was the victim of a vicious tornado which struck the Jackson, Mississippi, area even as this book was going to press.

The more I have worked with the artifacts from the *Cairo,* the more real to me have become the men who were her crew. The first item that impressed upon me their humanness was the signal board from the pilothouse. Nailed on it for good luck was a horseshoe. As I handled mess gear with names or initials etched on, I felt a personal tie with the owners. One man had cut a hole in his boot to ease a corn. Another had carved his initial on a deck swab. Thus, when I look at the men standing on the *Cairo's* deck in the only photograph of the vessel before her sinking, they seem especially close.

Which one of them was carving the little ship found in one of the holds? Who was studying the French grammar? Who had dug into an Indian mound for souvenirs? Some of the mysteries have been solved; some never will be. There were recovered numerous shoes of varying sizes for women and children. Why were they on the gunboat? Study of the records showed that the *Cairo*, while at Memphis in late 1862, had intercepted a small boat engaged in smuggling shoes across the Mississippi into Arkansas.

The *Cairo* and her men left an extraordinary and undisturbed record. Its examination created a complete fascination that took possession of me. The work has been long and hard and is not nearly over.

The assistance of many people is gratefully acknowledged. Museum Specialist W. E. Geoghegan of the Smithsonian Institution, Chief Naval Architect Clyde Leavitt of Ingalls Shipbuilding Corporation, and Regional Historian James Holland of the National Park Service read the manuscript, and each had a number of valuable comments which were incorporated in the study.

Technical questions about the vessel's construction were referred to Colonel Howard I. Chapelle and W. E. Geoghegan, who answered them promptly and graciously. Mrs. Sara Jackson of the Army and Air Corps Branch, National Archives, was very helpful in locating documents, as was Mrs. Evelyn Snyder of the Cairo Public Library. Miss Mary Sherard of the Vicksburg Public Library was always ready to secure books on interlibrary loan.

During the struggle to raise the *Cairo*, I depended on Ken Parks (as I had since 1959), Captain Billy Bisso, and Sam Bongiovanni for information as to what was happening below the surface. These men, although they were working from dawn to dusk, stood ready to answer all questions.

Without the contagious enthusiasm of Dr. Walter Johnston, the persistence of Ken Parks, and the determination and far-sightedness of the Warren County Board of Supervisors to see the project through, the *Cairo*, with her priceless artifacts, would still be buried in the mud of the Yazoo.

I am grateful to the following sources for their kind permission to reproduce some of the photographs included here: the Library of Congress, the Smithsonian Institution, the U.S. Army, the Mississippi Agricultural and Industrial Board, and the Ingalls Shipbuilding Corporation.

I wish also to thank those individuals who graciously permitted me to use pictures taken by them. These include Mrs. Annie Lee Sanders, of the Vicksburg *Evening Post;* Ken Parks, of station WJTV; John E. Warren, Clarksdale, Mississippi; William R. Wilson, Chicago; and D. B. Larr.

Mrs. Marye P. Smith of Vicksburg spent many long, hard hours typing the manuscript.

My wife Margie cleaned mud from artifacts, wrote several hundred letters tracking down identifications and information. She washed many pounds of mud from my clothes when I was helping wash the interior of the *Cairo* and pestered me until I finally wrote this book.

EDWIN C. BEARSS

Hardluck Ironclad

THE CAIRO
IS REDISCOVERED

W ARREN GRABAU shouted, "My God, stop the boat! The compass has gone wild! We've found the *Cairo!*"

This can't be the *Cairo*—it's too easy, I thought as Don Jacks wheeled the small boat around. But my heart was thumping as we started back over the place we had chosen as the optimum site. Again the compass needle swung wildly almost 180 degrees and as suddenly swept back to its original position.

"But it has to be the *Cairo!* This is exactly where she should be."

Our search for the sunken gunboat had its beginning in August, 1956. At that time I had been at Vicksburg a little less than a year, having been assigned the previous September as historian for the Vicksburg National Military Park. Several members of the Atlanta Civil War Round Table were in Vicksburg, Mississippi, at the time; and they asked me to take them to Snyder's Bluff, twelve miles northeast of the city, so they could use their mine detectors to look for artillery projectiles. While at the bluff, we spoke to several farmers who told us that if we were interested and returned when the water in the Yazoo River was low, we might see the wreckage of the *Cairo*.

"Where is the wreck?" we asked excitedly.

"Near the piers of the old bridge," was the reply.

This information did not check with accounts that I had read of the sinking of the Union ironclad, because they indicated that she had been torpedoed several miles below Snyder's Bluff. However, my curiosity was aroused. Within the next few weeks I discussed the subject with my friend Warren Grabau, who, besides being a professional geologist, is a Civil War buff. We finally decided to learn

3

what we could from the sources that mentioned the location of the first vessel ever to be sunk by mines. While Grabau checked maps and charts, I examined the official records of the Union and Confederate navies,[1] as well as old newspapers and the files of the U.S. Corps of Engineers.

From the official records I learned that the five-hundred-ton *Cairo* had gone to the bottom in a matter of minutes after being ripped by an explosion shortly before noon on December 12, 1862. I also discovered that, by the following January, rumors had reached Federal naval officers at Milliken's Bend, Louisiana, across the Mississippi from Vicksburg, that the Confederates were using a diving bell in an effort to salvage the gunboat. To verify this intelligence, Rear Admiral David D. Porter, who had come down from Cairo, Illinois, to supervise naval operations in the Vicksburg area, sent the tinclad *Rattler* and the rams *Queen of the West* and *Lancaster* up the Yazoo River on January 27. The expedition failed to discover any signs of Confederate salvage attempts; it also observed that the muddy waters of the Yazoo effectively concealed the resting place of the ill-fated ironclad.

After the fall of Vicksburg on July 4, 1863, Admiral Porter's thoughts turned to the possibility of raising the *Cairo*. That autumn, with a fall in the level of the Yazoo, Lieutenant Commander Elias K. Owen arrived to take charge of salvage operations. Because of the activities of Confederate guerrillas in the Yazoo Valley, Owen was unable to visit the site of the wreck. However, it was not too dangerous to send someone else; so he dispatched Ensign Phinis R. Starr, who had five years of experience as a Yazoo River pilot. Starr proceeded overland to Colonel Benson Blake's plantation and succeeded in locating the *Cairo*. The vessel lay in about twenty feet of water near the right bank of the river (when facing upstream) and about one and one-fourth miles below "Blake's lower plantation," a reference point used by Starr in his report. No part of the boat was above the surface of the river. Indeed, Starr reported that about three feet of water covered her wheelhouse. From A. J. Snyder and Benjamin Roach, who lived near Snyder's Bluff, Starr learned that the wreck had been in sight only once since the previous December, and, even then, only the top of the pilothouse had protruded above the surface. He was also informed that the chains which had hung over her bow had been removed by the Rebels and used in anchoring their rafts at Snyder's Bluff. Nothing else, he was told, had been removed from the hulk.[2]

Apparently, the idea of raising the *Cairo* was abandoned at this time. With the fall of Vicksburg and the surrender of the Confederate stronghold downriver at Port Hudson, Louisiana, the Federals gained undisputed control of the Mississippi River—a decisive factor in the final defeat of the southern states two years later. The war was over. The *Cairo* was not forgotten, however. In November, 1879, John N. Bofinger, as agent for the Nash Wrecking Company of St. Louis, wrote the Secretary of the Navy to propose that his company be allowed to raise the wreck of the gunboat. Since the Secretary of the Treasury had jurisdiction over hulks of naval vessels sunk in navigable waters, the Navy Department forwarded Bofinger's letter to that agency,[3] and on January 30, 1880, the Treasury Department signed a contract for salvaging the *Cairo*.[4] After deducting freight and other charges for selling the ironclad, the company was to pay into the Treasury of the United States one-fourth of the proceeds. The remaining three-fourths were to be retained by the company, out of which all other expenses and damages incidental to the salvage would be paid.[5] But protests were voiced when it was discovered that the Treasury Department had failed to let other companies file bids, and the contract was voided.[6]

After this episode, the *Cairo* was all but forgotten as the years passed. Colonel Blake pointed out the site of the sinking to his son, and the son to his son; each year the exact location became less certain, until at last it was lost. In 1956 D. C. Blake, grandson of the colonel, could say only that it was a tradition in his family that the *Cairo* lay somewhere along the river below the family's lower plantation. He had never seen it and doubted if anyone then alive had.

A study of Vicksburg newspapers turned up numerous stories regarding the supposed site of the sinking. In the 1920's many people, including several local historians, had visited Snyder's Bluff to view a portion of wreckage exposed by the falling water. Handwrought nails were secured from the broken planks and hailed as being from the *Cairo*. In the 1930's there was a move to raise this wreckage, which was presumed to be the *Cairo*.[7] A study of official records, however, satisfied Grabau and me that artifacts picked up along the river bank at Snyder's Bluff were from rafts the Confederates had placed across the river under the guns of the earthworks at that point and therefore could not possibly be from the gunboat since she had never been within range of these batteries.

I came across another clue to the position of the wreck in an 1874 report by the Corps of Engineers. At that time, the engineers said the *Cairo,* sunk six miles above the mouth of Chickasaw Bayou, constituted no hazard to navigation, as she had become deeply embedded in ooze. (Actually, the report erred so far as the position of the ironclad was concerned: the *Cairo* was only two miles above that point.)[8]

Our curiosity aroused, we decided to try to fix the site of the sinking. Maps of the Yazoo drawn during the 1860's were obtained from the Mississippi River Commission offices in Vicksburg. We were struck by the fact that the bends shown on the old maps matched almost exactly those of the modern river, and we had no trouble at all finding the location of Blake's lower plantation.

Here, however, questions began to arise. The salvage report stated that the wreck was "close to the right bank when facing upstream," but one of the old maps, purporting to show the position of the wreck, indicated the site as being on the left side when facing upstream. Map and account were thus thrown open to suspicion. After carefully analyzing stories of the sinking, the position of the vessel when the torpedoes exploded was fixed as closely as possible. It was assumed that her power had failed almost immediately, and that it would have taken her only a minute or so to lose way against the current. (In the modern stream, the current is about 1.5 miles per hour at a comparable stage of water.) According to the accounts, the *Cairo* was run into the bank but almost immediately slid off and sank.

It seemed reasonable to suppose that the first thing the pilots would do when the torpedoes exploded would be to swing the boat into the bank, while she still had some steerageway. With this information, and taking into account the speed and width of the stream, we plotted a hypothetical curve into the bank. If the boat's bow were driven into the mud at that point the current would swing the stern downstream, and the gunboat would slide off into deep water. This process would take several minutes; in fact, it took the *Cairo* about twelve minutes to go down. We reasoned that the pilots would probably choose the concave bank for two reasons: first, because the water there would be deep close to the shore, making it possible for the vessel to get near enough to the bank for the men to jump ashore; second, the current would tend to keep the ironclad pushed against the bank, at least for the critical few minutes necessary to get the men off.

The amount of guesswork in this reasoning began to assume formidable and depressing proportions. We projected these inferences onto paper, and placed a dot on a modern map in the position considered to be the most likely location for the wreck. To account for the possibility that the pilots had chosen the convex bank, a second curve was drawn, and another point was placed on the opposite side of the river. This site looked much less likely. The currents, the bottom configuration, and the shape of the bank looked very uninviting to one in the position of the pilots at the time of the disaster.

With the map in front of us, Warren Grabau and I weighed the possibilities. On the pro side of the argument were the map and the elaborate preparations that had led up to it. It all looked so logical! On the con side of the ledger was the fact that a lot of people had looked for the *Cairo* and failed to find it. On the basis of past experience, it seemed only too likely that we would join the company of those who had failed. Finally, we decided to go ahead: besides, it seemed a shame to quit without testing all our deductions. The question then became one of method. In view of the fact that the *Cairo* was an ironclad with much artillery and machinery aboard, it seemed likely that she would produce some sort of deviation in the magnetic field. This distortion, we hoped, could be detected with a dip needle, an extremely sensitive magnetic instrument. But, no dip needle was available in the vicinity, and so we were forced to use a much less sensitive pocket compass. To get as close to the wreck as possible in order to detect any magnetic changes, we waited until the water level in the river fell.

Waiting gave ample time for second thoughts. It occurred to us that the *Cairo* might have been swept far out of position by flood waters. Her timbers might have rotted to the point where very little remained but a pile of iron on the river bottom. Maybe she had been removed and no record kept. Our thoughts grew blacker as time went by.

In the meantime Don Jacks, an employee of the Vicksburg National Military Park, joined us. He contributed a small wooden boat with an outboard motor and, more important, an extensive knowledge and understanding of the river. He was reassuring: he said that once a wreck settled into mud it was there to stay, and that timber could be sunk in the river a long time without rotting, if no air reached it. It seemed clear that only the *Cairo's* pilothouse at most had been above water since that fateful day in 1862. So there was hope after all.

Finally, on November 12, 1956, a beautiful autumn day, the river gauge at Vicksburg fell to minus 1.9 feet. This was about as low as it could reasonably be expected to go, so we decided to see if our deductions would pay off. Even if nothing were found, we consoled ourselves with the thought that it was a good day for a boat ride.

We took the little boat well above the site previously selected as most likely, turned, and came down with the current, trying to hold some twenty-five feet off the bank. At first, Jacks had trouble holding the boat on the fixed course necessary for compass interpretation; but he soon developed a system that worked to perfection, and our search began in earnest. The compass was set in the bottom of the boat, in the lowest position possible. We hoped to get as close to the wreck as we could, believing that every inch might count. Then Grabau crouched over the compass, Jacks steered, and I watched the shore. The little boat slid downstream, barely maintaining steerageway.

At a point about one-half mile above the optimum site, the compass seemed to react slightly, so traverse after traverse was made. The deviation was so faint that we could not be sure it was there at all, but we went ashore and blazed a tree to mark the spot.

The downstream traverse was resumed, with everything quiet except the monotonous chatter of the motor. Suddenly Grabau yelled, "My God, stop the boat!" The compass needle had swung wildly halfway around the dial, then settled back to normal position a few yards farther downstream. Back went the boat, and this time there was no doubt about it. There was something in the river, and it was magnetic. The location was carefully plotted on the map, and it fell within about fifty yards of the optimum site. Excited, we hurried ashore and blazed another tree. Then, just to be sure, we crossed the river and carefully checked the second-best site, but the compass remained as steady as if it were frozen.

We then headed the boat downstream for Vicksburg at top speed. The next step was to probe, to see if any irregularities could be felt in the mud of the river bed. During the fifteen-mile trip to Vicksburg, we had time for sober reflection. After all, the Yazoo had carried countless boats in the old days, and this might be one of them, or even a pile of scrap iron that a planter had dumped over the bank. It had been much too simple. Everything had worked too well; nothing ever progressed as smoothly as this search! By the time the boat reached Vicksburg, the consensus was that it was hardly worth going back upriver to check. Our find could be almost anything—anything but the *Cairo*.

But stubbornness won out, and we went back with an iron bar about twenty feet long to use as a probe. At the site, we headed the little boat upstream and steered slowly and carefully toward the place where the magnetic disturbance had been strongest. The probe went down through fifteen feet of water and into blue clay. A few feet farther upstream, the probe struck solidly against iron and at a depth of only six feet. Back and forth we went, seeking to get some notion of the size and shape of the object under the water; but it proved impossible to control the boat well enough to obtain more than an impression of great size and lots of iron.

During the following weekends, we evolved a system of controlling the position of the boat, using an anchor in the channel and rope lines to a man ashore. By this means, an elaborate series of probe traverses over the site was made and carefully plotted. When these records were examined, a picture of a big, flat-topped, slope-sided object emerged. The sloping sides were iron; the flat top was wood; on the front of the wreck, near the bank, was a small iron tower with slanting sides. Everything checked! The slanting iron sides would be the armored pilothouse, and the flat top would be the unarmored spar deck. A scale drawing of the *Cairo* could be fitted perfectly into the probe records.

Close-range inspection seemed to be prohibited, for Mississippi was having a cold spell, and the muddy water of the Yazoo was icy cold. Robert Salassi, a Vicksburger with a soul of iron, offered to go down to see if he could feel anything that would corroborate the probe findings. The day of his descent was a bitter one. A fire was built on the bank so that he would not die of exposure when he surfaced. Down he went. On the top of the casemate near the bow, he found a loose bolt and managed to pull it out. On another dive the armor on the forward casemate was roughly measured and found to be about two and one-half inches thick. More confirmation. Later the water fell so low that it was possible for us to hang over the side of our boat and feel the top of the pilothouse, with its characteristic octagonal shape and slanting sides. It had to be the *Cairo!*

2

---•---

EADS BUILDS
THE IRONCLADS

Aᴘʀɪʟ, 1861, was a time of tremendous excitement for a divided nation, and nowhere was this more apparent than in St. Louis, Missouri. On the twelfth came news that the Southerners had fired on Fort Sumter off Charleston, South Carolina. This was followed the next day by word that the fort had fallen. President Lincoln called on the governors for seventy-five thousand volunteers to put down disturbances in the seceded states too serious for the law officers of the government to suppress. This brought a defiant answer from Missouri's Governor Claiborne F. Jackson, who branded it "illegal, unconstitutional, and revolutionary in its object, inhuman and diabolical." His state, Jackson said, would not furnish one man "to carry on such an unholy crusade." [1]

Missouri, like the rest of the country, was restless. Thousands, including the governor, urged secession. State guardsmen, whose sympathies were with the South, were called out and began drilling to be ready for the day the state convention would reconvene and declare Missouri's allegiance to the Union dissolved. As many people or more were equally determined that Missouri would remain in the Union. Among those was James B. Eads, who was known to every riverman on the Mississippi from the falls of St. Anthony to Head of Passes. Eads, a calm, introspective man, had retired at thirty-seven after making a fortune on the western rivers by salvaging wrecked boats. To carry out this work, Eads, a civil engineer, had designed and built a series of salvage boats.

The guns in Charleston harbor had hardly fallen silent when Eads wrote to his friend Edward Bates, now attorney general in Lincoln's cabinet. "Vigorous action must be taken to defeat the South," he said. A defensive war was not enough. Bates's reply electrified Eads. It read: "Be not surprised if you are called here suddenly by telegram. If called, come instantly. In a certain contingency it will be necessary to have the aid of the most thorough knowledge of our Western rivers and the use of steam on them, and in that event I have advised that you should be consulted." [2]

Before the week had passed, Eads received the anxiously awaited telegram. While en route by rail to Washington, he thought about the problems confronting the Union in the West. Like most westerners, he believed that the first and most important step in restoring the Union was to wrest control of the Lower Mississippi from the Confederacy. Detraining in the capital, Eads hastened to the office of the attorney general where he learned that Bates's idea was similar to his own: to regain control of the river, the government should build a fleet of gunboats.

A cabinet meeting was called by the President to hear Eads's recommendations, and the riverman tersely told of a plan he had conceived for creating an inland navy to spearhead an amphibious drive to recover the Lower Mississippi. All of the cabinet members were in favor of Eads's ideas except Secretary of War Simon Cameron, who thought the scheme absurd. However, Secretary of Navy Gideon Welles liked what Eads had to say and asked him to submit for consideration his thoughts on the "feasibility of effectually blockading the commerce of the rebelling States upon the Mississippi River." [3]

On April 29 Eads outlined his ideas for the Navy Department. As the first step in crushing the rebellion, he urged that a base of operations be established at Cairo, Illinois, supported by a strong river force and shore batteries "as will effectually control the passage of vessels bound up or down the Mississippi and Ohio Rivers." [4] The Missouri Wrecking Company (in which Eads was a stockholder), he continued, could supply a very strong boat capable of supporting a battery of 32-pounders. This was the *Submarine No. 7,* a salvage vessel which Eads had designed and built. It had a double hull with watertight compartments, and if armored with cotton bales, strategically placed, could be made "exceedingly effective for offense or defense" and could stop the erection of Rebel batteries on the banks of the Mississippi. Moreover, his firm had two smaller steamboats which could be outfitted for use on the lesser rivers.

The effect of closing the Mississippi, Eads predicted, would be disastrous to the South because it would effectually block the main channel through which flowed her food supplies. With the Mississippi blockaded, the only avenues of commerce open to the Confederacy west of the Appalachians would be the Tennessee and Cumberland rivers and the Louisville and Nashville Railroad. Except in periods of high water, these rivers could be navigated only by small steamers; and their mouths could be controlled by gunboats. The railroad at the same time could be sabotaged. Once these routes, along with the Mississippi, were sealed, Eads said, "starvation [would be] inevitable in less than six months." [5]

Secretary Welles thought enough of the presentation to ask Eads to expand on it before a board of officers headed by Commodore Hiram Paulding. They, in turn, approved; and Eads's memorandum was forwarded to Samuel M. Pook, naval constructor, for further study. At this point Secretary of War Cameron again intervened. Having had second thoughts on the subject, Cameron now reversed himself and announced that, as the navy had no authority over inland waters, the fitting out of river gunboats should be undertaken by the army. Cameron carried his point with the cabinet, and Eads was left to cool his heels in his hotel room while waiting to learn something from the secretary of war. When no messages came, he packed his bags and left.

A few days later Eads was back in Washington. During his brief absence from the capital, little had been done to bring order out of chaos—the city was still wild with excitement and confusion. At the War Department he asked about the projected inland navy, but Cameron was unable to give much encouragement. While still in Washington, Eads addressed a letter to Secretary of Navy Welles reiterating his plan to employ river gunboats to blockade the South. But that was now out of the Navy Department's hands. Baffled and irritated, Eads returned to St. Louis.

He had, however, forced the army's hand. Secretary Welles on May 14 referred Eads's plan to the War Department, "to which the subject more properly belongs." [6] Unwilling to make a decision about the matter without the knowledge and approval of the commander of the area in question, Cameron contacted Major General George B. McClellan, who had established his headquarters at Cincinnati, Ohio. McClellan was to consult Eads and such naval officers as the Navy Department mignt order to the Mississippi Valley. [7] Two days later, at the request of the War Department, Welles ordered Commander

John Rodgers, an experienced officer, to proceed to Cincinnati and report to General McClellan "in regard to the expediency of establishing a naval armament on the Mississippi and Ohio rivers, or either of them, with a view of blockading or interdicting communication and inter-changes with the States that are in insurrection." Since "interior nonintercourse" was a responsibility of the army, Rodgers would look to McClellan for his instructions. Naval armament and crews necessary to carry out the blockade would be forthcoming when called for, Welles promised.[8]

Rodgers, before reporting to McClellan, visited Cairo. There he was joined by Captain Eads, and the two men examined the *Submarine No. 7*. The naval officer vetoed Eads's plan to turn the big salvage boat into a cotton-clad gunboat and went on to Cincinnati to confer with General McClellan. (Subsequently, the *Submarine No. 7* was purchased by the army and converted by Eads into a powerful ironclad gunboat. Named the *Benton,* she served as the Western Flotilla's flagboat.) The general urged Rodgers to secure boats that would be useful on smaller rivers as well as on the Mississippi.

Unfortunately for himself, Rodgers concluded that gunboats were the navy's business, and used his limited authority to buy boats and material necessary to convert them. His charging the cost of three river steamers to the Navy Department earned him a prompt reprimand from Welles. Rodgers was to aid and advise the army, the Secretary wrote, but under their direction and at their expense. Welles would supply navy guns and crews but nothing more.[9]

When Rodgers replied that General McClellan had already approved the purchases, Welles, to make his position clear, wrote the naval officer that all movements on the Ohio and Mississippi rivers were under the control of the army. The effect of this was that Welles unwittingly established what became known in World War II as a unified command. For the next year and a half, naval officers on the western waters operated under the direction of army leaders.[10]

General-in-Chief of the United States Army Winfield Scott was seriously interested in exploiting the Mississippi and its tributaries to help bring the downfall of the Confederacy. In May, 1861, Scott asked his chief engineer, Brigadier General Joseph G. Totten, to prepare a study of boatbuilding facilities, distances, steamers for transportation, gunboats, coal supplies, and the like, on the Mississippi and Ohio rivers. Totten learned that there were about four hundred steamers on the two rivers. Secession had played hob with river traffic, and most of these vessels would be available for charter as troop transports by the government. At least four hundred coal barges and two hundred freight barges could be purchased or leased. Since an active campaign to open the Mississippi was planned, Totten recommended that the government take advantage of the June rise to employ a number of these barges to stockpile coal at Cairo.

Facilities for building boats on the Ohio River, his survey showed, existed at Pittsburgh, Pennsylvania; Wheeling, [West] Virginia; Cincinnati, Ohio; Madison and New Albany, Indiana; and Mound City, Illinois. Steam engines of all types could be secured at all these places except Mound City. Persons consulted estimated that the yards could get the boats ready within three months from the time the contract was closed, provided the matter was pressed.[11]

At General Totten's request, John Lenthall, chief of the navy's bureau of construction, had made a study of the possibility of constructing armed steam vessels for service on the Mississippi. Lenthall's report doubted that such vessels would be very efficient. The general depth of western rivers precluded a craft's being fitted with a propeller and an engine below deck. A boat designed for combat on the inland rivers would have to be a side-wheeler, built in the form of a flat-bottomed, double-ended bateau. Lenthall's vessel would be 8 feet, 10 inches deep and 170 feet long, and no wider than 28 feet. The bow and stern would be alike, each with a rudder—a forerunner of the double-enders. This craft, when armed with four 8-inch guns, would displace nearly 436 tons and draw 4 feet, 7 inches of water. Lenthall estimated the cost of such a hull and the necessary machinery at from $19,000 to $22,000. In addition, he suggested that the War Department consult naval constructor Pook, who was experienced in building warships.[12]

After studying Lenthall's paper, Totten informed General Scott that the design proposed could be a basis (on which modifications suggested by experience might be made) for the kind of craft needed to maneuver in western waters. It would be the government's role to determine how many boats of this kind would be needed and when. Totten believed that ten would be the minimum and twenty the maximum.

To undertake the task of constructing the gunboats, he suggested that several naval officers, at least one of whom had some rank and experience, be sent to the Ohio with authority to make the necessary contracts at sites along the river they thought best, keeping in mind production schedules and the builders' spirit of competition. The officer in charge would be given authority to consult Ohio River boat and engine builders as well as constructor Pook. Totten was opposed to advertising publicly for bids for building the boats because such an announcement would alert the Confederates to Union plans for carrying the war to them in the West. Because the gunboats would be placed under command of naval officers, he felt that it would be wise for the general in charge of the western theater of operations to call for these officers at an early date. Placing the men destined to command the boats in charge would assure "the very best means of securing a timely and complete outfit, as well as a faithful execution of contract." [13]

General Scott liked Totten's report. On June 10 he forwarded it to Secretary of War Cameron and recommended that measures be taken immediately to construct sixteen gunboats like those proposed by Lenthall. Each of these craft would be fitted with an engine, also built on the Ohio River, ready for service by the twentieth of the next September. Cameron transmitted the documents to the Secretary of the Navy with a request that Scott's recommendations be carried out. He urged that Commander Rodgers and Pook consult the principal western steamboat builders as to the proper design of the gunboats. Acknowledging Cameron's communication on June 12, Secretary Welles wrote that in view of the great demands upon it, the navy would be unable to furnish officers to superintend the building of gunboats and engines on the western rivers. As the gunboats would be "in many respects different from ocean steamers in their construction," Welles suggested that "it would be well to have them built by Western men, who are educated to the peculiar boat required for navigating rivers." The Navy Department would, however, be glad to authorize one of its naval constructors to advise and assist in building the gunboats in order to adapt the proposed vessels to war purposes. [14]

Cameron turned over the correspondence dealing with the construction of a fleet of river gunboats to Quartermaster General Montgomery C. Meigs, a forty-four-year-old former captain of engineers who, because of the war, had been promoted to general. After examining the material, Meigs and his staff forwarded the packet to Commander Rodgers with a request that he have Pook and engineers skilled in the building of boats on western rivers look over Lenthall's drawings.

The second half of June was filled with busy days for Rodgers and

Pook. After Pook had discussed the projected gunboats with most of the boat builders, engineers, and river captains in and around Cincinnati, he modified Lenthall's drawings extensively. The vessel he proposed was to be 175 feet long, have a 50-foot beam, and draw 6 feet of water. There were to be three keels, and the bottom was to be flat. The idea of a double-ender was abandoned. Atop the hull was an oblong casemate sloped up to a flat roof, forty-five degrees in front, thirty-five degrees on the side; its forward end was to be pierced for three guns, and its port and starboard beams for seven guns each, and its stern for three guns. Influenced by developments in Great Britain and France and by a study of the Crimean War, Pook proposed that the engines and boilers be protected by iron plates. On July 6 Commander Rodgers forwarded to Quartermaster General Meigs the specifications for the ironclad gunboats prepared by Pook. The drawings still on the drafting board were to be posted as soon as completed.[15]

Thirteen days later Meigs relayed to Secretary Welles plans and specifications of A. Thomas Merritt for the engines to be used on the gunboats. These were to be shown to the Navy Department's chief engineer, B. F. Isherwood; the army wanted his opinion regarding the engines before invitations for bids were published. Along with the drawings and specifications, Merritt had submitted a letter of explanation. The engines were to be placed transversely to the hull, and fitted into a space of less than sixteen feet. To cram them into this area, along with the driving wheel and pinion, it would be necessary that all connections be as short as practicable. Both engines were to be mounted side by side with a distance of six feet between the frames. An auxiliary engine would be placed about seven feet forward of the other engines, also transversely to the hull. The ends of the five boilers would be about three feet in front of the auxiliary engine.[16]

Three plans had been submitted by the army. Two were of paddle-wheel engines; the third was for a screw-propelled vessel. But Isherwood, like Lenthall, knew that a screw-propelled vessel would be extremely impractical in shallow, timber-filled rivers, and would often find itself aground. It was his opinion that the paddle-wheel engine usually employed on western rivers, "fitted with the usual cylindrical high pressure boilers, and employing the kind of engine valve in general use, will be found more reliable and satisfactory than any innovation is likely to prove."[17]

Even before plans and specifications for the hulls and engines had been approved, advertisements inviting bids to build the boats were inserted in the principal newspapers of the Ohio and Upper Mississippi river cities.

On July 15, three days before General Meigs drafted his letter inviting bids, three prominent residents of St. Louis, one of them Francis P. Blair (who, besides being a power in the Republican party, had a brother in Lincoln's cabinet), wrote Meigs they had learned from good authority that the government planned to build a number of gunboats for use in the West. Consequently, they wished to call to Meigs's attention the fact that Missouri was well supplied with all the needed materials and facilities to construct vessels of this nature.

These men pointed out that St. Louis and Cape Girardeau were admirably suited for building gunboats. St. Louis had drydocks, was a center for machinery manufacture, and could provide any number of skilled mechanics and machinists. Since the boats would operate on the Mississippi, the men argued that they should be built on that river, where they could "be got out at all seasons of the year, and not high up on the Ohio, where they may [be] tied up and of no use when needed." [18] The writers trusted that the War Department would give careful consideration to proposals for building gunboats that might be submitted by Missourians. Postmaster General Montgomery Blair, like his brother, urged Meigs to give careful consideration to bids filed by St. Louis contractors because, if the vessels were built on Ohio River ways, the water would be too low to enable the craft to reach Cairo in time to be of any use in the war. Like most people, North and South, Blair expected a short war.[19]

Captain Eads in the meantime had read the notice carried by the St. Louis papers. All he had for a guide in formulating his bid were the specifications of the hull and engines, with the general plan of the boats as drawn by Pook. When he drafted his proposal, Eads held it to the barest margin of cost and pledged himself to complete the boats in an almost unbelievably short time. On the designated day—August 5, 1861—Meigs and his staff opened the proposals which had been submitted. Of the seven bids, the one filed by James B. Eads was low. He proposed to build from four to sixteen boats and deliver them at Cairo on or before October 5 of that year. For each boat, he would charge the government $89,600. The boats were "to be completed including engines, boilers & iron plating," or Eads would "agree to forfeit $600 per day for every day over that time which may elapse before the completion and delivery of said boats, and said amount to be forfeited on *each boat* & each day until so delivered for 15 days." [20]

On August 7, in General Meigs's office, Eads signed a contract to construct "seven gun-boats, as described and referred to in the printed specifications." The boats were to be completed on or before October 10, 1861. If not, he was to forfeit $250 a day for each vessel delayed past the October deadline. He was to receive $89,600 in stipulated installments for each boat. Every twenty days superintendents designated by the government were to estimate the amount of work done in the preceding period, and the Treasury was to pay Eads 75 percent of the estimate.

To secure punctual performance, and to indemnify and protect the United States, the government was authorized to retain, until the agreement had been executed, 25 percent of "the moneys at any time due" the contractor, retaining the right to order suspension of work obligated under the contract at any time. Moreover, it was agreed that neither the contract nor any portion of it could be sublet.

The government was to name a project superintendent whose duty it would be to inspect the material used in constructing the ironclads and to reject all that he deemed defective. If all the vessels were not built in one yard, an assistant superintendent would be designated for each additional yard. A codicil was added to the document providing that "no deviation from the specifications shall be required by the superintendents which will delay [Eads] in completing his contract in the specified time." [21]

Plans for the type of vessel which Eads was to build called for seven ports to be cut into the port and starboard sides of the casemate, and three in each end. At the after end of the vessel, there was to be an opening eighteen feet wide, extending sixty feet forward to receive the paddle wheel. This aperture was to be "framed with an easy curve from the bottom up to the water line, so as to allow water to pass freely" to the paddle wheel. A plain cabin with two staterooms, two messrooms, and eight staterooms for officers was to be built into the after section of the casemate. The officers' quarters were to be fitted with berths, bureaus, and washstands. The contractor was to build suitable magazines, shellrooms, and shot lockers as directed by the superintendent.

Seventy-five tons of iron plating of sufficient thickness were to be used to protect the vessel's boilers and engines.²² Each boat was to be equipped with five boilers, thirty-six inches in diameter and twenty-four feet long. Atop each boiler was to be placed a connector, five inches diameter inside, to carry the steam to the steam drum. Beneath the boilers would be a fire box, with its bed lined with fire brick, and enclosed in good sheet iron. Two chimneys, forty-four inches in diameter and twenty-eight feet high, were to be placed in front of the boilers.

Each ironclad was to have two engines, whose cylinders were to be made of cast iron, mounted at a fifteen-degree angle, with a bore of 22 inches, and long enough for a piston stroke of 6 feet. A cast-iron piston was to be attached to a rod made of the best fagoted wrought-iron, 4 inches in diameter and 110 inches long.²³

The St. Louis *Daily Democrat* was delighted that the army had awarded the gunboat contract to Eads. Within two days of his return from the capital, the newspaper said, Eads had arranged to lease the marine ways at Carondelet (today part of the city of St. Louis), and had recruited a large force of mechanics and carpenters. Subcontracts were being negotiated for engines and machinery, and large orders had been placed with sawmills for lumber. Most of the white oak for which the specifications called had been secured from St. Louis dealers. It was rumored four thousand men would be employed in building the ironclads. With Eads in charge, the paper continued, "we hazard nothing in saying that the whole fleet will be ready to deal out death and terror to traitors by the 10th of October next, the time set for their delivery to the government." ²⁴

There was at least one man who was taken aback when the government awarded the contract to Eads. A. F. Temple of Madison, Indiana, who had filed one of the six unsuccessful proposals, wrote his senator, H. L. Lane, on August 14, that if the War Department wanted

gun Boats to prosecute this war, it would be better for them to get them built at some other point than Saint Louis, Mo., as it is impossible for them to be built at that point inside of four months or more, and Mr. Eaddes [*sic*], is not a builder—had no timber—no machinery, and no place of Building— And why should [the] Government award the contracts to him . . . when he had no legitimate right to bid at all, as the bids were to come from builders only—

If Boat builders, Ship wrights and other mechanicks [*sic*] are to be bartered and sold to speculators, such as Mr. Eaddes [sic], to grind them down to prices below ordinary wages in order that he may make a profit, it is time that the mechanics and working class should speak out.

Temple argued that Eads could never complete the ironclads in time for the autumn rise on the Mississippi, and that the government, if the vessels were to be of any use, would have to build them at some point other than St. Louis. Senator Lane sent Temple's letter to the office of the secretary of war, where it was filed and forgotten.[25]

Before work could begin on the hulls, superintendents and inspectors had to be designated to look after the government's interests. A. Thomas Merritt, who had designed the engines for the gunboats, asked General Meigs to name him superintendent for the construction of the ironclads, and Meigs acquiesced.[26] Commander Rodgers on August 8 appointed John Litherbury to oversee the construction of the Carondelet gunboats. He was to hasten to St. Louis and report to Captain Eads. In addition, he was authorized to name a sub-superintendent for each boat at a salary of $3 per day.[27]

The task of obtaining the guns to be mounted on the ironclads was undertaken by Rodgers. On August 10 the naval officer wrote Captain A. A. Harwood, chief of the navy's Bureau of Ordnance, that he needed thirty-five rifled 42-pounders and seventy 9-inch Dahlgren smoothbores to arm the seven vessels. This armament, he assured the captain, could be carried easily by the hulls.

Rodgers's request that the navy provide guns to be placed on the ironclads was temporarily denied by Captain Harwood. To discover a way out of this impasse, Rodgers wrote General Meigs on August 29 to see if the army could provide the "requisite nine inch columbiads, and forty two pounder rifles." [28] After reviewing correspondence in his files bearing on the problem, Meigs found that Secretary Cameron in June had promised that the army would provide the necessary 42-pounders. Secretary Welles in the meantime had contacted the War Department. As he recalled, the War Department had promised to provide thirty-five 42-pounder rifles, along with projectiles, for the Eads ironclads. If so, Welles requested that these guns be forwarded to St. Louis with the utmost dispatch. Other guns (8-inch cannon and 32-pounders) for these vessels, would be supplied by the navy from depots at Buffalo, Erie, and Sacketts Harbor; but because of the pressing wants of deepwater squadrons, Welles found it impossible to provide small arms for the gunboats being constructed for service on western waters.[29]

Commander Rodgers on August 26 announced that proposals would be received until the thirty-first for "naval gun-carriages for IX-inch guns and for 42-pounder rifled cannon, 74 of the former and 38 of the latter." The carriages were to be made of "seasoned oak, of the best quality, and the trucks of lignum vitae, or of oak two thicknesses and riveted together, with all the proper gun implements such as sponges, shot, ladles, scrapers, and worms." Carriages and implements were to be delivered at Cairo, ready for use, by October 10. [30]

The contract for building the gun carriages and implements was awarded the Eagle Iron Works of Cincinnati. Not being familiar with what the government desired, the factory's chief engineer caused one delay when he wrote Washington to secure a copy of the *Naval Ordnance Manual*.[31] Additional time was lost when the Navy Department notified the Cincinnati contractor that it knew of no such publication. The engineer therefore had to contact the officer in charge of the gunboats in order to secure plans of the carriages.[32]

Despite the optimism expressed by the *Daily Democrat* on August 14, all was not going well at Carondelet. A number of the artisans employed at the marine ways threatened to strike for more money, although they were being paid wages comparable to those received before the war. Pro-Southerners residing in the area had bragged in saloons that they would burn the hulls before they were launched. To prevent any such lawless act, demands were raised that a regiment be posted at Carondelet.[33] Commander Rodgers, on learning of this wild talk, became alarmed for the safety of the boats. He immediately requested that Major General John C. Frémont, who had recently assumed command of the vast Western Department headquartered at St. Louis, detail soldiers to guard the ironclads under construction at the Marine Ways.[34]

Eads used the *Daily Democrat* of August 22 to announce that more boat carpenters were needed. Wages would be $2 per ten-hour day, with 25 cents per hour for overtime. The *Daily Democrat* had greatly exaggerated in its report that four thousand would find work on the Carondelet hulls. According to Eads, only two hundred men were currently engaged on the four vessels being constructed though he planned to add another two hundred men to his working force during the next seven days. A large number of skilled craftsmen hired by him had come from boatbuilding centers on the Ohio River—Louis-ville, Cincinnati, Jeffersonville, and New Albany. Many of these people were of foreign birth.[35]

By August 25 most of the structural timbers were in place on the four Carondelet boats. Within three or four days, predicted people who had visited the ways, the hulls would be ready for planking. Meanwhile, Eads had decided to build three of the seven ironclads at Mound City and had worked out an agreement with Captain William L. Hambleton of the Mound City Marine Railway and Ship Yard to utilize that facility. By the latter part of August, more than 130 boat carpenters were engaged to augment the force already employed at the ways. The arrival of these men permitted work on the three hulls to commence immediately.[36]

On August 27 Eads forwarded to General Meigs's office the first estimate of work done on the gunboats. This small sum, $58,315.40, the contractor trusted, would not induce the government to conclude that work was "not being pushed with due vigor." As yet no estimate had been made on the three hulls under construction at Mound City, or for the iron plating (in which work two of the largest rolling mills in the Cincinnati area had been "engaged day and night for the past two weeks"), or for two sets of engines and boilers subcontracted to a Pittsburgh firm. The contractor notified Meigs at this time that, unless there was opposition and he was countermanded, he had selected names for six of the seven boats. In the order that they came off the ways they would be christened the *J. C. Frémont, Geo. B. Mc-Clellan, N. P. Banks, Nathaniel Lyon, M. C. Meigs,* and *John Rodgers.* As it turned out, none of these names was used.

Three days later Eads forwarded to Meigs's office the bonds re-quired by the government for his faithful performance of contract. At the moment, he said, he had about six hundred men and twelve sawmills at work on the seven hulls and had "no doubt I shall com-plete my contract in the specified time." Money, however, was all-important, and he trusted that the government would comply with its obligation to forward promptly the percentage of the first estimate to which he was entitled, thus enabling him to meet expenses.[37]

Two weeks later, on September 14, Eads forwarded to Washington the estimate of work accomplished during the past twenty days. This estimate dealt with the three Mound City hulls and with two sets of engines and boilers under subcontract to Hartupee and Company of Pittsburgh. He reminded Meigs that he had not received one dollar from the government on a contract (with extra work already ordered) involving an outlay of $700,000, and that he was "stringently bound under heavy forfeitures" to complete the contract by October 10. Despite the inconvenience to which he had been put by the government's failure to meet its obligations, he remained confident he would make delivery by the designated date.[38]

Because the government had not yet paid him the percentage of funds due on his first estimate, Eads could meet few of his debts. Hartupee and Company pressed him for its money. By the end of the second week of September, the engines and boilers were nearly ready for shipment. With more than $25,000 worth of work done under the subcontract, the company wired Eads for money and for information regarding whether the hulls were ready for the machinery. He did not acknowledge the telegram nor send a draft, and on the nineteenth the Pittsburgh firm notified Meigs of its difficulties with Eads.[39]

Eads then asked his friend O. D. Filley, a former mayor of St. Louis, to speak to the quartermaster general. During his forthcoming trip to Washington, Filley was to try to get the government to release the money due Eads in the two estimates.

In a covering letter to Meigs, Eads wrote: "The interest you have manifested for the early completion of the boats, and the fact that I am still without aid from the Government, assures me that you will do all in your power to save me from further distress." [40]

Before the week was over, Eads received some relief when he was paid the $43,736.55 due on the estimate of August 27. By this time, however, the date for posting another estimate was approaching. On October 2 he mailed to Meigs's office a second estimate on the engines subcontracted to Hartupee and the hulls for the Mound City gunboats —$32,000—once again begging Meigs to expedite payment. Only the day before, the contractor had received word that, on September 29, the quartermaster at New York City had made disbursements on the contractor's second and third estimates, totaling $111,000. Of this figure, the second estimate had been in arrears twenty-four days and the third a day less than two weeks. If these estimates, Eads complained, had been made "on a liberal basis I should have less cause to complain, but the whole amount paid to me up to this time is but $155,000." He felt safe in asserting that his contract was 80 percent completed, three-fourths of which would have entitled him to $200,000 more than he had yet received. For the past forty days, the contractor reported, he had been "cramped and annoyed for money," and within five days he would again be upon the "market as a borrower." [41]

The *Daily Democrat* on September 18 informed its readers that Eads, when awarded the contract to build seven gunboats in sixty-four days, had fully appreciated the "magnitude of the work to be performed in so short a time." Without a dollar in advance from the government, he had promptly organized his forces. Eads was known to have employed eight hundred hands, five hundred on the four boats building at Carondelet and three hundred on the Mound City hulls. One steamboat and four barges had been engaged in transporting lumber from the various points where Eads had mills cutting timber. Thirteen sawmills—five in St. Louis and eight elsewhere (Kentucky, Illinois, Ohio, and on the Missouri River)—were working exclusively for the project, cutting white oak into lumber.

According to reports reaching the *Daily Democrat,* the Carondelet boats were more than half completed; boatbuilders had been heard to remark that the work "is being done in a model manner, and according to the strictest letter of the contract." Moreover, Eads had accomplished all this without fanfare and ballyhoo.[42]

To complete the vessels by the date designated, Eads had placed his crews on a seven-day week. Night work was carried on where possible in the machine, blacksmith, and coppersmith shops, foundries, rolling mills, and sawmills.[43]

A correspondent for the *Missouri Republican* visited Carondelet, and the story which appeared on September 21 failed to present as bright a picture regarding the gunboats as did the article in its rival paper. The *Republican's* reporter observed that the four boats on the "Marine Railways at Carondelet," and those being built at Mound City, would probably not be ready until October 15—five days late. During the third week of September, 484 men (402 carpenters and 82 laborers) had been employed at the Marine Ways; but as the fourth week commenced, this force had been expanded to 700.[44]

Gaylord, Son and Company had signed a contract with Captain Eads to make and deliver seven hundred tons of iron sheeting for the gunboats. The iron was to be rolled in the company's mills at Portsmouth, Ohio, and Newport, Kentucky, into plates thirteen inches wide and of various lengths (from three and one-half to eleven feet), and two and one-half inches thick. To insure that the Gaylord company would not be delinquent in the shipment of the iron, Eads took a lesson from the government, and placed the firm under a forfeiture of two hundred dollars a day for every day's delay beyond the delivery date. The first lot of iron reached St. Louis one day ahead of the specified date!

Commander Rodgers and Superintendent Merritt decided to test the strength of the iron under artillery fire. For this purpose, they called on Lieutenant Adelbert R. Buffington of the St. Louis Arsenal for two rifled guns—10-pounder Parrotts. The artillery pieces and several sheets of iron were ferried across to the Illinois side of the Mississippi, opposite the Carondelet docks. Permission was received to use a sandy beach which had been uncovered by the falling river. The iron plates to be tested were bolted firmly to an oak block sixteen inches thick, and placed in a firm position at a thirty-five degree angle, the same inclination as the sides of the ironclads' casemates.

Buffington unlimbered his Parrotts at a range of eight hundred yards. The target was small for the distance, but with the aid of a spyglass "some good shots were made"; the first projectile struck "the iron under one of the bolts, tearing it out without injury to the iron, only making its mark in a raking way." After the Parrotts were advanced three hundred yards, two hits were registered—the first making "a very decided mark, indenting the iron one inch, while the other indented the iron and started all the bolts." Buffington now moved his cannon to within two hundred yards; the effect on the iron was the same, "a deep indentation being made, but not a crack or sign of breaking." Finally, to see if a projectile could hole the iron plating, the party set the target at a ninety-degree angle and placed one of the Parrotts at one hundred yards. Everyone claimed the solid bolt should go through. The projectile "hit fair in the center, knocking the target around out of its place, and shattering the ball in a thousand fragments, many pieces flying back to the gun." Buffington vetoed placing his Parrotts any nearer as too dangerous for the gunners, while Commander Rodgers declared that "the iron resisted beyond all expectations, and proved to be of a very superior quality." [45]

On October 6 Merritt notified General Meigs that Eads had just handed in "bills for work and materials furnished by him for the Gun Boats to the amount of $175,000." Of this figure, $20,000 was for iron plating currently en route from Cincinnati to St. Louis. According to contract, the boats were to be delivered at Cairo in four days, but, he continued, it would be at least a week before the first of the Carondelet hulls slid down the ways, and another one to two weeks before the contractor would be able to make delivery.[46]

When, on the eighth, Merritt forwarded the estimate of work on which the government was to make its fourth payment, he called to Meigs's attention a problem that had arisen regarding the iron plating. The specifications had called for seventy-five tons, but the area to be covered abreast the engines and boilers on each boat required ninety-one tons. If the forward casemate shield were to be plated as projected by the naval officers, an additional twenty-five tons of iron would be required for each boat.[47]

It was October 12, 1861, two days after the date designated in the contract for the delivery of all the ironclads at Cairo, that the first vessel was launched. A large number of people had gathered at the Carondelet Marine Ways on that Saturday afternoon to watch. At four o'clock the first ironclad built in the Western Hemisphere "was gradually lowered into the 'father of waters' upon the ways on which it was built, and such was the noiseless, and almost imperceptible manner of the operation," wrote one observer, "that we found the boat floating gracefully upon the water, and nobody hurt, and not even a lady frightened."

When launched, the boat, which was destined to carry the name Carondelet, was in an advanced stage of construction. The Daily Democrat reported that a few more days' work would suffice to get her ready for her trials. People familiar with river boats, on inspecting the craft, were delighted to see that the work had been "done in a very substantial, and smooth manner." [48] According to people close to Captain Eads, a second ironclad, subsequently christened St. Louis, was to be launched on the fifteenth, while the other two would be eased into the water by the end of the third week of October. The four Carondelet gunboats, it was confidently predicted, would be ready for service, with full armament, by the first of November.[49] The three other Eads gunboats were then building at Mound City. The Cairo was one of them.

3

THE CAIRO
ON PATROL DUTY

THE first of the Eads ironclads to be fitted out, the *St. Louis,* was in commission by the end of the year. The other six—the *Carondelet* (the first to be launched), *Cairo, Pittsburg, Louisville, Cincinnati,* and *Mound City*—were not commissioned until January, 1862, some three months after the delivery date specified.

In the meantime, Commander Rodgers, so concerned with laying the groundwork for the army's Western Flotilla that he failed to cultivate his punctilious superior, General Frémont, had been relieved of his assignment. His replacement was Captain Andrew H. Foote, another navy veteran. Foote assumed charge of the flotilla on September 6, 1861, establishing temporary headquarters at St. Louis. Other naval officers reached St. Louis and Cairo and were assigned various duties, afloat or ashore. Commander Henry Walke was rushed into duty by Foote to supervise the fitting out of one of the timberclads purchased by Rodgers. On October 5 Foote sent another new arrival, Commander Roger Perry, to Cairo to take charge of ordnance, quartermaster, and commissary supplies for the flotilla.

Foote soon discovered that he had inherited a number of problems with his new command. First, he needed money, powder, and small arms. Second, Eads was late in meeting the delivery date set for the ironclads. Third, the navy found it difficult to recruit men for service on the gunboats—up to October 19, only one hundred men had volunteered. Fourth, Foote saw many of his orders overridden by some of the general officers, hamstringing his efforts to get the boats ready. Letters of complaint to Welles and Fox pointed out that he should be named flag officer. Secretary Welles acted immediately

27

and issued an order appointing him "flag-officer in command of the U. S. naval force employed on the Mississippi River and its tributaries." [1]

It was Foote who decided, late in October, that the Eads ironclads would be named for cities and towns along the Ohio and upper Mississippi rivers, thus junking Eads's suggestion that they be named for Union military leaders. Also late in October Foote received news from Eads that the contractor would be compelled to "stop work to-night on the gun-boats for want of funds." [2] Foote's prompt appeal to Quartermaster General Meigs brought results; pressure exerted by Meigs won for Eads a much-needed $223,750 to which he was entitled by his fourth estimate. [3] Foote was hopeful that he might have the seven city-class vessels in his hands by December 1. But, he cautioned Assistant Secretary Fox, additional time would be needed, even after delivery, to equip and get the craft ready for service.

Frémont had ordered Foote to have the big guns and stores shipped to St. Louis because of a lack of storage facilities at Cairo. Now, with the Mississippi at low stage, these items would have to be transported to Cairo, as there was insufficient water over some of the bars on the river between St. Louis and Cairo to float the gunboats, if they were fully armed and equipped.

On November 15 Fox telegraphed Foote that five hundred seamen would leave Washington by rail for Cairo immediately. [4] When this wire reached Foote the next day, he promptly alerted Commander Perry, who would make arrangements to accommodate the men pending the arrival of the receiving boat *Maria Denning*. [5] If all went on schedule, the sailors should reach Cairo by Monday, the eighteenth. [6]

The week before, Foote had put Commander Benjamin M. Dove in charge of the *Maria Denning*. He was to see that ordnance stores and provisions assembled by the navy at St. Louis for the ironclads were loaded aboard his vessel, which would then proceed to Cairo and remain there to be used as a receiving boat. [7] At Cairo, Dove was to take on board the five hundred men then en route from Washington. [8] Until these men were assigned billets on the gunboats, they were to be organized into fatigue parties to assist Commander Perry in receiving and storing material for the ironclads. [9] When the boat reached Cairo on the twentieth, Dove was disappointed to discover that the men had not arrived.

On November 21 the bluejackets detrained in Cairo and were re-

ceived aboard the *Maria Denning*. There the easterners were greeted
by a number of "Western men, principally steamboat hands, with a
few Lake sailors." [10] At muster, Dove found that fifty-eight failed to
answer when their names were called out. The missing men had
apparently dropped off the train at various stops along the way.[11]

Three days later Fox cautioned Foote that he seriously questioned
the department's ability to provide any more sailors from the east
coast. Strenuous efforts were being made to ship recruits, but the
large number of vessels being added to the oceangoing squadrons
absorbed them almost as soon as the ink on their enlistment papers
was dry. Even so, Foote could rest assured that he would have first
call on any men who could be spared from the Atlantic coast.[12]

On November 19 Foote reminded Eads that earlier in the month
he had warned him that, because of falling water in the Mississippi
and the lateness of the season, it could be necessary to dispatch the
four Carondelet boats to Cairo by the twentieth. Since the ironclads
were still moored off the ways, he now felt called upon to renew his
instructions. The four boats would be sent to Cairo immediately, and
there be completed. An inspection had satisfied Foote that they were
in condition to undertake such a voyage. Guards would be provided
to protect the boats on the run down.[13]

News of the problems confronting the navy in getting the Carondelet ironclads down to Cairo spread like wildfire. The St. Louis
Daily Democrat of November 23 informed its readers that there was
considerable apprehension that "the gun-boats not quite finished, will
not be able to get out of the Mississippi river, unless they are sent
away within a few days." According to the latest reports from Hat
Island, there were only five and a half feet of water over the shoals;
and the gunboats reportedly drew five feet. Several days of cold weather
could be expected to lower the stage of the river by another foot,
and would trap the ironclads on the upper Mississippi.

The first two vessels to get under way were the *St. Louis* and the
Pittsburg. The *Pittsburg* grounded on the run down the river, and only
after much hard work she was pulled off the bar. She reached Cairo
around noon on the twenty-ninth and tied up at the levee near the
St. Louis, which had arrived the previous evening.[14] No time was
lost in getting the craft ready for active service. On the night of December 1, in a terrible snow storm, the *Pittsburg* was moored alongside the *Maria Denning* to receive her armament.[15]

Foote had written General Meigs on November 30 that the two remaining Carondelet vessels would start for Cairo on the first or second of December. Their engines had already passed inspection. Since the ironclads were nearly ready to be turned over to the government, Foote wanted "instructions as to the mode of accepting" them.[16] The *Carondelet* and the *Louisville* left St. Louis on the second. Foote wired Commander Dove to send the steamer *William H. Brown* to meet the vessels. Before starting upstream from Cairo, the steamer took aboard a 12-pounder boat howitzer and an armed guard of sixty men.[17] The vessels encountered no difficulties on their run downstream, and on the fifth they tied up near the receiving boat *Maria Denning*. Foote wired Secretary Welles that the four Carondelet boats were at Cairo and that he expected two weeks to elapse before the contractor would be finished with them. While Eads was completing his contract, time would not be wasted because the navy would employ this period to outfit the boats for combat.

Foote was still plagued with the problem of providing crews to man the gunboats. Eleven hundred men, in addition to those already sent, were needed immediately, he informed Welles. An air of urgency had been added to the situation by news that the Rebels had several strongly-armed and well-manned gunboats at Columbus, Kentucky, and were said to have an equal number on the Tennessee River. The Columbus vessels had reconnoitered the Mississippi below Cairo on the first, causing rumors to spread that the Confederates planned an early attack on the big Union base.

Foote wired General McClellan on December 6, informing him that the Western Flotilla consisted of twelve gunboats, of which three (the Rodgers timberclads) were in commission and nine still in the contractor's hands. Two of the latter were the converted *Benton* and *Essex*. If Eads turned over to the government by the eighteenth the seven city-class vessels, as he had promised, Foote felt he could have them in fighting trim in ten days, provided Welles dispatched the addditional personnel required to man them.[18]

A copy of this wire was forwarded to Major General Henry W. Halleck's St. Louis headquarters. (Frémont had been sacked and General Halleck had been placed in charge of the Department of the Missouri.) Foote also informed Halleck that the prospects for a Confederate thrust against Cairo had greatly diminished. But to assure Halleck, Foote revealed that two of the three timberclads, the *Tyler* and *Lexington,* were anchored off Fort Holt while the ironclad *St.*

Louis, though still in the hands of the contractor, was ready to defend herself.[19]

The *Cairo, Mound City,* and *Cincinnati,* under construction at Mound City, would not be finished for a fortnight, according to the latest word from Eads. Meanwhile, the task of fitting out the Carondelet ironclads was being expedited. Carpenters and engineers were busy from dawn to dark. Machinery had been adjusted, guns secured at their proper ports, and ammunition taken aboard.

On December 17 Assistant Secretary of Navy Fox shifted to the army the onus for finding personnel to man the ironclads. On that day he telegraphed Foote that General McClellan had issued orders for Halleck to detail eleven hundred unarmed soldiers stationed in St. Louis to serve aboard the gunboats. To command two of the new ironclads, Fox promised to send Lieutenants Nathaniel C. Bryant and Egbert Thompson.[20] Foote, who had previously promised one of the Mound City vessels (the *Cairo*) to his friend Lieutenant S. Ledyard Phelps, replied that if lieutenants junior to Phelps could not be sent to the Mississippi Valley, he would accept Bryant and Thompson.

Meanwhile, another serious problem had arisen. General Halleck, throwing a bombshell, notified Foote that officers of volunteer regiments slated to serve aboard the vessels of the flotilla must accompany the enlisted men. Army personnel were to be regarded as "marines," and were to be under the command of no naval officer, except the gunboat captains.[21]

On December 28 Foote notified Halleck that "volunteer soldiers" were needed on the gunboats as seamen. Since the complement of officers had been filled, there were no additional billets open, and no staterooms or other accommodations had been provided aboard the ironclads for additional officers. What the navy wanted was "men to fight the guns and work the boats." It was presumed that soldiers who had volunteered to go aboard the boats would be discharged by the army and would be reenlisted in the navy. Halleck was requested to send no more volunteers to Cairo until the subject was resolved.[22]

A copy of Foote's message to Halleck had been forwarded to the Navy Department. Answering the communication, Fox promised to see General McClellan at once and straighten out the problem of the army volunteers.[23] However, McClellan backed Halleck; so on the last day of the year, the Navy Department telegraphed Foote that enlisted army personnel could not be detailed to the gunboats "without their officers." General Halleck was authorized to discharge any soldiers who would volunteer for service aboard the ironclads.[24]

In the meantime, Superintendent Litherbury, on December 21, had inspected the city-class ironclads. In signing the inspection reports, Foote did not presume to release the contractor "from any obligation of forfeiture he may be under by terms of his contract in not completing the same within the time specified." The naval officer did not feel that the question of liability to forfeiture came under his jurisdiction. He likewise declined to accept formally the gunboats from Eads, as he considered the contract as obliging the contractor to "fully complete them for their armament, and therefore requiring him to do all extra work necessary to this end." [25]

While Foote appealed to the Navy and War departments for seamen to man the ironclads, Eads hastened to Washington to collect the unpaid balance on his contract ($148,925) and the $85,000 to which he believed himself entitled for extra work called for by Foote and Rodgers. Several days passed before he was able to see General Meigs, and then the interview proved most distressing. The ironclads had not been completed on time, Meigs held; therefore the government was entitled to damages.[26] But Eads tried again before returning to Cairo on December 29 and sent a note to Meigs, pointing out that it was "a matter of much importance to me and others to whom I am indebted, that I should know how soon I may reasonably look for the payment of the accounts left with you." [27]

Prior to his departure for the capital, Eads had notified Foote that the three Mound City ironclads should be ready to move downstream to the Cairo navy yard on Christmas. Two of the vessels (the *Mound City* and *Cincinnati*) arrived as promised. Foote was annoyed on learning that it would be the thirtieth before the *Cairo* came down. Addressing a note to Superintendent Litherbury, he warned, "I am waiting to put the guns on board the boats and can not wait longer than to-day." A steamer would be sent up to the marine ways early the next day to tow the *Cairo* down. If she were unready to send off, Litherbury was to draft a letter to be forwarded to Washington stating the cause. "The battery," fumed Foote, "must be put on board this week." [28]

The *Cincinnati* was commissioned on January 9 and the *Carondelet* the following day. Pulling out into the channel of the Ohio, the two ironclads anchored near the *St. Louis,* which had been in commission for several weeks. Telegraphing the good news to Secretary Welles, Foote pointed out that he had "but one-third of a crew" (sixty men) for each gunboat, while the carpenters and machinists had all but finished fitting out the vessels.[29]

President Lincoln, as expected, was tremendously interested in the progress being made in getting the ironclads ready for combat. Assistant Navy Secretary Fox notified Flag Officer Foote on January 10 that the "President desires immediately a full report of the number of your gunboats, armament, crews, etc." [30]

The next day Foote posted the requested data. He reported that of the twelve gunboats assigned to his flotilla, five (the timberclads *Tyler, Lexington,* and *Conestoga,* and the ironclads *St. Louis* and *Essex*) were in commission, with full armaments and crews. At the moment, the remaining seven craft (the sister ironclads *Cairo, Carondelet, Mound City, Pittsburg, Louisville, Cincinnati,* plus the converted *Benton*) were not yet "fully completed, or out of the contractor's hands." This latest delay had been caused by the necessity of moving the steam drums to the top of the boilers. On the run down from Carondelet, the engines of several of the city-class vessels had "worked water" instead of steam, endangering the engines. In addition, the carpenters had not completed the pilothouses. Foote in the meantime had seen that all the vessels were armed.[31]

The most pressing problem now was men. In response to an appeal, the Navy Department had answered that a Massachusetts regiment, without its officers, would be ordered to the Cairo Naval Station for service aboard the gunboats. These men, however, had not arrived; and the flag officer, if he were to man the seven ironclads, needed a thousand men immediately. If and when the requisitioned men arrived, he promised to have the boats ready for action within five days.[32] Foote again notified the Navy Department on January 12 that he had to have a thousand men to man the boats; meanwhile, he was "putting their ordnance and other equipments and stores on board." [33]

The next day he directed Lieutenant James M. Prichett to take temporary charge of the *Cairo,* pending the return of Lieutenant Phelps from a sweep up the Cumberland and Tennessee rivers with the *Conestoga* and the *Lexington.*[34] Prichett was to "attend to receiving and storing her ordnance and other equipment and stores" so she could be commissioned by January 15. [35]

Commanders Alexander M. Pennock and Roger N. Stembel, and Master Carpenter James R. McGee inspected the seven city-class ironclads on the fifteenth. The three-man team certified that the work on them had been "completed according to the terms of the contract with the Government, excepting the time at which they ought to have been finished and delivered at Cairo."[36] After examining the certificate filed by the team, Foote formally accepted the seven gunboats from Captain Eads.[37] Foote on the sixteenth placed the *Cairo, Mound City, Louisville,* and *Pittsburg* in commission. Chunks of ice were drifting down the Ohio as the boats pulled out into the channel and anchored beside their sisters. By the twentieth the vessels, except for the shortage of men to fill the billets, would be ready for combat.

On the day that the *Cairo* was accepted by the government, Foote wrote his friend Lieutenant Phelps that the Navy Department had ordered Lieutenants Egbert Thompson and William Gwin to report to the flotilla. Since they were junior to Phelps, this entitled him to command one of the ironclads; and the flag officer had earlier reserved the *Cairo* for him. "She is," Foote wrote, "of a light draft of water and promises to be one of the fastest of the boats." As soon as Phelps relieved Prichett, the junior officer would take charge of Phelps's former command, the timberclad *Conestoga.* Phelps was to report to Foote as soon as it was convenient and his accounts were in order so that he could be placed in charge of the *Cairo.*[38]

Phelps returned to Paducah on the eighteenth and learned that he had been assigned to the *Cairo.* After filing his report of the expedition up the Tennessee to within sight of Fort Henry, he thanked the flag officer for his "kindly interest." He hoped that in his new command, he might continue to merit Foote's approbation. Since he had some unfinished business aboard the *Conestoga,* Phelps indicated that it would be several days before he could take over the *Cairo.*[39] But before he could assume command of the ironclad, Lieutenant Nathaniel Bryant arrived at Cairo, and because Bryant was the ranking lieutenant in Foote's command, the flag officer was compelled to give him the *Cairo.* Foote wrote Phelps of this development: "I regret to inform you that it will not be in my power at present to assign you to the command of one of the ironclad steamers." However, to ease the hurt of this message, Foote informed his friend that within a "very few months you will be assigned to one of the armored gunboats."[40]

The *Cairo's* captain had been born into a shipbuilding family on March 27, 1823, at Nobleborough, Maine. In his early boyhood Bryant had attended Lincoln Academy and was subsequently sent to Augusta, where he completed his secondary education. At an early age he demonstrated an aptitude for mathematics and the languages which gained him a conditional appointment as midshipman in the United States Navy in December, 1837. After studying in Boston under the supervision of his uncle, Captain Joseph Smith, Bryant, at the age of fourteen, passed the necessary examinations and was issued his commission in October, 1838. The years immediately prior to the Civil War he spent at Mare Island Navy Yard. In April, 1861, he was ordered to duty with the home squadron; shortly thereafter he was assigned to the steam sloop *Richmond*.[41]

When Lieutenant Bryant assumed command of the *Cairo,* he was without a gunnery crew to man the ironclad. But by the end of the month, the situation had improved somewhat. Sufficient volunteers had been secured from the army to enable Foote to fill the billets on the *Cairo, Cincinnati,* and *Carondelet.*

Among the men who reported aboard the *Cairo* in January, 1862, was fourteen-year-old George R. Yost. He had signed up as a First Class Boy, and during the next eleven months he kept a journal. He reported that the commissioning ceremony was very impressive, "the officers, except for Lieutenant Bryant, and men being sworn into the U. S. Naval service at the same time."

For sixteen days thereafter, the ironclad lay at anchor off Cairo, taking aboard provisions and ammunition. Yost said of the activities:

. . . a large number of the crew were engaged in putting the finishing touches to the vessel. The entire boat was newly painted, the decks were holy stoned until they were white as a linen sheet, and everything made snug and clean from top to bottom, and from stem to stern. Daily exercises with "great guns," also with small arms was the invariable rule; so that long before we were in actual battle, every man was thoroughly at "home" in his special position. Our Executive Officer, Hiram K. Hazlett, assigned the crew to their several stations, and superintended them at drill. There were thirteen heavy guns, ranging from . . . [42-] pounder rifled to 32 pounder smooth bore, on the gundeck. Also a twelve pounder howitzer on the upper deck. In addition, there was a large supply of rifles, with sword bayonets; revolvers; double-edge cutlasses and boarding pikes, for every man; in the effective use of which, every member of the crew speedily became proficient. I was stationed at the starboard bow gun, (Powder boy) a . . . [42-] pounder rifle.[42]

Preparatory to leaving for the Tennessee River and the attack on Fort Henry, Flag Officer Foote on February 1 placed Commander A. H. Kilty in charge at Cairo.[43] When he moved against Fort Henry, Foote would have with him the *Essex,* three of the Eads ironclads (the *Cincinnati, Carondelet,* and *St. Louis*) and the three timberclads. Four of the city-class boats, including the *Cairo,* would be left behind. While Ulysses Grant and Foote were operating against Fort Henry, the *Cairo* was to anchor off Fort Holt, Kentucky. Bryant was to assume a position that would enable his guns to protect the approaches to the fort in case a Confederate column from Columbus, Kentucky, advanced and assailed that stronghold.[44]

But on February 5 Kilty received news from Bryant that the *Cairo's* engines were not functioning properly. Because manpower was at a premium, Kilty instructed Benjamin Dove, now in command of the *Louisville,* to proceed to the anchorage near Fort Holt. There he took aboard the crew of the *Cairo,* leaving Bryant only enough men to bring his craft to Cairo for repairs. The *Louisville,* for the time being, would remain anchored off Fort Holt.[45]

By the seventh the *Cairo,* with a skeleton crew, was back at her anchorage, about three miles below Cairo. "While we lay there, at anchor," George Yost noted in his journal, "the only incident of special interest which transpired, was the visit made by a Rebel boat bearing a flag of truce; we brought her to with one shot across her bows: then in answer to her signals we sent a boat with officer and an armed crew, under cover of our guns, to ascertain their desires. Their business, it turned out, related to a proposed exchange of prisoners." [46]

News of the victory scored by the ironclads at Fort Henry made the men aboard the *Cairo* curse the ill fortune that had caused their boat to remain behind. Three of the *Cairo's* sisters and a fourth ironclad, the *Essex,* in seventy-five minutes had hammered the seventeen-gun earthen fort guarding the Tennessee River so severely that the Rebels hoisted the white flag. Word of the fighting at Fort Donelson did little to chill the ardor of the *Cairo's* crew. During that battle, on the thirteenth and fourteenth, the flotilla underwent a tremendous pounding by the fort's water batteries. The damage suffered was severe enough to put half of the force out of action long enough to lose the fight for the Yankees. Indeed, the *Cairo's* men complained that had it not been for the breakdown, the *Cairo,* and not the *Louisville,* would have been present at Fort Donelson.[47]

Although the last of the ironclads had been commissioned on January 16, the government had not yet paid Eads the money he believed he was entitled to. His creditors were becoming impatient. The St. Louis shipbuilder had made another trip to Washington during the fourth week of January and again presented his case to General

Meigs. Once more he called attention to the government's lack of promptness in paying the estimated percentages. He pointed out that much time had been lost in meeting numerous change orders which had been issued by Litherbury concerning iron plating, and that weeks had been lost correcting variations from specifications in the vessels' machinery.[48] Although he gave a thorough airing to his grievances, his arguments failed to impress the Quartermaster General, who preferred to talk of Eads's failure to have the boats at Cairo on the designated date. Finding his words wasted on Meigs, Eads telegraphed Foote, "I can obtain no assurance of receiving a dollar and must return as I came." [49]

On February 5 Eads again contacted Meigs's office. This time, the contractor protested that, discounting his claims for extra work, as of November 2 he had done $10,500 more work than he had bargained for. He admitted that according to the contract he was liable to forfeit $1,750 each day on the seven boats, after the day stipulated for their completion, October 10. But, at the same time, he countered, the government had contracted to pay him a certain percentage every twenty days. "The Govt. failed to pay me according to agreement, and I failed to build the boats in time—Question, am I liable to forfeiture?" Eads wrote.[50]

General Meigs now decided that it might be wise to let a member of his staff, O. M. Dorman, make a study of the contract. Reviewing the contract and Litherbury's affidavit of December 21, Dorman found that the vessels were received by the government on January 15, 1862, ninety-seven days after the date stipulated. One important question involved in the case, however, could not be resolved by the attached documents; and this revolved around Eads's claim that "the failure to finish & deliver the Boats in the time specified in the contract arose from two causes, namely: the deviations from the specifications, and the failure [of the government] to make the payments according to contract."

Dorman felt that the considerable increase in the iron plating, which was not easily procured, lent some "probability, to the allegation that these changes may have occasioned some of the delay in completing and delivering the boats." But how much, he was unable to determine. It was unlikely, Dorman held, that the alterations required by Foote after the boats arrived at Cairo were contemplated to be done within the sixty-four-day period. Consequently, the "difference between the time of the delivery of the Boats at Cairo and their final acceptance" was twenty-five days; and for this period there could be no forfeiture on the part of Captain Eads.

An investigation of Eads's claim that the government's failure to make prompt payments on the estimates had delayed him in the performance of his contract demonstrated that the contractor was correct. Dorman found that there had been "delinquency on the part of both parties to the contract & yet . . . neither party declared a forfeiture," but went on as though there had been no delay; therefore, he felt that neither party could enforce a strict performance.

Should the government accept December 21 as the delivery date, as Dorman recommended, the forfeiture for seventy-two days would be $126,000; if January 15 were the day determined upon, the forfeiture for ninety-seven days would be $169,750. From the papers submitted, it was found that Eads, had his contract been fulfilled according to its terms, was still due $148,925.45. In addition to this figure, $85,856.86 in extra work had been approved by Flag Officer Foote.[51]

General Meigs forwarded to the Comptroller, on February 15, Eads's claims against the government for building the seven ironclads, along with Dorman's memorandum. Whatever was allowed on the contractor's claim was to be paid out "of the appropriation for gunboats on the Western rivers." [52]

Comptroller J. Madison Cutts, undoubtedly heartened by the electrifying news of the success just scored by the ironclads at Fort Henry, held that there had been no damage to the public interest by Eads's failure to have the vessels ready for service by October 10. In returning the correspondence to Meigs, Cutts observed, "I have no doubt of the legal right of Mr. Eads to payment from the Government of the amount reserved under the contract." United States bonds in the sum of $234,781.31 were issued to Captain Eads, and his account was marked settled.[53] Thus, for the better part of six weeks, the city-class ironclads, while officered by the navy and manned by mixed crews of soldiers and bluejackets, had operated against the Confederates with their title in dispute.

Flag Officer Foote returned to Cairo on February 16 to supervise the repair of the more seriously damaged ironclads and to see that the squadron on the Cumberland was reinforced by the *Cairo* and the mortar boats. He believed that if all went well, he would be back before Fort Donelson by the twenty-fifth. As his first order of business,

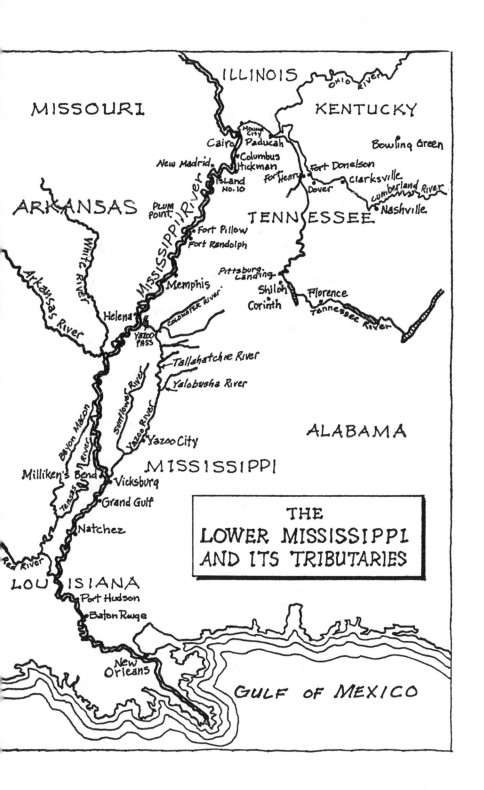

THE
LOWER MISSISSIPPI
AND ITS TRIBUTARIES

Foote, learning that the *Cairo* was now fully manned and ready for action, issued instructions for Lieutenant Bryant to start for the Cumberland immediately. Accompanied by six mortar scows and their tugs, the *Cairo* hoisted her anchors and started up the Ohio River. The convoy soon encountered a steamboat coming downstream with the news that the Fort Donelson Confederates had surrendered unconditionally to General Grant earlier in the day. As only a few men aboard the *Cairo* had heard a shot fired in anger, complaints were loud and long that the war would be over before they had a chance to burn any powder.

Within forty-eight hours Foote had completed his business at Cairo and was ready to return to the Cumberland. Boarding the *Conestoga* on the eighteenth, he headed back up the Ohio on the speedy timberclad. Foote reached fallen Fort Donelson early on the nineteenth and discovered that the slow-moving *Cairo* had arrived only a few hours earlier. Before many minutes had passed, the flag officer had spoken with General Grant and had drafted plans for a sweep up the Cumberland to Clarksville, Tennessee. Foote would take with him on his reconnaissance the *Cairo* and *Conestoga*.[54]

As it was well known that the *Cairo* would be unable to keep up with the timberclad, Lieutenant Bryant requested and received permission to get under way while the *Conestoga* was waiting for Foote to return from his meeting with Grant. Even with the head start, the *Conestoga,* which was one of the "racer breed of boats and walked the water like a thing of life," soon overtook the lumbering ironclad.[55]

In mid-afternoon the gunboats rounded a sharp bend in the river opposite Linwood Landing, several miles below Clarksville. Directly ahead loomed a high bluff, its crest scarred by a recently erected earthwork—Fort Defiance. As the bluejackets manning the *Cairo's* bow battery trained their guns on the fortification, the lookouts saw a white flag snapping in the breeze. The stronghold had been evacuated the day before. On the boats steamed, passing the fort's silent guns. As they approached the confluence of the Red and Cumberland rivers, the Federals sighted a second earthwork, Fort Clark. Here no flag was flying. As the *Cairo* and *Conestoga* were heaving to, a "very dirty white flag" crept slowly up the staff. Flag Officer Foote sent a party led by Lieutenant Phelps to take possession of the fort and to raise the Stars and Stripes. From the townspeople, the sailors learned that at Fort Clark a strong wind had blown down the white flag and it had been soiled by the heavy rain of the previous evening.[56]

Reaching Clarksville at 3 P.M., Foote sent for the "city fathers"; Judge Thomas W. Wisdom, Cave Johnson, and the mayor responded to the flag officer's summons. From these three, the naval officers learned that the Rebel military, advised of their approach, had evacuated the city after setting fire to the vital bridges which carried the tracks of the Memphis, Clarksville, and Louisville Railroad across the Cumberland and Red rivers. Further questioning by Foote revealed that two-thirds of the citizens had fled from the place panic stricken. To calm the populace, Foote assured his visitors that "we came not to destroy anything but forts, military stores, and army equipments." [57]

Landing parties from the Cairo and Conestoga visited the telegraph office. There they found a copy of a dispatch signed by W. H. Allen, who had been in charge of the small Confederate force in Clarksville. Allen had notified Nashville that the gunboats were coming and that a demolition team had set fire to the railroad bridges, but that the one spanning the Cumberland was burning so slowly the fire would "probably go out before it falls." [58]

After questioning the Clarksville inhabitants, the Federals became satisfied that the Nashville populace was in a state of panic and that the capital city would be surrendered without a fight if a squadron of gunboats ascended the Cumberland River. According to the citizens, Confederate General Albert S. Johnston, after evacuating Bowling Green, Kentucky, was concentrating his troops at Columbia, Tennessee.

The next morning (the twentieth) Foote, leaving the Cairo to hold Clarksville, returned to Dover, intending to organize a task force consisting of two or three ironclads, one timberclad, and six mortar boats. With this force he proposed to go to Nashville, capitalizing on the Rebels' fear of the gunboats.[59] But on reaching Dover, he was shown a telegram that Grant had received from General Halleck ordering the gunboats not to "go higher than Clarksville." After the Clarksville railroad bridges had been destroyed, the mortar boat flotilla and all the gunboats, except one, were to return to Cairo.[60] The reason for this urgent message was a decision by the Washington authorities to use the fleet for the reduction of the "Gibraltar of the West"—Columbus, Kentucky.[61]

Foote was disappointed because the Cumberland River was high and he and Grant thought they could take Nashville without difficulty. The flag officer had the Conestoga take him downriver to Paducah, where there was a telegraph line to Cairo. He remained at Paducah until the twenty-second, trying to get the Washington authorities to change their minds. While waiting to hear from Washington, Foote asked Grant to "hold on to the gun and mortar boats till you hear further from me." If the boats were already at Clarksville, so much the better because if permission for the move on Nashville were given, they would be closer to the objective, whereas if authority to proceed against Nashville were denied, the vessels could be rushed down to Cairo. If this were the case, Grant was authorized to retain for his use the ironclad *Cairo*.[62]

Hearing nothing more from Washington, Foote decided he had better not delay any longer. Before proceeding to Cairo, he dispatched a message to the Union authorities at Fort Donelson. They were to send "down to Cairo, with the utmost haste, and in tow of steamers, all the mortar boats" and one of the ironclads, either the *Louisville* or the *Cairo*. Foote would prefer to have the *Cairo,* if she could get under way as soon as the *Louisville*.[63] But the *Cairo* was still at Clarksville, so Grant ordered the *Louisville* to accompany the mortar boat flotilla downstream.

On February 19 Grant had alerted Brigadier General C. F. Smith to hold his division ready to occupy Clarksville. According to the news he had received from the navy, Grant informed Smith, there were no Confederate troops at Clarksville. But General Johnston might try to reoccupy that strategic point; so Smith should move there as rapidly as possible. Rations to last ten days would be taken along by the division quartermaster and issued to the troops before they went ashore.[64]

Two days passed before four regiments from Smith's division boarded steamboats at Dover and were dispatched up the Cumberland to Clarksville. With the *Cairo* standing by in case of trouble, Smith's infantrymen landed early in the afternoon. Patrols sent out by General Smith visited the warehouses, where they found considerable amounts of army stores, chiefly flour and bacon. The troops camped about the forts on the north bank of the Cumberland.[65] Meanwhile, working parties from the *Cairo* had been turned to wrecking sections of the railroad bridges that had escaped the flames and dismantling the batteries in the Clarksville forts. A large supply of coal was found at the steamboat landing, and Lieutenant Bryant saw that his vessel's bunkers were refilled.[66]

A number of Nashville citizens chartered the steamer *Iatan* on February 23 and had the captain take them down the Cumberland to Clarksville under a white flag. The group's leader told General

Smith that they had brought surgeons to attend Confederates wounded in the desperate Fort Donelson fighting. But Smith got the impression that the real object of their mission was to receive some assurance that their property would be protected when the Federals occupied Nashville. The spokesman told Smith that General Johnston and his army had fallen back from Nashville to Murfreesboro, after destroying bridges and commissary stores, and the artillery which could not be carried on the retreat.

When the *Iatan* started back to Nashville, she was accompanied by the *Cairo*. General Smith, having learned that Brigadier General Don Carlos Buell's vanguard was approaching the city, felt that the *Cairo* would be of assistance covering the Army of the Ohio as it crossed the Cumberland River.[67]

Sixteen steamboats carrying Brigadier General William Nelson's division of the Army of the Ohio were at this hour chuffing up the Cumberland River. Nelson's soldiers, who had been slated to reinforce Grant's army before Fort Donelson, had boarded the transports at West Point, Kentucky, on February 17. The suddenness of the Confederate surrender threw General Buell and his staff into a quandary about what should be done with Nelson's division. Several days were lost before Buell determined to rush Nelson's troops to Nashville by water.

The crowded transports began reaching Clarksville several hours after the *Cairo* had left for Nashville. While the first steamers to arrive were waiting for the others, two Union horsemen galloped into town with a dispatch from General Buell at Bowling Green. They had been twenty-five hours in the saddle. At the time that Buell drafted the dispatch Brigadier General O. M. Mitchel's column had not entered Nashville. The retreating Confederates had burned both bridges spanning the Cumberland at Nashville, as well as the steamboats at the wharf, so Buell felt that Nelson's fleet would probably have to ferry Mitchel's troops. Nelson was to push forward as rapidly as possible.[68]

He needed no urging—it was sufficient that his division might be the first Union troops in Nashville. Although some of the boats had yet to reach Clarksville, Nelson gave the order to shove off. Above Clarksville, the Cumberland was in full flood. Frequently the steamers "would for a shorter route leave the main channel and pass over farms, and by houses with the first story filled with water and the family in the upper, with their boats cabled to the building." [69]

A five-gun water battery was spotted late in the afternoon on an island at the head of Harpeth Shoals. Since it was known that the *Cairo* had left Clarksville for Nashville earlier in the day, Nelson determined not to stop to reconnoiter. That night there was no moon, but the sky was clear, so Nelson resolved to push on. Two hours later, the *Cairo* was sighted, laboring heavily upstream, towed by the *Iatan.* At 9:30 P.M. the *Cairo* pulled into the bank and tied up for the night. In compliance with his instructions, which were to follow the ironclad, Nelson reluctantly gave orders for the fleet to anchor. People familiar with the Cumberland told the Federals that they were within fifteen river miles of Nashville.[70]

February 25 dawned bright and beautiful on the reaches of the Cumberland below Nashville. Preceded by the *Cairo,* the convoy got under way. Seven river miles below Nashville, the lookouts on the ironclad spotted a high bluff on the left bank of the river crowned by the parapets of Fort Zollicoffer. Nelson signaled for the transport *Woodward* to come up to his flagboat. Calling to Colonel Jacob Ammen, the general told him to land several companies from the 36th Indiana and examine the earthworks. While the *Cairo* stood by, her crew at battle stations, Ammen led the men ashore. When they entered the fort, they found it a shambles. Several of the oak barbette carriages were still smouldering. Thirteen guns, ranging in size from 32-pounder smoothbores to 6½-inch rifles, had been dismounted or spiked. Scattered about the stronghold's interior were thousands of bars of railroad iron, many of them badly twisted by the terrific explosion that had shattered the magazine they had been intended to shield. Cotton bales used to reinforce the parapets had been burned.[71]

Ammen recalled his troops and returned to the river, where he reboarded the *Woodward* to resume the run up the Cumberland. With the *Cairo* in the lead, the convoy rounded a wooded point, and across a bend in the river the eager Federals caught their first glimpse of the smoke and spires of Nashville. Many of the buildings near the river displayed white flags, but though the officers and men strained their eyes, no Stars and Stripes were seen, and no United States flag floated over the State House. The crew of the *Cairo* and Nelson's soldiers knew that they would be the first Yankees in the city.[72]

Becoming impatient with the slow-moving *Cairo,* General Nelson ordered the captain of the *Diana* to pass the ironclad and make for Nashville at full speed. It was 9 A.M. when the flagboat touched the wharf, where a disorderly mob had collected. The *Cairo* stood with her guns trained on the city as the soldiers filed ashore.[73]

The Federals learned that Confederate cavalry had evacuated Nashville even as the first of Nelson's troops were scrambling ashore. Small squads of horsemen were reportedly still lurking in the outskirts, watching for an opportunity to cut off and capture unwary Union patrols.

Meanwhile, General Nelson prepared to cross the Cumberland and meet General Mitchel. Leaving Ammen in charge in the fallen capital, Nelson crossed the river. Reaching Mitchel's command post, Nelson was surprised to find his superior—General Buell. Buell had arrived the previous evening on the north bank of the Cumberland opposite the city with Mitchel's division, nine thousand strong. He had learned from his scouts, a few of whom had crossed the river, that Rebel cavalry was still in Nashville. Accordingly he had decided not to cross the Cumberland until he could do so in sufficient force "to run no great hazard." Observing the arrival of the *Cairo* and Nelson's division early on the twenty-fifth, Buell deemed it unwise to recall them lest it embolden the Confederates and have a bad effect on his troops' morale.[74] Now, protected by the guns of the *Cairo,* Buell began crossing Mitchel's division to the left bank of the Cumberland.

The Union had moved promptly to capitalize on its victories at Fort Henry and Fort Donelson. Within a month, units from General Grant's Army of the Tennessee were moving up the Tennessee River toward the vitals of the Confederacy. The advance of Grant's army from Fort Henry to Pittsburg Landing, twenty-two miles from Corinth, Mississippi, would be by boat. At Pittsburg Landing, Grant's soldiers would take position and await the arrival of Buell's Army of the Ohio, which was to march southwestward from Nashville.

Confederate General Albert S. Johnston at the same time was massing a powerful army at Corinth. Skillfully employing the railroads, which for a brief span of time made Corinth the most strategic point in the Confederacy, Johnston and his generals laid plans to smash Grant's army before Buell's troops could join him.

On March 16, the same day that his advance division went ashore at Pittsburg Landing, Grant addressed a note to his and Buell's immediate superior, General Halleck. Grant felt it would be wise to have an ironclad support the expedition he had sent up the Tennessee. Since the river was very high and still rising, there would be no danger of the vessel grounding.[75]

Halleck telegraphed Buell on the eighteenth, "If one or both of the gunboats in the Cumberland can be spared they should be sent to the

Tennessee." Halleck had previously asked Flag Officer Foote to dispatch four gunboats to the Tennessee for convoy duty, but because of the operations against Island No. 10 Foote had been able to send only two—the timberclads *Lexington* and *Tyler*.[76] At the same time, Halleck instructed Grant that all transports sent up the Tennessee were to be convoyed by a gunboat. Reports had reached St. Louis that the Confederates were sending troops from Corinth to attack steamboats plying the river between Savannah and Fort Henry.[77]

Grant informed Halleck on the nineteenth that General Smith had been directed to have one of the timberclads patrol the Tennessee between the Danville railroad bridge and Savannah.[78] Smith felt it would be imprudent to spare a gunboat at that time. But on the receipt of Halleck's communication of the eighteenth, one of the timberclads made a sweep from Fort Henry to Savannah, Tennessee, and returned on the twentieth. Henceforth, this operation would be repeated daily. In view of the high stage of the Tennessee, Grant assured his superior that there were "but few points on the river where light artillery could be taken to annoy our transports." [79]

On the same day Buell notified Halleck that he had detained only one gunboat, the *Cairo,* on the Cumberland, but that he had released her several days before in compliance with a request from Grant.[80] Much to his embarrassment, Buell discovered on the twenty-third that the *Cairo* was still on the Cumberland. He sent word to Lieutenant Bryant to take his ironclad up the Tennessee and report to General Grant.[81] The *Cairo,* along with the timberclads *Tyler* and *Lexington,* would have a dual mission on the Tennessee. Besides furnishing fire support to Grant's Army of the Tennessee, they were to keep Confederate partisans from attacking unarmed Union transports operating on the reaches of the river between Fort Henry and Pittsburg Landing.

The ironclad entered the Tennessee on the morning of the twenty-eighth and reached Savannah, seven miles below Pittsburg Landing, on the evening of March 31. Grant, who maintained his headquarters at Savannah, lost no time in putting the *Cairo* to work. Previously, he had contacted Brigadier General William T. Sherman, directing him to organize a landing party to send against batteries the Confederates had emplaced at Chickasaw, Alabama, and Eastport, Mississippi. Sherman was not to engage any force that might make a stand against him, but if the batteries were unsupported by infantry or cavalry, he was to destroy them. The *Cairo* and the timberclads *Lexington* and *Tyler* were to accompany Sherman's command.[82]

By daybreak on April 1, 1862, Sherman had loaded his troops on board the transports *Empress* and *Tecumseh.* Lieutenant Bryant at 6 A.M. notified Sherman that the gunboats were ready to cast off. Before the fleet had gone very far, it became apparent that if the *Cairo* did not have assistance, it would be dark before she reached Eastport. Hailing Lieutenant Shirk of the *Lexington,* Bryant told him to get a line aboard the lumbering ironclad. Thereafter, the fleet made better progress.

As the vessels approached the Eastport batteries, Bryant had the line cast loose. "General Quarters" sounded aboard the gunboats, and guns were loaded and run out. With the *Cairo* leading and the transports bringing up the rear, the gunboats closed with the batteries. At 1:30 P.M. the *Cairo* and the timberclads began hammering the battery above the mouth of Indian Creek. There was no reply. Followed by the *Tyler* and *Lexington,* the *Cairo* proceeded up the river cautiously, shelling all points where Rebel batteries had been pinpointed earlier. The run up to Chickasaw took slightly over an hour. As soon as the gunboats drew abreast of the Chickasaw battery and found it deserted, Bryant signaled for the vessels to cease fire.

Sherman now ordered his soldiers ashore. The steamer with the battalion of the 77th Ohio aboard pulled into the landing at Eastport, while the craft with the 57th Ohio proceeded to Chickasaw. Colonel William Mungen's soldiers of the 57th Ohio thronged ashore to find that the Chickasaw battery had been abandoned for some time. Recent high water on the Tennessee had flooded the low ground to the rear of the emplacement and had compelled the Rebels to remove the guns to Eastport, where the batteries were on elevated ground, accessible at all seasons from the country to the rear. All that he saw satisfied Sherman that Chickasaw had little importance as a military position.

Abandoning Chickasaw, Sherman went ashore at Eastport to discuss the situation with Colonel Jesse Hildebrand of the 77th Ohio and reconnoiter the area. Eastport Landing earlier had been under twelve feet of water, but with the river falling, the landing was the best he had seen on the Tennessee. The levee had been cleared of trees and snags, and hundreds of boats could tie up without confusion. Moreover, the soil was of sand and gravel and very firm, and the road leading inland was improved.

Colonel Hildebrand told Sherman that he had sent out scouts who had encountered Confederate cavalry after advancing about two miles. Not wishing to chance an engagement with the large force of Southerners reportedly based at Iuka, eight miles away, Sherman recalled the patrol and ordered Hildebrand to reembark his foot soldiers. The expedition returned to Pittsburg Landing, where it arrived well after dark.[83]

On March 26 news that the Tennessee River was falling reached Flag Officer Foote, who was on the Mississippi directing operations against Island No. 10. Alarmed that the *Cairo* and the two timberclads might be stranded, Foote forwarded a note to Commander Alexander Pennock in charge of the Cairo Naval Station to warn the captains of the three vessels. Before leaving the Tennessee, the captains were to consult General Grant.

Reports had reached Foote that the Confederates recently had completed thirteen gunboats at New Orleans. He feared that these vessels would be rushed up the Mississippi to reinforce the four or five gunboats below New Madrid. Along with the ram *Manassas,* this force could be expected to attack Foote's flotilla. Should the Federals be defeated, Pennock must hold the gunboats currently operating on the Tennessee ready to protect the Union bases at Cairo and Columbus.[84]

Foote's orders recalling the *Cairo* from the Tennessee reached General Grant shortly after the ironclad had returned from the expedition to Eastport and Chickasaw. Casting off from Pittsburg Landing on April 3, the *Cairo* proceeded to the Cairo Naval Station, where she arrived on the fifth. As the gunboat chugged along, the crew saw that the stage of the Tennessee was falling rapidly. On the day after the ironclad tied up at Cairo, the battle of Shiloh opened. At first, the Confederates swept everything before them. Driven from their camps, the Yankees, fighting desperately, fell back toward the landing. Late in the day a new line of defense was established, and, supported by the fire of the gunboats *Tyler* and *Lexington* and recently arrived troops from General Nelson's division of the Army of the Ohio, Grant's soldiers finally checked the Rebels' onslaught. Once again, as at Fort Henry and Fort Donelson, the *Cairo* had missed being at the right place at the right time.[85]

4

ACTION
OFF PLUM POINT

LIEUTENANT BRYANT kept his officers and men occupied during the six days his ironclad was tied up at Cairo. Eight weeks before, on February 14, four of the city-class gunboats had been battered by the Fort Donelson water batteries. The Rebels had scored damaging hits on the pilothouses of the *Louisville* and *St. Louis*, killing or wounding several men, among them Flag Officer Foote, who had been struck in the ankle by a flying piece of iron. In an attempt to avoid having the *Cairo* crippled by similar hits, Bryant determined to have the pilothouse altered.

Carpenters were put to work strengthening the three front panels, as they would be most exposed on the bows in fighting for which the ironclads were designed. Another course of white oak was added, increasing the thickness of the backing on these panels from twelve to nineteen and a half inches. No longer would the pilothouse be a perfect octagon; and when it was reassembled additional iron plating had to be added at the points where the reinforced panels joined the others. To help shield those in the cramped pilothouse from deadly fragments and splinters loosened by a projectile striking the armor plate, the carpenters lined the interior of the structure with pine paneling. Blacksmiths fashioned eight iron flaps; through the center of each a hole the size of a silver dollar was drilled. These flaps were hung on hinges which had been placed above the pilothouse ports. While engaging the foe, the flaps could be dropped, providing the personnel with additional protection but, at the same time, greatly increasing the difficulties of the pilots.[1]

By nightfall on April 10 Executive Officer Hazlett reported that the pilothouse had been reassembled. The *Cairo* was ready to rejoin

49

the fleet. Bryant opened the sealed orders, handed to him the previous evening, and found that he was to report to Foote at Island No. 10.

After a seven-hour trip downriver the next day, the *Cairo* reached the anchorage, and in response to a command, anchored near the powerful flagboat *Benton*. At 5 P.M. the signal to cast off was hoisted by the *Benton,* and the assemblage of transports, tugs, towboats, mortar boats, and gunboats got under way. The fleet dropped down the Mississippi several miles and anchored off New Madrid, Missouri, having passed the wrecks of two steamers scuttled by the Rebels during the operations that had preceded the fall of Island No. 10. [2]

Foote went ashore to iron out with Major General John Pope final details of the projected downriver expedition against Fort Pillow and other strongholds guarding the river approaches to Memphis. He was miffed on learning that not all the soldiers had embarked.[3] Pope told him that the last of the men would be aboard by the thirteenth. From Pope he also learned that seven Rebel gunboats were at anchor fifteen miles below New Madrid.[4] Foote felt that the vessels would flee at the approach of his flotilla and take cover under the guns of one of their downriver forts. Pope's headquarters informed him that the next point on the river where Confederate opposition would be encountered was Fort Pillow, Tennessee, eighty to ninety river miles above Memphis. The Rebels had forty heavy guns at the fort, and twelve hundred Negroes were working to strengthen the batteries commanding the river and the rifle pits covering the land approaches.[5]

On the morning of April 12 Foote decided not to wait for the army. Before hoisting the flags to get under way, he got in touch with Bryant. Since there was a chance the Rebel gunboats might fight, he did not want to be encumbered with the unwieldy mortar scows, each mounting a 17,000-pound, 13-inch mortar. Therefore he told Bryant to hold the *Cairo* at New Madrid for several hours before bringing down the mortar boats. At the designated hour the tugs lashed onto the scows and the *Cairo* weighed anchor.[6]

Although the lookouts kept sharp watch, no Confederate gunboats were seen as the ironclads made their trip down to Hale's Point, about fifty river miles below New Madrid. It was nearly dark before the *Cairo* and her brood reached the anchorage.[7] At daybreak on the thirteenth the sailors sighted a heavy smoke cloud approaching from upstream. Within the hour a large number of transports crowded with thousands of soldiers from General Pope's Army of the Mississippi appeared on the reach above Hale's Point.

At eight o'clock several Union soldiers chanced to be looking down-

re photographs in the National Archives show Eads ironclads under construction in
Carondelet, Missouri, shipyard near St. Louis. Timbering is well along and the five
lers are in place on one of the vessels. A picture of the *Cairo* in this stage would be
rly identical.

Only existing photograph of the U.S.S. *Cairo* taken before her sinking in the Yazoo River on December 12, 1862.

The *Cairo's* pilothouse clears the surface of the Yazoo, September, 1960. The structure's exterior was sheeted with 1¼-inch-thick iron plating, backed with many inches of wood—nearly 20 inches on the three front panels.

New England Naval and Maritime Museum diver Dick Suschena retrieves a mess plate from the sunken *Cairo*, October, 1962.

A 32-pounder naval gun comes out of th[
October, 1963.

Several giant logs had to be dragged out of th[
before the first lift wire could be slipped
under the *Cairo's* bow in the early phase of sal[

Barges in position alongside the sunken hulk during the 1963 operations. Th[
Cairo lay between the two, her bow to the bank, where she had been run i[
by her captain.

Cairo's casemate breaks water just before lift cables sliced into the gunboat's
ships, October, 1964. Paddle-wheel spiders can be seen above the surface in the
kground.

High point in the salvage, October 17, 1964. The Cairo is still intact.
Standing are Senator H. V. Cooper, Captain W. A. Bisso, Jr., author
Bearss, diver Ken Parks; seated, diver Sam Bongiovanni.

The casemate shield on the deck of a barge, November, 1964. Considerable damage was done to this portion of the *Cairo* during lifting operations; part of the port casemate fell back into the river and was lost.

The derrick *Cairo* prepares to place the ironclad's midships on a barge. The bottom of the vessel was flat, contrary to the belief of many of those involved in the raising. The 2½-inch-thick armor extends 55 inches below the ironclad's knuckle.

A rudder and rudder post rest on the bank of the Yazoo, November, 1964.
The city-class gunboats carried two such rudders.

The *Cairo's* cooking range was damaged when the midships collapsed
during lifting. Three of the vessel's boilers are in the background.

The stern portion after beaching in December, 1964. This portion, like the case-mate, suffered severe damage while being raised, when it slid back into the water, but luckily still in its lifting slings.

Ken Parks inspects the forward starboard hold, where enlisted men's personal gear was found.

river, as the leading gunboat of Confederate Captain Thomas B. Huger's fleet rounded the bend. During the night the Confederate ram *General Sterling Price* had spotted the Union ironclads, and Huger had decided to engage the enemy. By the time the Union fleet could weigh anchor, five additional Rebel gunboats were in view. The first ironclad to get under way was the *Benton,* closely followed by the *Carondelet* and *Cincinnati.* As they opened at long range with their bow guns, the leading Rebel vessel, the *Maurepas,* replied with a 9-inch Dahlgren, but the shell fell short. Huger saw that he had stirred up a hornet's nest, and signaled his boats to break off the engagement. Coming about, the Confederate boats started down the Mississippi at full speed. After the Federals had fired a number of shots, it became apparent to Foote and his officers that unless the Confederates ran aground, they were in little danger of being overtaken.[8] Aboard the *Cairo,* Lieutenant Bryant and his men chafed at the dull but necessary assignment—guarding the mortar scows—which kept them from joining in the affair.

The Union ironclads pursued the Confederate gunboats to within range of the Fort Pillow guns. At 11 A.M. Foote told his pilots to head back upstream. As soon as the *Carondelet, Cincinnati,* and *Mound City* joined the *Benton,* Foote took the four vessels to within a mile of the fort, so that he and his officers could study the works through their glasses. Beyond observing that the fortifications were extensive, with guns of the heaviest caliber, they were unable to learn much of the nature of the Rebel defenses. As the ironclads rounded to and started upriver, several of the fort's guns roared; the Southerners, however, overshot their marks. The Union boats headed for Plum Point on the Tennessee shore, where they tied up well out of range.[9]

Escorting the mortar scows and transports, the *Cairo* trailed the flotilla down the Mississippi. It was mid-afternoon before the convoy reached Plum Point. The army transports made for the Tennessee shore, while the *Cairo* and the mortar scows anchored on the Arkansas side of the river in the bend above Craighead Point.[10]

General Pope, accompanied by some of his staff, boarded the *Benton* to discuss the situation with Foote. The naval officer briefed Pope on the fort's strong position, cautioning him that an attack by the fleet could result in loss of most of the ironclads. Several citizens, whom he and his officers questioned, had warned that the people in the area were strongly secessionist in their feelings and that the fort would make stout resistance.

As the initial step in reducing Fort Pillow, the Federal leaders determined to have Captain Henry E. Maynadier, in charge of the mortar flotilla, moor his boats against the Arkansas shore, within range of the Confederates' big guns; the ironclads would protect the scows from a sudden dash by the Rebel gunboats. General Pope was to land his troops about five miles above Plum Point, advance across the neck, and assail the fort from the rear.[11]

Early on April 14 the tugs took seven of the mortar scows in tow and moved down to within a half mile of Craighead Point. As soon as the scows could be anchored, men were put to work felling trees whose limbs might get in the way of the 200-pound shells as they were hurled from the squat, ugly 13-inch mortars toward Fort Pillow, thirty-eight hundred yards away. The *Cairo* and several of her sister boats stood by with crews at battle stations and guns shotted to protect the scows and tugs in case the Confederate gunboats attempted to interfere.

Several hours after the last of the scows had been placed in position, fire broke out on the *Erebus*. Within a few minutes the tug was enveloped in flames. "She spun around in the river like a pyrotechnic grasshopper," an eyewitness recalled, "threatening to fire some mortar boats, the transports, and the magazine boat *Judge Torrence*, then lying below on the Arkansas side."[12] Three or four tugs and the *Cairo* rushed to her assistance, but could do nothing beyond rescuing the crew. One of the tugs succeeded in getting a line aboard the *Erebus* and towed her into shore, where she burned to the waterline.

At 2 P.M. there was a flash and a puff of black smoke followed by a loud roar as one of the mortars lofted a shell toward Fort Pillow. Captain Maynadier kept his men at the mortars for the next six hours, expending eighty rounds before he passed the word to stop firing. The bombardment of Fort Pillow by the mortars, except when foul weather or a sortie by the Rebel fleet compelled a suspension, was to continue for the next seven weeks.

Patrols sent out by the army to reconnoiter the land approaches to the fort and to find a way to bypass the Rebel stronghold were unsuccessful. Meanwhile, General Halleck had decided to redeploy Pope's army from the Mississippi to the Tennessee River. Pope was to move his army to Pittsburg Landing, leaving enough troops with Foote "to land and hold Fort Pillow should the enemy's forces withdraw."[13] If feasible, Halleck hoped that the Mississippi flotilla would continue to bombard Fort Pillow; if the Confederates abandoned the post, Foote was to take possession or proceed downriver, depending on what course of action he thought best.[14]

Foote and Pope learned of Halleck's plans on the evening of April 16. News that Pope's army was to be sent to the Tennessee discouraged Foote, because this move ruined the careful and hopeful plans hammered into shape in the campaign aimed at the capture of Fort Pillow and Memphis.[15]

Before casting off, Pope designated the two-regiment brigade led by Colonel Graham N. Fitch to remain behind. Though not under Foote's command, Fitch was to "render him every possible assistance in his operations upon the river." Fitch's men were to continue exploring the bayous and swamps on the Arkansas side, to determine if a practicable passageway for boats could be opened to the Mississippi below the fort.[16] The next day twenty transports crowded with Pope's soldiers started for the Tennessee River, as soon as there was light enough to see.

Meanwhile, the bombardment of Fort Pillow continued. Among the hundreds of sailors who watched the action was First Class Boy Yost of the ironclad *Cairo,* who recorded his thoughts:

I frequently saw as many as a dozen shells in the air at one time, crossing each other's fiery tracks; some of them burst in mid air, some landing in the water, others in the heavy woods on the Arkansas shore. One shell, a very large one passed directly over our upper deck, where I was sitting, missing our wheel house about twenty feet, and dropping into the water twenty yards away, where it burst, making a tremendous splashing of the water.[17]

At noon on the sixteenth, Captain Maynadier received orders to fire a shell every minute. Six of the mortar boats were towed into position, as the *Cairo, Carondelet,* and *St. Louis* stood by. Moments after the bombardment began, the Confederates replied with several of their big 8- and 10-inch columbiads mounted in an emplacement half way up the bluff.

The Confederate cannoneers served their pieces with uncanny accuracy. A 128-pound plunging shot from a 10-inch columbiad grazed hammock nettings on the *Carondelet* and pitched into the Mississippi next to her casemate, cascading water over sailors standing near the railing. A shell burst a few feet above the *St. Louis'* spar deck, and another struck the *Cairo.* However, these projectiles did little damage and inflicted no casualties.

The skill of the Rebel gunners forced the ironclads to keep constantly in motion. Lieutenant Bryant, as well as the captains of his sister vessels, could see that their boats were in danger of receiving a plunging shot through their unarmored decks. Such a projectile would have encountered little resistance in passing through the gun-deck and hull. Bryant and his brother officers swore at their inability to return the foe's fire with their guns. Though the big 42-pounder rifles would have had no difficulty hurling their 87-pound shells into Fort Pillow, the intervening trees effectively screened the Rebels.

Pained as he was by his Fort Donelson wound, Foote continued seeking ways and means of carrying out a successful attack on Fort Pillow. In a letter to Secretary Welles on April 23, he complained that "the capture of this place was predicated upon a large land force cooperating with the flotilla, or its being turned by the army marching upon Memphis from the east." [18] If Washington would only take into consideration the difficulty and danger involved in moving the slow ironclads downstream, Foote felt certain there would be no surprise at his apparent inaction.

He warned that the Rebels were strongly fortified and had eleven gunboats anchored below the fort. That very morning, a civilian had come from Fort Pillow with disconcerting news: he told Foote that the Confederates had increased the strength of their squadron to thirteen; although seven vessels were only river steamers with boilers and machinery sunk into holds for protection, all were armed with four to eight heavy guns, some rifled. The other boats were ironplated or protected by cotton bales. In addition, rumors were spreading that the steamer *Louisiana* (said to carry sixteen to twenty guns) was expected momentarily from New Orleans.

About this time Foote received news that a deepwater fleet led by Flag Officer David G. Farragut had entered the Mississippi and was preparing to attack the forts below New Orleans. Foote was depressed by this information, and became impatient for his flotilla to push on past Memphis, to meet the oceangoing ships before they got past New Orleans.

On the twenty-seventh of April a supply vessel arrived from Cairo with several 30-pounder Parrotts recently received from the East. One of these long-range weapons was allotted to the *Cairo*. Although it was Sunday, Lieutenant Bryant turned out a large fatigue party. Laboring under the supervision of Executive Officer Hazlett, the men mounted the rifle with its semicircular carriage on the forward section of the upper deck. By nightfall the task had been completed, and Yost boasted, "We are now in readiness for offensive and defensive warfare."[19]

As the days passed, Foote suffered more and more from the effects of his Fort Donelson wound. By mid-April he had become concerned enough to convene a three-man medical survey board. The doctors concluded that his condition was such that if neglected "it would probably soon totally unfit you for the performance of your important duties as flag-officer."[20] They suggested that he be permitted to return home to recover.

The report of the board of medical survey was forwarded to Washington. In an accompanying letter Foote informed Secretary Welles, "I place this matter solely on the grounds of what will best promote the efficiency of the flotilla, not on personal grounds, as I am ready, if called upon, to sacrifice my life in vindication of the flag of my country."[21] Foote then wrote Welles a personal note concerning his successor, and recommended Captain Charles H. Davis. The one-time Harvard student had seen duty with the South Atlantic Blockading Squadron. Earlier he had been a junior member of the Board of Detail, an agency established by the Navy Department and detailed the task of ascertaining the best way to get back the forts and harbors which had been taken over by the Rebels.[22]

Welles, after studying the correspondence bearing on Foote's injury, sent a telegram to Captain Davis, on temporary duty in New York, directing him, on completion of his assignment, to proceed to Cairo without delay and report to Flag Officer Foote.[23]

Welles also addressed a message to Foote. Under no circumstances, he wrote, did he wish to detach the flag officer as commander of the Mississippi flotilla, because it would boost Confederate morale to know that he had been disabled. If necessary, upon Davis' arrival in the West, Foote could go to Cairo or St. Louis for treatment, while retaining command of the flotilla.[24] The same boat which took Davis downstream from Cairo carried another dispatch from Welles, authorizing Foote to consult his own feelings about where he wished to travel to recuperate. Foote was again reminded that for the time being he would not be detached from his command.[25]

Davis reported to Foote aboard the *Benton* on May 8, a day filled with excitement. Union lookouts at daybreak sighted a smoke cloud rising from the river below Craighead Point. Soon three Rebel rams

—the *Sumter, General Bragg,* and *General Earl Van Dorn*—rounded the point, and the leader made for the area from where the mortar boats were in the habit of firing. As chance would have it, the Confederates had cast off too early to accomplish their mission, because at this hour the mortar boat assigned to shell Fort Pillow during the day was still anchored near the *Judge Torrence.* The ammunition boat and her brood were tied up to the Arkansas shore, a short distance above the *Cairo, Cincinnati,* and *Mound City.*

As soon as they discovered that their attempt to capture a mortar boat had been foiled, the Rebel gunboats came about, just as the three ironclads opened with their bow batteries. The range was too great for the 42-pounder rifles, and the shells struck the water well behind the rapidly retreating Confederates. Seeing this, Flag Officer Foote signaled the ironclads to cease fire.[26]

It was soon apparent that the emergency had passed. Two of the scows, accompanied by the *Cairo,* dropped down to their accustomed firing station. The *Cairo* stood guard while the gunners of *Mortar Boat No. 16* worked feverishly. By noon the Yanks had plastered the fort with sixty shells, and during the afternoon Captain Maynadier had his men slow their rate to three shells per hour. The Confederates' efforts to employ their guns to harass the Federals failed. Along toward dusk, the mortarmen secured their piece and the vessels returned to their anchorage.[27]

Foote was in such pain by this time that he could not concentrate on military affairs; now that Davis had arrived, he decided to heed the advice of the board of medical survey. On May 9, he took leave of his officers and men and boarded the transport *De Soto.* As the *De Soto* pulled away, "the officers and men pulled off their caps and gave three loud and hearty cheers" as a token of their esteem.[28] During Foote's absence, Davis was to perform all the duties of flag officer, and his orders were to be obeyed by the personnel assigned to the squadron.[29]

The first engagement between the Rebel and Union fleets occurred almost immediately after Davis came aboard the flag-steamer. At 3 P.M. that day a small steamer flying a white flag was observed coming upriver. Rounding the point, the Rebel stopped, and the tug *Jessie Benton* was sent down by Davis to communicate with her. After a short time the tug returned to the fleet with two Union surgeons who had been captured by the Southerners at Belmont, Missouri, the previous November and who were now being offered for exchange. A number of the Federals, both officers and enlisted men, were suspicious of this action on the part of their foe. Yost that evening jotted down in his diary: "I do not know the subject of the conference, but I suspect their *object was to observe* the positions and gauge the strength of our fleet." [30] How correct this view was, the events of the next day disclosed.

That night a council of war was held by the officers of the Confederate River Defense Fleet, including colorful Brigadier General Jeff Thompson of the Missouri State Guard. The Confederate leaders determined to attack the Yankees in the morning and destroy the ironclad which had been guarding the advance mortar scow near the head of Craighead Point.

Captain J. Ed Montgomery got the rams under way at 6 A.M. Breasting a five-mile-an-hour current, the vessels chugged past Fort Pillow, the crews exchanging cheers with the heavy artillerists manning the guns. The boats had been ordered to stay together until they sighted the Yankee ironclads. Then the fastest were to take the lead, and thus be unhampered by the slower ones—a mistake, the Confederate officers were to learn. Just above Fort Pillow, the Mississippi made a sharp right-angle turn around the head of Craighead Point; the River Defense Fleet rounded it slowly in formation. Thompson aboard the *General Bragg* sighted through the haze a long line of flat-topped pyramids on rafts—the city-class ironclads. The command was given for full speed ahead. A converted two-master from the Gulf trade, the *General Bragg* took the lead, cutting the wind with her tall spars "like the swoop of an eagle," as she made for the picket ironclad.[31]

Before Foote's departure, the Federals had been warned by refugees that the Rebels planned to attack the fleet with rams. Foote had ordered the captains of the ironclads to keep up steam, and to be prepared for action at any moment. This order, however, had not been followed to the letter by several of the vessels, including the flagboat.[32] He had given no special instructions relating to the formation in which the Confederates were to be met, or to the plan of attack. What appeared to be an oversight on Foote's part might have been an unwillingness to try to outguess the Rebel leaders. It appears that Foote had decided to rely on the experience and discretion of the gunboat commanders.[33]

As on the previous day, when Foote had taken leave of the flotilla, the *Benton* and two of the ironclads, the *Carondelet* and *Pittsburg,* were anchored off Plum Point, while the *Cairo, Mound City, Cincinnati,* and *St. Louis* were moored on the opposite side of the Mississippi. The *Cairo's* crew rested on their arms, and sentinels scanned the horizon for a sign of the foe.[34] At 4 A.M. *Mortar Boat No. 16* was towed downriver to Craighead Point to begin the daily bombardment of Fort Pillow. The *Cincinnati* followed to protect her in case the Confederate fleet attempted a dash upstream.[35]

At about 6 A.M. the Union lookouts sighted a heavy smoke cloud moving upstream toward the point. Lieutenant Bryant on the *Cairo* shouted for his crew to man their battle stations. The leading vessel in the Confederate fleet rounded the point at 7:25 A.M. She was followed by seven others, all hugging the west bank of the river, as they chugged along breasting the powerful current. At this, the *Cairo* slipped her hawser to the "bare end," ready for orders to go ahead.

Richard E. Birch, a pilot, was the only officer on the deck of the *Benton* at the time. After alerting Captain Davis, who was in his quarters, Birch called for the *Carondelet* and the *Pittsburg* to head downstream without waiting for the flagship. At the same time, a signalman aboard the *Benton* hoisted the "general signal" to get under way, but the morning was so hazy that the signal was not seen by the *Cairo* and the other two ironclads of the second division.[36] The *Cincinnati* was now lying just above *Mortar Boat No. 16,* tied fast to the trees, with all hands turned to holystoning the deck.

The eight Confederate vessels were now barely three-quarters of a mile below the *Cincinnati*. Eight minutes would bring them alongside. To make matters worse, the *Cincinnati* had hardly enough steam to turn her giant wheel. The rest of Davis' fleet, not one boat of which had a sufficient head of steam to hold herself against the current, lay three miles away. It was horribly apparent to the crew of the *Cincinnati* that the Rebels had surprised the ironclad and might sink or capture her, destroy the mortar boat, and withdraw before the fleet above could come to her rescue.

Commander Roger N. Stembel bellowed for his men to slip the cables, and the *Cincinnati* slowly swung out into the stream. Engineers threw oil and anything which was inflammable into the fires, in an effort to raise the necessary head of steam to enable the pilots to handle the boat. Stembel shouted for the pilots to make for a bar, where the water would be too shallow for the deeper draft rams to follow. As the lumbering ironclad came about, the gunners manning the bow battery opened up on the leading vessel in the Confederate fleet, the *General Bragg*.[37]

Aboard *Mortar Boat No. 16* the gunners were ordered to switch targets. Cutting their powder charges and fuses to the minimum, they sighted their 13-inch mortar on the oncoming rams. Though they failed to score any direct hits, the men were able to burst several of their big 200-pound shells directly over the rams, showering the superstructures with jagged scraps of iron.[38]

As soon as Pilot Birch had given the word, the *Carondelet* slipped her hawser and made for the enemy. Meanwhile, Captain Davis and the rest of the officers had come up on the spar deck. The pilot told the captain that the *Cincinnati* was in peril and that it would be several minutes before the *Benton,* still without a full head of steam, could get under way. Davis, observing that the *Carondelet* was moving, grabbed a trumpet and told Commander Henry Walke to go ahead, and not wait for the flagboat. Walke, his fighting blood up, called for his engineers to keep the fires under the boilers roaring, and, picking up speed, the *Carondelet* headed downstream to the rescue.

On the west side of the Mississippi, the captains of the *Cairo* and the other two ironclads of the second division had not seen Davis' signal to cast off. But Commander Kilty of the *Mound City,* had spotted the oncoming smoke cloud and started his vessel downstream about the same time as the *Carondelet.*

Walke's and Kilty's ironclads had proceeded about a mile before the flagboat was able to raise sufficient steam to start moving. The *Pittsburg* and the *St. Louis* ran into difficulties. At the time the *Benton* cast off, the *Pittsburg* was not yet clear of the bank, and the *St. Louis* was putting out a boat to cast off her hawsers. While the crew of the *St. Louis* was struggling to get under way, the *Cairo* followed the *Mound City.*[39]

The *Carondelet* and *Mound City* opened on the oncoming *General Bragg* with their bow batteries at range of three-eighths of a mile. Kilty held his craft parallel to the west bank; Walke sheered his ironclad across the river. The two gunboats were soon compelled to cease fire, for fear of damaging the *Cincinnati,* as the Rebel rams closed with her.[40]

Not wishing to ram the *Cincinnati* bows on, Captain H. H. Leonard maneuvered the *General Bragg* to crash into the ironclad's starboard beam. As he did, the Yankees at a distance of not more than fifty yards sent a broadside from their starboard battery—four 32-pounder smoothbores—smashing into the enemy ram. Cotton bales tumbled and splinters flew, but on she came, "her great walking-beam engine driving her at a fearful rate." [41] When the *General Bragg* had closed to within less than fifty feet, the *Cincinnati's* pilots succeeded in swinging her bow around, and the two vessels came together with a fearful crash. The *Bragg's* starboard paddle wheel climbed the *Cincinnati's* sloping casemate, almost upsetting the ram.

Fortunately for the Federals, the Confederates had given the ironclad only a glancing blow on the starboard quarter, and not the one she intended, which would have sunk the *Cincinnati*. Even so, it tore a piece out of the ironclad's midships six feet deep and twelve feet long, flooding the forward shellroom and knocking over mess chests, chairs, tables, stoves, and bottles throughout the boat. The *General Bragg's* armored beak remained embedded in the hull of the *Cincinnati* for a few moments, during which time she received a second broadside which slightly damaged her. The ram backed water frantically. As she came about, she received another broadside which cut her tiller ropes, making it impossible for Captain Leonard to maneuver his craft.

The seriously crippled *Cincinnati* retreated upriver. As soon as the two vessels parted, the *Carondelet* and *Mound City* reopened fire on the *General Bragg* with their bow guns. Now, two more rams, the *General Sterling Price* and the *Sumter,* closed on the *Cincinnati*. Aboard the *Carondelet* and *Mound City,* gun captains shouted frantically for their crews to concentrate on these new threats. The flagship *Benton,* commanded by Lieutenant Ledyard Phelps, had now arrived within range and her heavy guns roared.

The *Sterling Price* struck the *Cincinnati* first. She smashed into the ironclad a little abaft amidships on her starboard beam, tearing away the rudder, sternpost, and a large piece of the stern. Water gushed into the ironclad through the splintered timbers.

The *Sumter* then struck the *Cincinnati* a fearful blow in her stern which threw the bows under. Now her fires were drowned and the magazines and shellrooms were flooded. The gunners had only one round of ammunition left for each gun.[42] At close quarters, sharpshooters on the *Sumter* swept the ironclad's decks with a hail of Minié balls. One of these missiles struck Commander Stembel in the back near a shoulder blade and, passing through his neck, came out under his chin. Stembel was carried below decks; all believed him dead or mortally wounded,[43] although he was to recover and later return to duty.

Now began the grim fight to keep the stricken ironclad afloat long enough to work her into shallow water.[44] Once again, the *Mound City* and *Carondelet* had been compelled to hold their fire to keep from hitting their sister boat as the Rebels closed in for the kill. As the two rams dropped downstream after smashing the *Cincinnati*, the Federals put their bow guns back in action. Walke maneuvered his vessel to bring his port broadside guns into play.[45]

The *Van Dorn*, Captain Isaac D. Fulkerson commanding, had followed the *Price* and *Sumter*. Fulkerson aimed his ram at the *Mound City*, whose bluejackets sent shot after shot skipping along the water toward the *Van Dorn*. Holding a collision course, the ram bore in on the *Mound City* amidship. Commander Kilty waited until the last moment before swinging his vessel hard aport, but when the ironclad sheered to the left, the *Van Dorn* struck her a glancing blow, smashing a hole four feet deep in her starboard forward quarter. Fulkerson realized that his boat was isolated, as she had by this time passed above three of the ironclads, and called for his pilots to come about. The *Cairo*, which had followed the *Mound City* downstream, and the *Benton* moved in to protect the crippled ironclad. The *Cairo's* bow guns were rapidly fired "full in the face of the foe" as she hurried to protect her damaged sister. Suddenly a 32-pound ball from the *Van Dorn* struck the angle of the *Cairo's* center bow gunport, "bounded to the muzzle of the gun, and glanced off without doing any damage." Yost was standing within ten feet of the spot. Had it struck the opening fairly, he reported, "great loss of life and serious damage would have resulted." [46]

Lieutenant Phelps, seeing that the ram *Little Rebel* was bearing down on the *Mound City,* maneuvered the flagboat between the two. As Phelps recalled, "The rascal, afraid to hit us, backed off." As she did, the gunners manning the *Benton's* port bow rifled 42-pounder sent an 87-pound projectile crashing into her, hitting a steam-pipe or cylinder. A cloud of steam enveloped the vessel, as she retreated downriver. Escorted by the *Cairo*, the *Mound City* started upstream. Within a few minutes, the executive officer informed Kilty that he was experiencing considerable difficulty in keeping the boat afloat.[47]

Soon after the *Van Dorn* had rammed the *Mound City*, Captain Montgomery saw that the ironclads were taking positions where the water was too shallow for his rams. As his heavy ordnance was "far inferior to theirs, both in number and size," Montgomery had the signal to retire hoisted from the jackstaffs of the *Little Rebel*.[48]

As the dense smoke that filled the battle area began to rise, the Federals saw the Confederate rams retreating rapidly, in great confusion. The *Carondelet* dropped down to within a half mile of Craighead Point, firing as she did so at the withdrawing Rebel fleet with her bow battery. When the Southerners were almost out of range, the *Benton*, her forward guns roaring, passed the *Carondelet*. Montgomery's squadron had now entered the reach of the river commanded by Fort Pillow. Not wishing to chance an engagement with the shore batteries, Captain Davis (who during the action had calmly smoked a cigar in the *Benton's* pilothouse) ordered his gunners to cease fire. Rounding to, the *Benton* and *Carondelet* headed back to the fleet anchorage.[49]

The *St. Louis* reached the battle area after the Confederates had broken off the engagement and joined the *Cairo* in assisting the crew of the *Mound City* in the unsuccessful battle to keep their vessel afloat. The *Mound City*, "her bow pretty much wrenched off," was run onto a shoal opposite Plum Point, where she sank.[50]

The *Cincinnati*, attended by the *Pittsburg* and a tug, limped toward the Tennessee shore as the water kept inching up inside her hull. Suddenly, she gave a convulsive shudder, and went down bow-first in eleven feet of water.[51]

At Plum Point, the Yankees had been caught napping. The naval officers had failed to station a picket boat near the head of Craighead Point which could have given timely warning of the approach of the Confederate ram fleet. Not even the guard boat *Cincinnati* had a sufficient head of steam to enable her to protect herself, let alone *Mortar Boat No. 16*. Except for the *Carondelet* and *Mound City*, the other ironclads failed to close with the foe and, before they were in position to counterattack effectively, the rams had inflicted considerable damage. The Confederates withdrew as planned, as soon as they were threatened by a superior force.[52]

Aboard the ironclads the battle was the principal topic of conversation for the next several days. Crews on four of the vessels were critical of the performance of the *Cairo, Pittsburg*, and *St. Louis*, for, they complained, these vessels had been slow to get under way and had made no effort to close with the enemy. Officers of the "Old

Navy," who were well acquainted with Lieutenant Bryant, felt he had the "slows."

From the first to the last shot, one hour and ten minutes had elapsed. The engagement was sharp but not decisive; both sides claimed victory. Casualties to personnel were negligible. The Confederates listed their losses as two killed and eight or ten wounded, while the Federals reported four casualties, one dead and three wounded.[53]

Plum Point was one of the few engagements in the Civil War that could be called a "fleet action." Moreover, it was the only one in which the Confederates felt that they were sufficiently prepared to take the offensive. At Plum Point they more than held their own in an attack on a superior force.[54]

5

DEFEAT AT MEMPHIS

THE battle off Plum Point had clearly demonstrated to the officers of Davis' flotilla that the armor of their vessels needed to be strengthened. Therefore, Davis ordered the captains of the ironclads to reinforce their craft at the waterline, and by May 28 all had been "secured as far as possible" against another attack by the rams.[1] Railroad iron was attached around the bows and sterns, and buttresses of cypress logs were slung where there was no protective plating on the port and starboard beams.

To offset partially the temporary loss of the *Mound City* and *Cincinnati,* which had been refloated and sent to Cairo for repair in the navy yard, Captain Davis summoned the *Louisville,* anchored off Hickman, Kentucky, to join his fleet. Commander Benjamin Dove brought the *Louisville* to the flotilla on May 13. [2]

There was considerable dissatisfaction in the fleet with the performance of the *Cairo* and the *Pittsburg* in the Plum Point fight. When Lieutenant Phelps wrote his friend Flag Officer Foote, he commented: "Captain Dove is here with the *Louisville.* Now we have the *Cairo, Pittsburg,* and *Louisville* to 'count' among the six vessels of the fleet. I would rather have either one of the other two [*Cincinnati* and *Mound City*] than all three. Kilty did handsomely in the fight. Neither the *Pittsburg* nor *Cairo* got into it, and the *St. Louis* can hardly be said to have done so." [3]

Writing Foote a little later, Phelps reported that Lieutenant Thompson was getting the *Pittsburg* secured, "so that when the rebels come around the point again he can pitch into them." As for the *Cairo,* nothing was known "except that she was heard of to-day as wanting

64

coal, being about out of that commodity and pretty much run ashore for provisions." With another officer, Lieutenant W. McGunnegle, in charge of the *St. Louis,* Phelps was satisfied that when the next engagement occurred, she would do her part.[4] After her damage was repaired, the *Mound City* rejoined the flotilla on May 22.

The shelling of Fort Pillow had been resumed almost as soon as the Confederate fleet pulled out of the Plum Point engagement, but not before Captain Davis made some changes in operating procedures. Two ironclads would be detailed to guard the scow or scows on firing stations. Each morning at daybreak, as the tugs maneuvered the scows into position, the guard vessels would drop downstream to remain with the barges throughout the day. Shortly before dark, the tugs would tow the mortar boats upstream for the night, and the ironclads would rejoin the fleet.[5]

On the thirteenth the Rebels had begun a short-lived war of nerves designed to keep the flotilla on edge. A Confederate vessel would appear, show itself only long enough to alert the enemy, and then wheel about and disappear. This action was sufficient to cause Captain Davis to direct Maynadier to take his mortar boats out of battery for a day.[6]

There followed an eight-day interruption of the bombardment caused by bad weather and an ammunition shortage. Then, on the twenty-first, orders were issued for the *Cairo, Carondelet,* and *Pittsburg* to escort two of the "bombers" down to the point. As soon as the scows could be secured to the bank, the mortars zeroed in on the fort to resume their pounding. By 7 P.M., when they secured for the day, the mortarmen had lofted fifty-four bombs into the Rebel works. During the exchange, however, several of the Confederates' shells burst too close to the flotilla for comfort.[7]

At the end of the fourth week of May a number of Confederate deserters turned themselves in to the Federals. They told the Yankees that their comrades at the fort were in need of food. The morale of the garrison was low and the fire of the enemy's mortars was becoming increasingly effective.[8] In spite of this heartening news, Davis expected the Rebel rams to come up again, and wrote Secretary Welles, "If there are rams, as I understand there are, being fitted up under the direction of the War Department, at Pittsburg [*sic*], Cincinnati, or elsewhere, for service in this river, now is the time to make them useful." [9] Consequently, on May 25, Colonel Charles Ellet, with nine rams and two floating batteries, reached the Plum Point anchorage.

The fifty-two-year-old Ellet was a civil engineer and a father of the idea of using steamboats as rams. He had, with the approval of the War Department, quickly converted into rams four side-wheelers, the *Lancaster, Monarch, Queen of the West,* and *Switzerland,* all weighing 400 tons; and five stern-wheelers, the *Mingo, Lioness, Dick Fulton, Sampson,* and *T. D. Horner,* from 175 to 300 tons. He had chosen these craft for their speed and maneuverability, modifying them to deliver crushing blows that could cave in the side of an enemy boat.[10]

Although the flotilla had been reinforced, no orders for an attack on the Confederate River Defense Fleet could be formulated, because Captain Davis and Colonel Ellet were unable to agree on a plan for joint action. The aggressive Ellet wanted to dash past Fort Pillow with his rams and engage the Rebel boats, with the ironclads following in support. But Davis considered this plan too rash; he wanted his ironclads to take the lead at the moment of attack. Ellet became so exasperated with Davis that he wrote Secretary of War Edwin Stanton on May 30 that if the naval officer continued to be obstinate he would attack on June 2 with the ram fleet.[11]

Before the hour scheduled for the attack arrived, Ellet postponed it until the third; meanwhile, the two officers continued to quarrel. During these exchanges, Ellet cited orders from the War Department which gave the ram fleet freedom of action under certain circumstances.[12]

Having won his point with Davis, Ellet prepared to push matters. On the evening of the second, he put ashore a small party, accompanied by a detachment of infantry from Colonel Fitch's brigade. The patrol advanced down the levee to check and see if the Rebel patrol gunboat still lay off Craighead Point. If she were there, they were to ascertain if the rams could get at her without being subjected to a raking fire from Fort Pillow. The men were disappointed to find the boat gone. Two of them crept over to the tow head. Studying Fort Pillow closely, they concluded from what they saw and heard that the Confederates actually were evacuating.[13]

On June 3 the *Cairo* and *Mound City* were sent to guard the two mortar boats on bombardment duty. About 11 A.M. a party of men was seen on the Arkansas shore, about three hundred yards off the *Cairo's* starboard beam, waving a white flag. Lieutenant Bryant dispatched the tug *Jessie Benton* to pick up the Rebels and take them to the flagboat.[14] Ellet during the day sighted a Rebel gunboat, the *Jeff Thompson,* lying under the guns of Fort Pillow. The colonel had been disturbed to learn that his men had been talking with the men from the ironclads. Stories exaggerating the strength of the Rebel rams spread like wildfire. To check these tales, Ellet determined to move against the Southern vessel with two rams. Although he realized the undertaking might be hazardous, he deemed the object sufficient to warrant the movement.

The vessels he designated to participate in the attack were the *Queen of the West* and *Monarch*.[15] Colonel Alfred W. Ellet, Charles Ellet's younger brother, was in command of the *Monarch*. As soon as the crew of the Confederate boat sighted them, her men slipped the lines. Meanwhile, the Fort Pillow cannoneers raced to their emplacements and within a few moments had eight guns in action. After seeing that the boat had escaped and having secured valuable information on the location and strength of the gunpits, Alfred Ellet ordered the two rams back to their anchorage.[16]

Soon after the rams returned, lookouts spotted a smoke cloud moving upstream. Lieutenant Bryant and Commander Kilty ordered the *Cairo* and *Mound City* ready for action. The Rebel fleet soon rounded the point, and the *Cairo's* bow battery spoke. After several near misses, the Confederates retreated without returning the *Cairo's* fire.[17]

Patrols from Colonel Fitch's Indiana Brigade had been reconnoitering the Tennessee side of the Mississippi as well as the Arkansas shore. By June 1 army scouts had worked their way forward to a position near the area where Cold Creek emptied into Flower Island chute. Here they were within thirty yards of the outer line of Fort Pillow rifle pits. Colonel Fitch and his men ascertained that not a single gun in the fort's batteries could be registered on the sector where they planned to force a crossing of Cold Creek. Better yet, the ridges behind and overlooking the fortifications would give the Yankees a covered line of approach. Fitch relayed this news to Davis; the army officer was satisfied that his men in one working day could open a covered approach to the creek. A joint attack on Fort Pillow was scheduled for the morning of June 5. On the third Colonel Fitch told Major T. H. Bringhurst of the 46th Indiana to take three companies and open a road down the left bank of the Tennessee, parallel with Flower Island chute. By nightfall on the fourth, the men had built a bridge and opened a road to within three hundred yards of the Rebel entrenchments covering Cold Creek.[18] Bluecoats from the 43rd and 46th Indiana then moved forward into position, ready to storm the rifle pits. They would begin their move by 7 A.M. the next day, and the ironclads would drop downstream and begin hammering the fort.[19]

A week earlier the fort's commander, Brigadier General John B. Villepigue, had been ordered by General P. G. T. Beauregard to evacuate.[20] Villepigue, having held the fort for over six weeks, felt he could continue to make a successful defense and asked for reinforcements.[21] But on receipt of the distressing news that no men were available, he began moving out soldiers and matériel, so that by the morning of June 3 the fort was almost empty.

Rebel Flag Officer Montgomery employed the vessels of his fleet in the evacuation. Learning that the army would be unable to remove many of their big guns, he secured four of them (42-pounders) and mounted them on four of his rams. Along toward dusk on the fourth, his vessels got under way and reached Memphis at noon the next day.[22]

Under cover of darkness on the fourth, Villepigue's demolition teams began to apply the torch; shortly after dusk considerable smoke was seen rising above the trees over Craighead Point. Within a few minutes, the sky had taken on a reddish glow, and the men aboard the Union ironclads soon realized that Fort Pillow was burning. As the evening advanced, they saw flames spread steadily downriver—the entire series of fortifications had been set afire.

Nevertheless several of the naval officers were skeptical. They argued that the fires were a ruse to induce the Federals to send several of their gunboats below Craighead Point to investigate. To see if the Confederates were abandoning the fort, Davis sent Lieutenant Phelps on the tug *Jessie Benton* down to the point. When he returned, Phelps told his superior that the fort was engulfed in flames. About the same time, a patrol which had been operating on the Arkansas shore returned with news that the Rebel fleet was lying off Fulton. This intelligence satisfied Davis that the Confederates planned to dispute the passage of the river, and, if they were unsuccessful, they would scuttle their boats.[23]

Meanwhile, Colonel Fitch's scouts had brought in a Confederate deserter, who told the Federals that his former comrades had pulled out of Fort Pillow. Hours seemed like days, as the Northerners waited for dawn. Davis, Fitch, and Ellet each hoped that his command would reach and take possession of the fort first. Colonel Fitch canceled his plan to march his column down the recently opened road to Cold Creek. Instead, he and a picked detachment boarded the transport *Hetty Gilmore.* Preceded by two open rowboats, the *Hetty Gilmore* at 3 A.M. dropped slowly down the Mississippi.[24] As the steamer passed the *Benton,* Colonel Fitch hailed Captain Davis and said that he would give a blast on the whistle if the Rebels were gone. Few men aboard the *Cairo* slept that night. All had grown weary of the "protracted and fruitless siege, and were burning with a desire to do something or see something done." Orders had been issued by Davis for the ironclads to be ready to move before sunrise. Long before the designated hour, her crew climbed out of their hammocks and turned "anxious looks toward Craighead Point, which had so long and so vexatiously shut out from their view the vision of Fort Pillow." [25]

At 4:10 A.M. the Western Flotilla moved downriver—the *Benton* leading, followed by the *Cairo, Mound City, Louisville,* and *St. Louis.* Four of Colonel Ellet's rams hailed the ironclads as they rounded Craighead Point. Ellet, seeing that Fitch's transport would reach the landing in front of the fort ahead of the lumbering ironclads, called for his engineers to pour coal to the fires. Picking up speed, the rams overtook and passed the gunboats. Arriving in front of the fortifications ahead of the *Hetty Gilmore,* the rams hove to, while Colonel Alfred Ellet and a handful of men from the *Monarch* scrambled into a yawl, reaching the landing moments ahead of the *Hetty Gilmore.* Colonel Fitch was chagrined as he led his cheering soldiers ashore, only to find that Ellet had beaten him and that the Stars and Stripes were already snapping in the breeze.[26]

While the *Cairo* and the other ironclads were anchoring across the channel, Colonel Alfred Ellet reboarded the *Monarch.* Three of the rams then resumed their run downstream, hoping to overtake any laggard Confederate vessel. At Fort Randolph, twelve miles below fallen Fort Pillow, the younger Ellet and a small detachment went ashore. They found that the guns had been dismounted. Bales of cotton used to strengthen the earthworks were still smouldering.[27]

Captain Davis in the meantime had sent Lieutenant Phelps to make a quick inspection of Fort Pillow. He found that most of the buildings and their contents had been burned and the fort's guns put out of commission. The water battery, which was embrasured for ten guns, had been damaged by high water when the Mississippi had crested. Union officers who had been at Forts Henry and Donelson and Island No. 10 pronounced the defenses "equal, if not superior" to those of the other fortifications.[28]

The expedition was ready to push on to Memphis by noon on the fifth. The *Pittsburg* was left to discourage any Rebel attempt at re-occupying the fort, now in the hands of Colonel Fitch's detachment. The *Mound City* was detailed the task of convoying the transports, which were not yet ready to move. The *Cairo, Benton, Carondelet, St. Louis,* and *Louisville* were soon steaming downstream, followed by the mortar flotilla and supply boats. The transports with Fitch's brigade did not get away from Fort Pillow until the next morning. As the fleet passed Fulton, where the Confederate rams had been anchored the previous afternoon, the naval officers swept Fort Randolph with their glasses. On the parapet they saw the United States flag raised earlier by Colonel Ellet.[29]

Very few people were seen along the shore, as the *Cairo* and the other vessels pushed on toward Memphis. Houses and plantations appeared silent and abandoned. Occasionally groups of Negroes gathered on the levees and waved their hats and kerchiefs at the gunboats. "Our reception, if not cordial, was very genteel, absent of all demonstration," Yost recalled.[30] At many points along the Arkansas and Tennessee sides of the river, the invaders saw that the Southerners were destroying their cotton, "the deposed Rebel King, who was never aught but the King's fool," wrote a correspondent. The surface of the Mississippi was flaked with tufts of floating cotton, pitched into the river by retreating Confederates. Cotton bales stacked at the landings and the gin houses went up in smoke.[31]

The bluejackets on the *Cairo* marveled as their boat chugged along that no ambitious butternut shot at them with his rifle or shotgun. Instead they were treated "as if we were the ancient priests of Isis descending the Nile." [32] Several citizens, who rowed out in small boats to the flotilla, told the Yanks that Memphis was nearly deserted, that all the cotton, sugar, and tobacco had been burned, that a number of houses had been fired by the mob, and that the city had been saved only with difficulty.

That evening the fleet lay at anchor near Memphis. The vessels were stationed in order of battle—the ironclads at the lower end of Island No. 45, a mile and a half above Memphis; the mortar scows, tenders, and supply boats at Island No. 44; the Ellet rams eighteen river miles above Memphis.[33] From their anchorage the sailors aboard the *Cairo* could see the lights of the city twinkling brightly on the bluffs.[34]

As they had just seen the Confederate squadron abandon Fort Pillow, where it could choose its mode of attack, most of the Union naval officers did not expect Montgomery and his captains to make a stand at Memphis. The sights and sounds reported by the watch reinforced the officers in this belief.[35]

Confederate Flag Officer Montgomery's River Defense Fleet arrived at Memphis about noon on June 5. As his vessels were running short of coal, and none was available from the usual sources of supply, he requested that the citizens contribute whatever quantities of fuel they might be able to spare. Some of the suppliers heard Montgomery and several of his captains boast that they would return upriver to Island No. 44 to engage and destroy the hated ironclads.[36]

Shortly before 10 P.M. the Confederate tugs on picket above Memphis reported sighting the Yankee fleet. Although the Confederates tended to discredit this news, Montgomery anchored in mid-channel, cleared for battle. At dawn on the sixth, he took the eight rams of the River Defense Fleet upstream to attack the Yankees.[37]

At 4:30 A.M. Flag Officer Davis, on the *Benton,* joined the *Cairo, Carondelet, St. Louis,* and *Louisville.* The *Benton* and *Louisville* took the lead in the downstream trip. Commander Walke steered the *Carondelet* into her battle station on the flagship's port beam, while the three other ironclads took position to the flagboat's starboard—the *St. Louis* on the left, the *Cairo* in the middle, and the *Louisville* on the right.[38]

The river seemed clear. No boats were visible until the ironclads drew abreast of the northern fringes of Memphis, but the lookouts saw that the news of their coming had spread rapidly. Although the hour was early, the levee and bluff were crowded with anxious spectators, routed from their beds before dawn.

The Federal crews sighted several ocher-colored boats lying alongside the Memphis levee, with steam up. Ten minutes later, these boats began to drop downstream; eight rams were counted. Captain Davis decided not to press matters, for he wanted his men to eat a hearty breakfast before going into action (he believed that men fought better on full stomachs). So obsessed was he with this idea that he signaled his vessels to come about and ascend the river.[39]

Before the ironclads had proceeded very far, a dense smoke cloud was sighted coming up the Mississippi, and a vessel identified by her profile as the *Little Rebel* rounded the head of Rail Road Point. A number of the naval officers could not believe that the Confederates planned to make a stand here, and were of the opinion that the object of the *Rebel's* mission was to present a truce flag from the city. Three more Rebel rams now rounded the point, causing the Union officers to have second thoughts. Aboard the *Cairo,* the officer of the day noted the time: it was 4:50 A.M. Not wishing to engage Montgomery until the *Mound City* and the Ellet rams joined him, Davis signaled his captains to continue the run up the Mississippi. To the Confederates it appeared that the Yankees were wavering, and they pressed on to make a bold attack. A puff of smoke lifted from the bow of the *Little Rebel,* and a ball whistled over the *Benton,* striking and skimming along the water beyond. No reply was made by the ironclads as they continued to lumber upriver. A second shot from the *Little Rebel* also overshot Davis' flagboat. Still the Western Flotilla steamed on, and a third time the foe discharged a gun without effect at the big Yankee ironclad. Davis, finally realizing the Rebels' intent, abandoned the idea of a before-battle breakfast and ordered his flotilla into action.

The *Cairo* was the first of the ironclads to come about. She opened fire with her starboard bow 42-pounder rifle. An 87-pound projectile struck the water within a few feet of the *Little Rebel.* The other ironclads first fired their stern guns, and then, as they rounded to, opened with the powerful guns mounted in their bow batteries. Since Memphis was behind the Rebel boats, the gun captains cautioned their men to be careful where they pointed their pieces.[40]

Colonel Charles Ellet had gotten his rams under way at daybreak. Four of his most powerful steamers, the *Queen of the West, Monarch, Lancaster,* and *Switzerland,* took the lead: the other rams, which were towing barges, lagged. As they approached Memphis, the men on watch sighted the ironclads deployed across the channel ahead. Ellet had the *Queen of the West* made fast to the Arkansas shore, because he planned to take a small boat out to the *Benton* to confer with Captain Davis before deciding his next move. The other rams hove to, while awaiting word from the flag steamer. Several minutes after the crew of the *Queen* had put her lines ashore, they heard a dull boom, and a projectile passed overhead. This was the first shot discharged by the *Little Rebel.* Colonel Ellet, who was standing on the hurricane deck of the *Queen,* sprang forward and waved his hat to attract the captain of the *Monarch,* calling out, "It is a gun from the enemy! Round out and follow me! Now is our chance." As the flag steamer rounded to and headed downstream, one of the crew ran up the Stars and Stripes, the signal Ellet had prescribed for going into action.

The morning was clear and perfectly still. A heavy wall of smoke had formed across the river, so that the position of the ironclads could be seen only by the flashes of their guns. With her engines pounding wildly, the *Queen* passed between the Arkansas shore and the *Louisville* and bore down upon the foe. Only the tall chimneys of the *Queen* were visible as she entered the wall of smoke. As she emerged from the smoke, those standing on the *Monarch's* deck could see Colonel Ellet standing on the *Queen's* hurricane deck, waving his hat to show them which of the Rebel vessels he wished them to attack.

As the flagboat closed with the oncoming fleet, Ellet saw that they were rams, but that, unlike his, they were armed with heavy guns. He told the pilots to steer the *Queen* toward two Rebel rams which were about in mid-channel, very close together, and supported by a third, a little in their rear and somewhat nearer the Memphis shore.[41]

Ellet expected that his vessel would be followed by the *Monarch, Lancaster,* and *Switzerland.* Although he was unaware of it, only the *Monarch* had followed the *Queen* on her dash down the Mississippi. Aboard the *Lancaster* several of the officers became excited and confused. Though the engineers did their duty, the pilot erred in his signals; the engines were reversed at the wrong moment, and the vessel backed into the bank under a full head of steam, disabling the rudder. The captain of the *Switzerland* "construed the general sailing order to keep a mile in rear of the *Lancaster* to mean that he was to keep half a mile behind her in the engagement." Consequently, he stopped his boat, as soon as his lookouts reported the *Lancaster* hove to and did not get into the fighting.[42]

The fleets had now been in contact for about twenty minutes without material damage to either side. Montgomery and his captains sighted Ellet's rams as they passed the islands "Paddy's Hens and Chickens." Realizing that the arrival of these reinforcements made the odds too great to continue the battle with any hope of success, Montgomery signaled his captains to fall back. This order was obeyed with considerable reluctance by the individualistic steamboat captains. As they dropped downstream, the pilots kept the bows of their vessels pointed toward the *Cairo* and the other Federal vessels, while the gunners kept up a vigorous fire.[43]

By the time the River Defense Fleet arrived off Beale Street, it was no longer in line of battle. As luck would have it, the cry "Lookout for one of the rams!" was raised. Out of the smoke which clouded the river came Colonel Ellet's flag steamer *Queen of the West,* dense black smoke belching from her twin chimneys.[44]

Ellet, who stood behind his pilots, saw that the two Confederate rams *Beauregard* and *Lovell* were aiming their armored bows toward the *Queen.* The colonel was in a quandary, for it was impossible for him to tell his pilots upon which to direct their attack. The distance between the boats was rapidly narrowing. Moments before the vessels collided, the two Confederate captains rang frantically for the engineers to reverse the engines. As the Rebel rams backed water they began to turn, thus exposing their broadsides. Since the *Queen* was pounding ahead at forced draft, Ellet only had a few seconds to select his target. He pointed at the nearer vessel, the *General Lovell.* To try to make the Yankee alter her course, Confederate gunners aboard the *Beauregard* charged their 32-pounder with grape, but the charge went wide of its mark. Ellet's pilots sent the *Queen's* bow crunching into the *General Lovell's* broadside, crushing her hull; many of the crew, fearing their vessel was going to sink, leaped overboard.

The bow of the *Queen* was so deeply embedded in the *General Lovell* that she had a difficult time freeing herself. Ellet and his crew were fighting to back her free when the *Beauregard* rammed into her starboard wheelhouse, breaking the *Queen's* tiller rope, crushing in her wheel and a portion of her hull, and leaving her all but helpless. Ellet was struck in the leg by a pistol ball fired by one of the *Beauregard's* crew. The blow delivered by the *Beauregard* had knocked the *Queen's* bow free of the *General Lovell,* which listed and within a few minutes disappeared below the churning waters of the Mississippi. Aboard the *General Lovell* the crew was wild with fear, and "their agony made it a terrible scene" as the boat went down.[45] Rescue boats were launched by the *Benton,* the *Cairo,* and some of the rams, and six or seven exhausted sailors were pulled in; but the current was so powerful that few of those who swam for shore reached it. After being disabled, the *Queen* worked her way slowly over to the Arkansas shore.[46]

The *Monarch,* which had followed the *Queen* on her dash toward the Confederate fleet, passed in front of the Memphis bluffs under a full head of steam. Now she was confronted by the *Beauregard* and the *General Price.* So intent were the captains of these two vessels in dealing the Yankee a fearful blow that they forgot about each other. At the last possible moment, Captain David Dryden maneuvered the *Monarch* so as to avoid the *Beauregard,* which surged on to strike the *General Price,* seriously crippling her. She was run aground on the Arkansas side of the river, her crew escaping ashore.[47] Dryden then drove the *Monarch's* bow full into the *Beauregard.* By this time the *Cairo* and the ironclads were closing in for the kill.[48] As soon as the two had separated, the ironclads opened up on the Confederate ram, nearly sinking her outright.

Captain Dryden, seeing that the *Beauregard* was sinking, got a line aboard the stricken craft to tow her to the Arkansas side, but she quickly sank. Fortunately for the surviving members of the crew, the vessel's texas and chimneys remained above water, and, like so many ants, the crew crowded onto the texas, waving anything that was white and calling for help.[49]

The *Little Rebel*, although sinking, still flew her colors, and several of the ironclads, including the *Cairo*, fired on her in a futile effort to make her surrender. The *Little Rebel* was run onto a bar off Hopedale and abandoned by officers and crew before the *Monarch* could reach her.[50]

The surviving rams of the River Defense Fleet, the *Jeff Thompson, General Van Dorn, Sumter,* and *General Bragg,* now broke off the engagement and headed downstream at forced draft, their captains and crews aware that their only hope was in retreat. The Rebel vessels should have easily outdistanced the slow-moving ironclads, but the *Cairo,* along with the *Carondelet,* now demonstrated the advantage of her superior speed. The heavy protective timbers which had been added were cut adrift, and the *Cairo* rapidly forged ahead.[51]

During this chase, the *Jeff Thompson,* on fire, was run aground and abandoned; the *Sumter* was disabled and abandoned; and the *General Bragg,* also burning, was run ashore. Prize crews were able to board the *Sumter* and *General Bragg,* but the *Jeff Thompson* finally disappeared in a tremendous explosion.[52] The *Van Dorn* had gradually pulled away from her pursuers, and Captain Davis called off the chase. The *Cairo* still followed her, but after about fifteen miles, Bryant ordered the craft about to return to Memphis, where she anchored in mid-stream at 11 A.M. While en route upriver, Davis hailed two of the swift Ellet rams, the *Monarch* and *Switzerland,* and told their captains to see if they could overtake the *Van Dorn.*[53] But the Confederate had too great a head start and they failed. Davis' ironclads returned to Memphis in triumph and anchored off shore keeping their heavy guns run out and trained on the city.

After the surrender and occupation of Memphis, the bluejackets from the *Cairo* and the other ironclads found five large Mississippi steamers, the *Victoria, H.R.W. Hill, Kentucky, New National,* and *Acacia,* with C.S.A. painted on their wheelhouses. As these vessels had been chartered by the Confederate government, they could be sent to a prize court for adjudication and sale, the proceeds to be distributed among personnel of the Western Flotilla. In addition, a large wharfboat and a considerable amount of cotton fell into Yankee hands.[54] Several Memphis citizens of pro-Union sentiment told the Yankees that Confederate Flag Officer George Hollins' fleet, now under Commander Robert F. Pinkney, and consisting of four vessels, had left Memphis the day before for Vicksburg.[55]

Confederate casualties totaled about one hundred killed and wounded and one hundred fifty taken prisoner. The Federals repaired and added to the Western Flotilla four of the Confederate rams, the *General Price, General Bragg, Sumter,* and *Little Rebel.*[56] Aboard the Yankee rams, the only casualty was Colonel Charles Ellet. The gallant colonel was ordered home to recover from his leg wound. Blood poisoning developed, however, and he died at Cairo early on the morning of June 21. [57]

6

A NEW CAPTAIN
COMES ABOARD

For six days following the surrender of Memphis, the ironclads lay at anchor in front of the city.[1] On June 12 Captain Davis called for Lieutenant Bryant. The lieutenant was to take the *Cairo* back to Fort Pillow, where he would contact Lieutenant Thompson of the *Pittsburg* regarding the big guns emplaced at Fort Randolph, some of which were reportedly still mounted. These pieces, as well as those which had been tumbled off their carriages, would be transported by fatigue parties to the landing and loaded on a scow for shipment to Cairo. After this project had been completed, the *Cairo* was to take station at Fort Pillow—to guard the public property and keep track of Confederate movements ashore.[2]

The *Cairo's* crew was hardly jubilant over leaving the flotilla and the area of active operations. They would spend three months at Fort Pillow, demolishing fortifications, patrolling on either side of the river, and strengthening their boat.[3] The *Cairo* reached her new station on the thirteenth and Executive Officer Hazlett with a selected landing party went ashore to examine the fortifications. About four miles east of the fort, Lieutenant Bryant located an abandoned sawmill. Here several of the crew, who had worked in sawmills, prepared a large quantity of heavy timbers which were used to erect an effective barricade around the *Cairo's* engines, steam drums, and boilers. These barricades were reinforced with railroad iron salvaged from the Fort Pillow fortifications, thus making the ironclad quite invulnerable to a projectile such as the one which had decimated the crew of the *Mound City* at St. Charles, Arkansas, on June 17. [4]

In the weeks that followed, working parties from the *Cairo* became

77

very familiar with the Fort Pillow fortifications. They found that the batteries which had held the flotilla at bay for fifty-four days consisted

of sixteen distinct sections, advantageously placed, and mounting all told fifty-four guns, ranging from 13 inches down to 6 inches in diameter. We found 15 guns still in their places; they having been disabled by spiking, bursting of the breech, burning of their supports, &c. Large quantities of shot; furnaces for heating shot; bombproof casements [sic] and "rat holes" for the gunners to take refuge in; bombproof magazines; and all the essentials of a strong defensive fortress were in evidence.[5]

Fatigue parties from the *Cairo* also visited Fort Randolph, where they loaded the big guns aboard steamboats for shipment upriver.

A mail boat which reached Memphis on June 20 had some interesting news for Flag Officer Davis. As she was passing the mouth of Forked Deer Creek, the crew had sighted a smoke cloud up that stream, such as given off by a steamer. Davis sent a note on the next north-bound mail boat asking Bryant to investigate this report.[6] Bryant accordingly took the *Cairo* up the Mississippi to the mouth of the creek. A small boat party then went up that stream several miles but was unable to learn anything concerning the craft the mail boat crew believed they had seen. Bryant relayed this news to Davis, along with an inventory his men had made of the captured ordnance at Fort Pillow.[7]

Davis, after starting for Vicksburg on June 29, realized that the *Pittsburg* was still at Fort Pillow and in need of repairs. Knowing that many days would pass before he returned to Memphis, the flag officer hailed the *Mound City* and *St. Louis,* which were returning from the disastrous White River expedition, and asked them to carry a message to Lieutenant Bryant at Fort Pillow. Bryant was to send the *Pittsburg* and the captured steamer *General Pillow* to Cairo. As soon as the *General Pillow* had been outfitted as a light-draft gunboat, she was to report back to Bryant.[8] After reaching Vicksburg, Davis reconsidered his plan. He knew that the *Cairo* drew too much water to explore the Mississippi's tributaries on cotton gathering and guerrilla hunting forays; consequently, on July 2 he wrote the commander of the Cairo Naval Station to see that the former Rebel flagboat *Little Rebel* reported to Bryant.[9]

July and August of 1862 were difficult months for the Western Flotilla. The Confederates held firm at Vicksburg; in engagements with their ironclad *Arkansas,* the Union vessels *Carondelet, Tyler,* and *Lancaster* were heavily damaged and had to be sent upriver for repairs. The *Essex* and *Sumter* had accompanied Farragut's fleet on its recoil from Vicksburg. Davis' squadron, following the retreat of the oceangoing fleet, had retired from the Vicksburg area to Helena, Arkansas. Over on the Tennessee River, Rebel partisans were becoming bolder. Flag Officer Davis in mid-August was compelled to increase the strength of the force operating on the Tennessee. The *Little Rebel* was accordingly ordered to this new danger point.

Repairs on the *Pittsburg* were completed at the Cairo navy yard on July 22, but her crew had been so debilitated by sickness that she was unable to get under way. It was August 7 before the fifty vacant billets on the *Pittsburg* had been filled. Davis by this time had other work for the ironclad; instead of rejoining the *Cairo,* she would join the fleet at Helena.[10]

Meanwhile, the *Cairo* continued to be responsible for guarding the reaches of the Mississippi above and below Fort Pillow. At 8 P.M. on July 9 she was hailed from the shore by a man looking surprisingly like a Union naval officer. A small boat was cast off and soon returned with the man, who proved to be one of Farragut's officers, en route to Cairo. He reported that the steamer *Shingiss,* in which he and a number of sick and wounded from the combined fleets had taken passage from above Vicksburg for the hospital at Mound City, had struck a snag and sunk seven miles below Fort Pillow.

The crew and passengers of the *Shingiss* had been safely landed ashore near the place where she went down. Lieutenant Bryant had to wait more than six hours before a head of steam could be raised, as the *Cairo's* fires had been out for several days. Just as he was preparing to get under way for the rescue mission, the steamer *Tycoon,* on her way upriver, pulled alongside. Bryant, knowing that she could move much faster than his ironclad, told Pilot Thomas E. Young to board the *Tycoon* and take her downstream and rescue the survivors. This was done, and within a couple of hours the entire party was aboard the *Cairo.*

About 6 P.M. the hospital boat *Red Rover* was spotted coming downriver, and the *Cairo* signaled her to come alongside. Sailor Yost recorded in his diary: "No notion being taken of our signal, a shot was fired across her bow, which quickly brought her alongside." After taking on board those bound for the hospital, she continued on downriver. A "bell-boat" was rushed up from Memphis. For the next four days, while divers raised the *Shingiss* and the damage control crew effected temporary repairs, a large number of armed men from the *Cairo* patroled the area to ward off attacks by guerrillas.[11]

While at Fort Pillow, the *Cairo's* crew had to cope with a number of problems. The most vexing of these was how to contend with Rebel guerrillas. Almost daily, citizens who had taken the loyalty oath came aboard the ironclad to complain of harassment and ask Lieutenant Bryant for protection. Since the partisans kept well inland, there was little the naval officers could do. On several occasions, lookouts aboard the *Cairo* caught sight of armed mounted men ashore. When a landing party questioned these people, they explained that they were hunting Negroes. By early July the Confederates became bolder. Fifty bales of cotton, scheduled to be shipped North, were burned at Fort Randolph.[12]

Flag Officer Davis was kept advised of these developments. On July 13 Davis wrote Bryant that he was sorry to learn of the harassment of "loyal citizens in the interior," but unless the army saw fit to post a strong garrison at Fort Pillow, it would be impossible for the navy to intervene in these citizens' behalf. Nevertheless, Bryant was to continue to do everything in his power to sustain and encourage the Union sentiment. Shipment of cotton by planters would be furthered, while in the future no fugitive slaves were to be received "promiscuously" aboard the vessels of the Western Flotilla.[13]

On September 9 Lieutenant Bryant, on orders from Flag Officer Davis, headed downstream and rendezvoused with the flotilla at Helena on the following day. Bryant had been in ill health for several months. When he failed to respond to treatment, a board of medical survey recommended that he be granted an extended sick leave. Secretary Welles approved the board's findings, and orders were issued relieving Bryant of his command. On September 12 Officer Hazlett turned out the crew of the *Cairo,* and while the officers and men stood at attention, Bryant, thin and pale, bade them goodbye. As Bryant was getting ready to salute the *Cairo's* colors for the last time, his replacement, Lieutenant Commander Thomas O. Selfridge, was piped aboard by the bos'n.

Selfridge, the crew observed, was much younger than their departing captain. He was said to be ambitious, and it was known that he had important connections, having been born into a seafaring family —the son of a ranking naval officer. He had graduated from the Naval Academy in 1854 at the head of his class. Immediately before his assignment to the Western Flotilla, he had been in command of the experimental submarine *Alligator*. When the Navy Department was finally satisfied that the submarine was of no value, Selfridge and his fourteen volunteer crewmen were ordered to report to the commandant of the Cairo naval base. Within a few days Lieutenant Commander Selfridge was handed his orders to replace Bryant as captain of the *Cairo,* and early in September he and his crewmen from the *Alligator* had boarded a Helena-bound steamboat.[14]

Later in September the *Cairo* and her new captain drew as their assignment a brief chore guarding prisoner-of-war transports. This resulted from a meeting at Haxall's Landing on the James River in July. Major General John A. Dix, representing the Union, and Confederate Major General Daniel H. Hill had signed a cartel at that time providing that "all prisoners of war now held on either side and all prisoners hereafter taken shall be sent with all reasonable dispatch to A. M. Aiken's, below Dutch Gap, on the James River, Va., or to Vicksburg, on the Mississippi River, in the State of Mississippi, and there exchanged or paroled until such exchange can be effected." [15]

Both North and South moved promptly to carry out the terms of the Dix-Hill agreement. Confederate prisoners from camps west of the Appalachians were to be concentrated at Cairo, where they would be loaded aboard steamboats for the trip down the Mississippi to Vicksburg. Flag Officer Davis would be called on to provide vessels from his flotilla to convoy the transports.

The first Rebel prisoners scheduled to be exchanged in the West were those confined at Camp Morton, Indiana. Trains carrying 3,900 of these men rolled into the Cairo yards during the fourth week of August. As soon as they had clambered off the cars, the Rebels were marched aboard one of the four transports designated to carry them to Vicksburg.[16] Davis, when called on by Captain Henry M. Lazelle, the agent for the exchange of prisoners of war, said that he would "with the greatest readiness furnish the convoy required." [17] Since he was at Cairo, Davis proposed to employ his new flagboat, the *Eastport,* to escort the transports to Vicksburg. The vessels sailed on August 28. Because of low water, the *Eastport* grounded several times on the run down to Helena, where the convoy arrived on September 5. [18] Davis now realized that with the low stage of the Mississippi, he would be courting further delays to continue with the *Eastport.* He accordingly drafted orders assigning Commander Benjamin Dove the task of escorting the fast transports with the prisoners the rest of the way to Vicksburg. In addition to his own vessel, the *Louisville,* Dove would be assisted by the ram *Monarch.*[19]

Trains, each one carrying about a thousand prisoners guarded by a company of soldiers, began reaching Cairo from Camps Douglas and Butler during the first week of September. Confederates confined at the Alton Military Prison were sent to Cairo by boat. All these men, numbering over six thousand, were jammed aboard six transports. On the run downstream to Helena, the steamers were escorted by the timberclad *Lexington.*[20] When the convoy stopped at Helena, Davis on the sixteenth notified Lieutenant Commander James W. Shirk of the *Lexington* that the *Cairo* and the ram *Queen of the West* would help guard the transports as they pushed on to Vicksburg. As soon as the prisoners had been exchanged, the transports were to head back upstream under convoy of one or more of the gunboats.[21]

At the last minute it was learned that the *Queen* was not available, and Davis, so as not to further delay the convoy, told Shirk to proceed without her. Early the next morning, the steamboats with the thousands of Rebel prisoners and the two gunboats cast off. Instead of the Stars and Stripes a flag of truce whipped in the breeze from the *Cairo's* jackstaff as she chugged along behind the transports.

On September 21 the fleet hove to off Young's Point. On the trip down from Helena, there had been some excitement. The steamers that had inaugurated the prisoner exchange in the West were encountered coming upriver with about a thousand happy Union soldiers aboard. These men, who had just been released from Rebel prison camps, cheered and jeered the Vicksburg-bound vessels. The *Cairo* grounded several times on submerged sandbars, and had to be pulled off by the steamers.[22]

After a flag of truce had been exchanged, the six transports ran on to Vicksburg to land the happy prisoners. While awaiting the steamers' return, Commander Selfridge on the twenty-third eased his ironclad downstream to a position near the upper entrance to Williams' Canal. From this vantage point, the officers and men could look across the neck of De Soto Peninsula and see Vicksburg. Near the head of the peninsula, Confederate working parties could be seen felling timber for an abatis and clearing fields of fire for the big guns emplaced on Wyman's Hill.[23]

When the transports returned from Vicksburg, they carried a number of exchanged Union prisoners. According to a man of pronounced Union sympathies, these men "presented evidence of rough life during

Ready to fire. Fused twelve-pounder howitzer shells found in the *Cairo's* passing room.

The *Cairo's* bell.

A white oak naval gun carriage still sou after its long submersion.

An 8-inch naval gun and length of anchor chain.

Heavy guns from the *Cairo* after being carefully disarmed, then cleaned.

Pile of black powder. Black powder had to be hosed into the river as it was still inflammable when dry.

Top left, stand of grape.

Bottom left, charge of canister.

WILLIAM R. WILSON

Leather powder-passing buckets, shoes and officers' boots. Boots became soft and pliable again after treatment with a preservative.

J. D. Callihan's watch. Mess gear, comb, knife marked against theft. Identification stamps.

Section from a box addressed to a member of the crew by his family.

GI pistols found on the gundeck.

Grease cup, fife, GI knife, officer's and enlisted man's belt buckles.

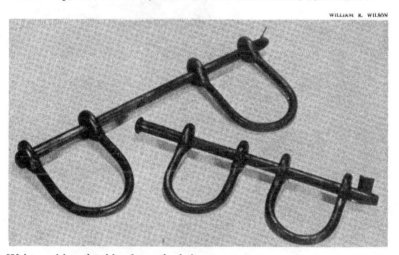

Wrist and leg shackles from the brig.

A bed pan.

Coffee pot.

Ironstone bowl and pitcher.

Glass lampshades, bottles recovered unbroken. Brushes, razors, and other items.

their captivity, but not one of them was half as dirty as the most cleanly rebel prisoners sent down in exchange for them." [24]

The steamers were convoyed as far as Helena by the *Cairo* and *Lexington*. On the run up, Commander Selfridge and Chief Pilot Oscar B. Jolly argued. Jolly became so incensed that he resigned, and on October 4 took passage on a northbound boat. "Captain Selfridge," diarist Yost commented, "is a splendid fighter, but some of the boys are not accustomed to his strict discipline." [25] Jolly, who was considered one of the best pilots on the river, was succeeded by his assistant Charles Young.

In July, Congress took the command of the Western Flotilla away from the army and assigned it to the navy, thus ending a system in which, as Andrew Foote had complained, every brigadier could interfere. The actual transfer took place on October 1. Secretary of Navy Welles at the same time replaced Davis as commander of the flotilla, recalling him to Washington as chief of the Bureau of Navigation.[26] David D. Porter was named to take his place, with the rank of acting rear admiral.[27] Porter assumed command of the Mississippi Squadron, as the Western Flotilla henceforth would be officially designated, at Cairo on October 15.

Besides the clash between captain and chief pilot, there had been other problems aboard the *Cairo* on the passage up from Young's Point. The fire linings had deteriorated so thoroughly that the vessel twice caught fire; each time, the blaze was put out without much trouble. Selfridge, after consulting Engineer J. W. Hartupee, decided that until the linings were repaired it would be foolhardy to risk taking the *Cairo* on another downriver patrol. Requisitions for fire linings and fire brick were forwarded to the Cairo Naval Station. Three weeks passed, and the materials had not arrived, so on October 18 Selfridge wrote Davis. (News that Porter had replaced Davis had not yet reached Helena.) The commander informed his superior that he had learned that "the fire brick, and the masonry can be tended to in Memphis." As a trip to Memphis would require an absence of not more than five days from his station, Selfridge recommended that the *Cairo* be ordered there for repairs, rather than having the brick forwarded from Cairo, and having him risk "the chances of finding a proper mason amongst the soldiers here." [28]

Selfridge two days later inspected his vessel's magazines, and found that all except sixty of the fuses used to detonate the big shells had been ruined by dampness. These fuses were of army pattern, so they contained no seals to protect them from sweating when stored in the lead-lined shellrooms, which were below the water line. Writing to his new chief, Admiral Porter, Selfridge observed that if plans called for supplying the squadron with shells and fuses manufactured to naval specifications, he would prefer to wait for them, rather than replace the defective fuses by a requisition upon the ordnance boat.[29]

Commander Selfridge, while waiting to hear from Porter, assembled thirty-three Negroes and placed them aboard a Cairo-bound boat; orders had been received from Secretary of Navy Welles authorizing the enlistment of Negroes. Selfridge in a covering letter to Admiral Porter explained that circumstances beyond his control kept him from sending the number requested. (The army was unwilling to release any able-bodied Negroes currently working on the Helena fortifications, while the navy could not send any more without interfering with the efficiency of the squadron.) In addition, Selfridge complained, bread and flour were running short aboard the vessels at Helena, and the navy was now dependent on the army for these items. The coal stockpile, down to four thousand bushels, was also becoming a problem. Except for these difficulties and the activities of Confederate guerrillas, he reported that all was quiet at Helena.[30]

Commander Walke reached Helena with the *Carondelet* on October 23. Walke was under instructions from Admiral Porter to take charge of the vessels stationed there, and to provide fire support to the army in case the Confederates attacked the Helena perimeter. The day after his arrival at Helena, Walke issued orders for the ordnance steamer *Judge Torrence* to proceed to Cairo for repairs. The *Cairo* would accompany the ammunition boat as far as Memphis.[31]

The run up the Mississippi to Memphis took the better part of two days; the *Cairo* tied up at Memphis on Sunday, the twenty-sixth. On the following morning, the *Judge Torrence,* escorted by the *Baron De Kalb* (the former ironclad *St. Louis*), resumed her run upstream. Commander John A. Winslow, before leaving Memphis, told Selfridge that he was to remain there until he received further orders from Porter. While at Memphis, Selfridge resolved to see that needed repairs were made to the *Cairo*. The quartermaster was rushed ashore to purchase new linings and grate bars for the fire boxes. He soon returned and reported that he had been unable to procure these parts. When Selfridge forwarded a request to Cairo for these repairs, he also informed Porter that he needed another anchor to replace the one whose shank had broken recently.[32] Before the items arrived from Cairo, a second visit to the Memphis warehouses turned up the needed fire linings and grate bars.[33] A squad of boilermakers and brick masons boarded the *Cairo* on the twenty-eighth, and working under Chief Engineer Hartupee's supervision began repairing the boilers and fire boxes.[34]

Selfridge kept his officers and men occupied while the *Cairo* was tied up for repairs. Twice daily the crew was called to quarters for inspection. October 30 was spent by Executive Officer Hazlett exercising the men at the heavy guns and in small-arms drill. Commander Selfridge, who watched the men closely, commended their quickness and accuracy.[35]

When Selfridge wrote Admiral Porter on November 7, the repairs to the *Cairo's* machinery and boilers had been completed. Selfridge reported the gun deck's planks were so worn that the "dumb trucks" caught in the decking, rendering it difficult to point the guns. As plenty of oak planking was available at the Memphis sawmills, he informed Porter he planned to replace the defective planks and cover the deck, which was made of soft pine, with an inch of oak sheathing.

Although the *Cairo* had been tied up for repairs for eleven days, Selfridge and his bluejackets kept a close watch on trade passing between Memphis and the Arkansas shore. All boats plying the river were required to check with Selfridge and submit to an examination before being allowed to cross. Two of the *Cairo's* small boats, fully manned, patrolled the river at night with orders to intercept all smugglers.[36] The *Cairo's* cutter on the night of the third overtook three men in a skiff, as they were trying to slip across the Mississippi. When asked for their papers, the men were unable to produce any and were turned over to the army for investigation.[37]

At 7 P.M. on November 5 the deck watch hailed and brought alongside the steamer *Blue Wing,* which was about to start downriver. An inspection by the bluejackets disclosed that the steamer was loaded with unmarked provisions and merchandise. Bills of lading shown to the searching party by the captain indicated that his cargo was to be landed at points below Helena, in an area known to be in Confederate hands. Equally suspicious was the knowledge that the merchantman had been loaded only at night. Since the captain and most of his crew were known secessionists, Selfridge had them placed under arrest, and the boat and cargo held as a prize.

Within less than seven hours, an order arrived from Major General William T. Sherman, who commanded at Memphis, directing that the navy release the *Blue Wing* and her crew.[38]

Despite the vigilance of the navy, Selfridge complained to Admiral

Porter, large quantities of contraband continued to be landed on the river banks, the traders having secured certificates from the Memphis board of trade. This body was responsible to General Sherman; consequently, Selfridge would like the admiral's opinion as to whether the navy should continue to honor permits signed by the board of trade.[39]

Selfridge's letter was read and answered by Porter on the eighth. Any additional repairs to the *Cairo* which Selfridge wished to undertake at Memphis were authorized. Porter wanted his captain to make the ironclad as efficient as possible, because an active campaign on the Mississippi was about to begin. Selfridge, in carrying out his instructions to control smuggling, was directed to pay no attention to the permits signed by the Memphis board of trade. To break up illicit traffic on the river banks, the officers from the *Cairo* were to board and examine any craft that seemed suspicious. Since almost everything had been classified as contraband, Selfridge should encounter no difficulty in supervising the blockade. As long as the Rebels could get supplies, Porter admonished, they would continue to fight, and it would do no harm "to put them to all the inconvenience we can." [40]

The *Cairo* on the thirteenth steamed upriver a few miles, and the crew spent several hours firing at targets with the big guns. Returning to Memphis, the ironclad found that the *Blue Wing* had returned "from her supposed contraband expedition, loaded with cotton received in exchange for her cargo of merchandise." Since cotton was selling for a dollar a pound, Yost noted in his diary, "somebody is making money." [41]

On November 17, while the gunners were being exercised at the guns, Commander Selfridge called upon Third Assistant Engineer George Aiken, who was on duty watch in the engine room. Selfridge told Aiken "to have a working power of steam at noon," as he intended to have a trial of the engines in the afternoon. A few minutes after 11 A.M., off-duty Fireman Andrew Lusk noticed that the boilers were giving off an unusual amount of heat. Glancing at the steam gauge, Lusk was horrified to see that the needle registered 205 pounds, and with the fire doors closed and dampers open, pressure was increasing rapidly. Unable to locate Aiken, Lusk rushed up onto the deck and reported his discovery to another engineer. The officer raced below, and after taking action to correct the situation, went to the steerage, where he found Aiken playing dominoes.

When Selfridge learned what had happened, he cited Lusk for his prompt action, which probably saved the vessel and crew from disaster. In a letter to Admiral Porter on November 17, Selfridge recommended Lusk for promotion and reported that he had suspended Aiken from duty.[42]

Upon receipt of Porter's message of the eighth authorizing him to "break up the general traffic on the river banks," Selfridge put his crew to work. By November 15 he was able to report that all fishing camps to a distance of fifteen miles above and below Memphis had been broken up, and all skiffs and flatboats seized. Patrols stopped and checked all boats, large or small, crossing the river from Memphis to Arkansas. Everything beyond the bare necessities of life, including salt, coffee, shoes, quinine—in fact, any article which the *Cairo's* officers felt might bring aid or comfort to the foe—was confiscated.[43]

On November 18 Commander Selfridge sent the *Cairo's* two largest boats, with an armed party led by Officer Hazlett, up Wolf River. When the expedition returned Hazlett reported that his men had scuttled between forty and fifty skiffs.[44]

On the seventeenth, Selfridge began compelling all people crossing the river, except those holding passes from the military, to take the oath of allegiance. He hoped that these measures would meet with Porter's approval and that "the rebels in Arkansas . . . [would] soon cease to regard the Mississippi as a source of supplies." [45]

While the navy was doing all in its power to blockade the Confederates, Selfridge complained, its efforts were being frustrated by the army which permitted the landing of large quantities of contraband at Memphis, Columbus, and other river ports in Union hands. He estimated that no less than $100,000 worth of merchandise was landed daily at Memphis.

Porter, having received reports concerning the defective fuses aboard the *Cairo* and a coal shortage at Memphis, wrote Selfridge on the fifteenth. If Selfridge would send the admiral a list of the type and caliber of projectiles required, he would see that a shipment was forwarded to Memphis. As to the coal, a barge load had been dispatched downstream a short time before. "Under no circumstances must anyone be allowed to take our coal hereafter excepting our own vessels," Porter cautioned his subordinate.[46]

7

RENDEZVOUS
WITH HISTORY

In the fall of 1862 the Union command initiated a second attempt to capture Vicksburg and seize control of the 260 miles of the Mississippi River still held by the Confederates. To accomplish this, the Army of the Tennessee under Major General Ulysses S. Grant in the first week of November commenced an advance southward down the Mississippi Central Railroad from Grand Junction, Tennessee. By the end of the third week his troops were in possession of Holly Springs, Mississippi, and the Confederates under Lieutenant General John C. Pemberton had dug in behind the Tallahatchie River to dispute Grant's march.

On November 12 General Sherman wrote Admiral Porter from Memphis regarding the situation in north Mississippi. He suggested a thrust by the navy up the Yazoo and Yalobusha to Grenada to attempt to destroy the railroad bridges at that point. Pemberton's army would then be confronted by a dangerous situation, with Grant's army to its front and an unfordable river to its rear.

Sherman learned that there were four feet of water over the bars below Yazoo City, Mississippi, and that several of the smaller Red River packets had emerged from their hiding place in the Delta and were operating from Vicksburg to the mouth of the Red River and back, bringing sugar and cattle from Louisiana. Sherman's informant had assured him that "many planters along [the] Yazoo are tired of war, and are actually praying for the coming" of Union gunboats.[1]

Porter at the same time inquired of Sherman, "Can you tell me whether you think he [Grant] will attempt to reach Vicksburg alone, or without the aid of gunboats? If he does, he will not act wisely."

The admiral wished to cooperate in every way, and he hoped that Sherman would let him know Grant's plans. If Grant were moving south, Porter would move down the river, "ready to be of any service to the army." [2]

Sherman replied that "a perfect concert of action should exist between all the forces of the United States operating down the valley"; and that he was of the opinion that Grant's troops could handle Pemberton's army. According to Grant's plans, the infantry columns were to strike Grenada and then advance down the watershed separating the Yazoo and Big Black rivers, to cut off Jackson from Vicksburg. The fleet should in this scheme "be abreast or ahead of the army." [3]

On November 19 Admiral Porter alerted the commander of his advance flotilla, Captain Walke, to prepare to start for the Yazoo.[4] Two days later Porter issued orders for Walke to take his entire force (except the *Benton* and *General Bragg*) to the Vicksburg area. If it were feasible, Walke's vessels were to enter the Yazoo and destroy any Rebel batteries encountered. Should the water be too low to get his ironclads over the bar at the mouth of the Yazoo, Walke was to send in the tinclads *Signal* and *Marmora* to keep the lower reaches of the river clear of Confederates, so that Federal infantry could be landed to assault Vicksburg.[5] The tinclads would then continue up the Yazoo and enter the Tallahatchie and Yalobusha rivers. If successful, this sweep would enable the navy to sever rail communications between the Confederate army opposing Grant's drive down the Mississippi Central Railroad and its base of operations at Jackson. As it developed, the unseasonably heavy autumnal rains caused a marked rise in the stages of the Mississippi's eastern tributaries, thus making the normally shallow streams and bayous navigable, and facilitating Porter's plan.[6]

On the morning of November 25, 1862, Walke's advance contingent, consisting of the ironclads *Carondelet* and *Mound City* and the tinclads *Signal* and *Marmora,* cast off from Helena en route for the mouth of the Yazoo. Because of low water on the Mississippi, several vessels which earlier had been ordered to report to Walke had been delayed. Among these were the *Pittsburg* and *Baron De Kalb.*[7] Because of low water, the flotilla traveled only during the daylight hours; the *Marmora* and *Signal* ranged far ahead of the ironclads.

The gunboats anchored off Milliken's Bend, Louisiana, at 3:30 P.M. on November 28. Within the hour, one of the tugs dropped down toward the Yazoo's mouth with a scouting party; before the tug had gone very far, she was fired on by a Rebel sharpshooter. One of the officers was wounded, and the tug returned to the fleet, so that the injured man could receive a surgeon's attention.[8]

On the morning of the twenty-ninth, Walke determined to send a strong force to reconnoiter the lower reaches of the Yazoo. The flotilla cast off as soon as it was light. Not wishing to risk grounding his ironclads, Walke hailed the captain of the *Marmora*, Lieutenant Robert Getty, and told him to take his boat and the *Signal* and enter the Yazoo. As the tinclads crossed the bar, soundings were made; eighteen feet was recorded here. The two vessels steamed slowly upriver, making soundings as they did. Off Willow Bayou, one mile above the mouth, a depth of seven feet was found. Three miles farther, at White House Shoals, the men on the lead lines reported only five feet of water. This was the only bar discovered that the ironclads would be unable to cross. At Snyder's and Drumgould's bluffs, whose sides were scarred by recently constructed Confederate earthworks, Union observers carefully scanned the position and strength of the Rebel fortifications; the light-drafts then returned to the mouth of the Yazoo.[9]

The *Mound City* had grounded during the morning's run down the Mississippi. As it was clear that the river was continuing to fall, Walke led his flotilla back to the anchorage off Milliken's Bend. As soon as the Mississippi started to rise, he vowed to drop back down and send another expedition up the Yazoo.[10]

On the last day of November, several vessels were sighted coming downstream. The newcomers proved to be the timberclad *Lexington* and the steamer *David Tatum*. Walke was delighted to learn that the steamer was loaded with a cargo of fresh provisions for his flotilla. Early the next morning the transport *Metropolitan*, crowded with nine hundred Confederate prisoners en route to Vicksburg to be exchanged, and the ironclad *Pittsburg* hove to off Milliken's Bend. Walke signaled Commander J. W. Shirk of the *Lexington* to convoy the *Metropolitan* to Vicksburg.[11]

By December 4 coal and food were in short supply aboard the vessels of the advance flotilla, so Walke sent the *Signal* upstream with a message to be forwarded to Admiral Porter reporting what the patrol up the Yazoo had disclosed. Walke also informed his superior that he was in need of several rams. According to information picked up by his men, the Confederates had several large steamers at Vicksburg, and Walke was afraid they might try to surprise his flotilla as Montgomery and his River Defense boats had the previous May at Plum Point. He further informed Porter that one of his pilots had learned the Confederates had assembled a force of from five hundred to six hundred mechanics at the Yazoo City Navy Yard. Several rams similar to the *Arkansas* were said to be on the ways, while a number of large steamers were being converted into cotton-clad gunboats. If he could get his gunboats past the forts at Snyder's and Drumgould's bluffs, he assured Porter, "we might make a good haul on them." [12]

Hardly had the *Signal* disappeared from view, before one of the city-class gunboats and three transports were sighted rounding the head of Island No. 102. A glance at the yellow recognition bands showed that the ironclad was the *Baron De Kalb*. Lieutenant Commander John S. Walker of the *De Kalb* told Walke that his vessel had grounded three times on the run down the Mississippi from Cairo, but little difficulty had been encountered in getting her off. Walke was disappointed to learn that there was little coal in the *De Kalb's* bunkers. While the strength of his flotilla had been increased, the fuel shortage had been accentuated. Though there was no need to do so—for from the cheers and jeers and stench the bluejackets had already guessed—Walker explained that there were Confederate prisoners (about twelve hundred) aboard the three steamers (the *Dacotah, Tecumseh,* and *Sallie List*) that his ironclad had escorted down from Helena. [13]

Several hours later the *Lexington* and the steamer *Metropolitan* came upriver from Vicksburg. Crowded aboard the transport were several hundred jubilant Union soldiers who had been exchanged for the Confederates carried on the run down. Realizing that Commander Shirk was familiar with the exchange routine, Walke signaled him to have his big timberclad stand by to convoy the three recently arrived transports and their Rebel prisoners to Vicksburg. [14]

Admiral Porter had anticipated Walke's call for rams. The admiral on November 24 had issued orders for the *Queen of the West* and *Switzerland* to proceed to Helena and report to Captain Walke. Coal was in short supply at Memphis and Helena, so Porter urged the officer in charge of the two rams, young Colonel Charles R. Ellet, to go downriver from Cairo at low speed. At Memphis, the rams would stop and take aboard some of the coal the crew of the *Cairo* had salvaged from a sunken barge. [15] By the time the rams joined Walke's flotilla on the sixth, the gunboats had again moved downstream and anchored off the bar at the mouth of the Yazoo. [16]

Porter on November 22 had issued orders for Commander Selfridge to proceed to Helena with the *Cairo* and report to Captain Walke.[17] The previous day the admiral had notified Walke that the *Cairo* was to join his expedition.[18] Selfridge was taken aback when he read his superior's orders, because if he were to honor other commitments it would be impossible to start down river for several days. Within the past several days, Selfridge had learned that a coal barge had sunk on the Arkansas side of the Mississippi. Coal was very short at Memphis, since all the barges had been sent down to Helena, so he had organized a large working party from the *Cairo's* crew. With the river falling rapidly, the barge was now above water, and he had turned his men to removing the coal. By nightfall on the twenty-fourth the sailors, using baskets, had removed about seven thousand bushels of coal from the barge, leaving another five thousand bushels that could be salvaged.

Obtaining ammunition for the *Cairo's* guns would likewise be a problem. Selfridge questioned the wisdom of requisitioning ammunition from the ordnance boat *Great Western,* because the shells had been aboard her for a long time. An inspection had shown that the fuses were "merely protected by a piece of brown paper," and he doubted their reliability. If he were to take the *Cairo* downriver, Selfridge would like very much to have shells with navy fuses. He was also concerned about the three ancient rifled 42-pounders. By carefully watching the powder charge, he believed, these pieces might "do very well in ordinary service," but if employed in a protracted bombardment they would be likely to burst.[19]

General Sherman, upon learning that the *Cairo* was under orders to go to Helena, informed Selfridge he was extremely anxious that a gunboat remain at Memphis until the garrison was reinforced. To underscore his point, Sherman explained that he planned to march with three divisions on the twenty-sixth to join General Grant. Upon his departure only three regiments would be left to hold the extensive earthworks guarding the approaches to Memphis. Relaying this information to Porter on the twenty-fifth, Selfridge pointed out that he had assumed the responsibility of remaining at Memphis for the time being.[20]

Porter fumed when he read Selfridge's letter on the twenty-eighth. "With every disposition to oblige the army officers," Porter wrote, he would feel better if he were allowed to deploy the vessels of his squadron as he thought best. Unless events justified a subordinate in not carrying out his orders at once, he was "taking upon himself more responsibility than he is called upon to do." This time, however,

Porter would let Selfridge judge whether the *Cairo* was required at Memphis until relieved by another vessel, though it would interfere with the expedition Walke was leading down the Mississippi.[21]

Selfridge kept his crew busy removing coal from the beached barge and sending it across the Mississippi to Memphis. Some of the coal was stored in the *Cairo's* bunkers, so the ironclad would not be delayed when her replacement showed up. On the afternoon of the twenty-fifth, Hazlett turned out a twenty-man detail, and taking the cutter, the sailors made a short patrol up the Mississippi. About three miles above Memphis, the cutter sighted and chased a skiff whose occupants ran their vessel aground, jumped out and disappeared into the brush. When the Federals searched the small boat, they found and seized seventy-four pairs of shoes, one box of cavalry boots, and twelve boxes of cotton cards.

Two days, November 27 and 28, were spent by the *Cairo* tied up near the foundry. A quantity of railroad iron was carried aboard the ironclad, and used as further reinforcement for the casemate protecting the boilers and machinery.[22] As soon as the carpenters had finished strengthening the boat's casemate, the *Cairo* pulled out into the channel and anchored with her bow upstream. The watch on the afternoon of December 2 sighted mounted Confederates riding through the woods on the Arkansas shore. Fearful lest the Rebels planned to attack the men guarding the coal barge, Selfridge sent his crew to their battle stations. The port guns were cast loose, and a couple of shells sent the Southerners scampering to cover.[23]

The *Cairo* was finally relieved on the morning of the fourth by the *General Bragg* and by mid-morning had passed the Chickasaw Bluffs. Darkness overtook the ironclad above Helena, and Selfridge, aware of the low stage of the Mississippi, tied up for the night. When the *Cairo* got underway the next morning, snow was falling. The flakes increased rapidly in size, and by the time the ironclad reached Helena, visibility on the river was almost zero. Selfridge tied up to the Helena wharfboat and waited for the weather to clear. From the citizens, Selfridge and his crew learned that snow was rather unusual in this latitude.[24]

At 1 P.M. on the sixth the snow had ended, and the *Cairo* cast off and headed downstream. Toward dusk the ironclad grounded on a sand bar. Selfridge and his men worked throughout the night (starting and reversing the engines, shifting stores and guns, and finally putting lines ashore) before they were able to free the *Cairo*.

The morning of the eighth found the *Cairo* anchored off Illawara plantation on the Louisiana side of the Mississippi. The weather was unseasonably cold, and the sailors had used all the kindling to fire the pot-bellied heating stoves in the quarters. A landing party of armed men was sent ashore to secure wood; a good supply was brought aboard, and the gunboat resumed her run downstream. Shortly after noon, the channel bore over toward the Mississippi shore. Yost at this time was standing on the port side of the spar deck next to "one of our best sailors, William Smith." Suddenly and without warning came a volley of small-arms fire. Smith let go a yell and clutched his left elbow with his right hand. While Surgeon J. Otis Burt and his assistant attended to the wounded man, the rest of the crew raced to their battle stations. The guns in the port battery raked the clump of woods from which the shots had been fired. Pilot Young chanced to be standing near a stack of muskets. Quickly snatching up one, he fired, and Yost saw a Confederate fall. Thick undergrowth concealed the rest of the Rebels. To take out his frustration, Selfridge had the big guns turned on a nearby house.[25]

The lookouts aboard Walke's flotilla sighted the *Cairo* at 2 P.M. In response to a signal from Walke, Commander Selfridge anchored his vessel off the mouth of the Yazoo. As soon as the lines had been secured, Selfridge had the launch lowered and reported to Walke aboard the *Carondelet*. While the officers talked, the men manning the launch mingled with the *Carondelet's* crew. As in all wars, rumors were plentiful. Sailors from the flag steamer told the newcomers that in the morning the flotilla would enter the Yazoo and attack the eight-gun battery—known as the Snyder's Bluff Battery—the Rebels had thrown up at Snyder's Bluff. It was after dark when the *Lexington* and the three steamers that had carried the exchanged Confederate prisoners to Vicksburg rounded Kings Point and anchored near the flotilla.

Soon after daybreak on the ninth, Walke signaled Commander Shirk of the *Lexington* to convoy the steamers to Helena. Before she started upstream the *Lexington* came alongside the *Cairo,* and the wounded William Smith, whose injured arm had been amputated above the elbow, was placed on a litter and carried aboard the timberclad by six of his shipmates.[26]

During the morning Walke and his officers were cheered by the return of the *Signal* from Helena. The tinclad was accompanied by the steamer *Champion* towing several barges loaded with coal. The run down from Memphis had all but exhausted the coal in the *Cairo's* bunkers, so Walke authorized Selfridge to have first call on one of the barges.

The next morning Walke advised his captains that the ram *Switzerland* would be dispatched to Helena with the fleet's mail. This news caused considerable excitement. Men who could write dashed letters off to loved ones, while the captains and their officers prepared requisitions for needed supplies. Accompanied by the steamer *Champion*, the ram left for Helena at 4:30 P.M. Meanwhile, the *Cairo's* launch had been sent ashore with a detail to gather firewood. The fatigue party had been working about two hours when the signal "Call your men off the shore" was hoisted by the *Carondelet*. Confederate partisans had been spotted lurking in the woods near the working party. The bluejackets scrambled into the launch and returned to their boat.

At 11:30 P.M. Selfridge decided to test his crew. General Quarters sounded. "It took the first division (every man being asleep when the alarm was given) exactly 3½ minutes to be ready for action," diarist Yost proudly recorded, while "the other divisions reported in from 6 to 10 minutes. At 12 midnight we left our positions at the guns, after securing them in proper Man of War style, brought down our hammocks and were soon fast asleep." [27]

The next morning Walke sent the tinclads *Marmora* and *Signal*, up the Yazoo. The *Marmora*, accompanied by a tug, had made several sweeps up the river earlier. Each time Lieutenant Getty returned with news that there was insufficient water over White House Shoals to float the deeper draft ironclads and rams. Further knowledge of the Confederate fortifications at Snyder's and Drumgould's bluffs was gleaned from a runaway slave, who informed Captain Walke that the Rebels had no rams or gunboats up the Yazoo, but that they had a heavy timber barricade at or near the fort, twenty-three miles above the mouth of the Yazoo, which mounted ten guns.[28] Walke wanted confirmation of this.

Arriving within sight of the Confederate earthworks at Drumgould's Bluff on the morning of December 11, the sailors "were apprised of the presence of a number of torpedoes by the unaccountable number of small scows and stationary floats of various kinds along the channel of the river." [29] One of the sailors aboard the *Marmora* picked up a musket and fired at one of the objects, which blew up with a tremendous explosion that rocked the boat from stem to stern. Carefully avoiding more of the "infernal machines," the two gunboats began to turn about, preparatory to heading downstream. While the *Signal* was performing this maneuver, difficult in the narrow river, another mine detonated near her. A geyser of water drenched the tinclad's decks. Satisfied that the area was unhealthy, the two little stern-wheelers fled downriver to carry the unwelcome news regarding the mining of the channel. Near Old River, the gunboats were fired on by Confederate snipers lying in ambush, but no one was injured.[30]

The captains of the tinclads informed Walke that they could destroy all the torpedoes with perfect safety if he would have them protected by one or two of the ironclads, "as there was water enough to admit them, and the river was rising." [31]

Walke and his officers were familiar with Confederate torpedoes, having encountered them at Fort Henry and Columbus. They had also read with interest of the efforts of the Rebels on the Atlantic Seaboard to destroy Union warships with "infernal machines." Although the Southerners had failed to sink or seriously damage any vessels, Walke was worried, and well he should be. The outbreak of the Civil War had found the Confederate authorities confronted with a number of vexing problems. None of these was more critical than the defense from forays by the Union navy of the South's long and exposed coastline, with its many navigable rivers penetrating the hinter-land. Lacking the industrial capacity to build a navy that could compete on numerically equal terms, the Confederacy tried to overcome Yankee superiority by two means which have concerned small navy powers throughout history: the invincible warship, and novel and untried secret weapons that might destroy the foe at one stroke.

The invincible warship was tried on the Atlantic coast with the *Virginia,* but she was neutralized by the *Monitor;* in the West, the *Arkansas* fought the combined fleets of Flag Officers Farragut and Davis but, when her engines failed, the Confederates were compelled to scuttle the vessel to keep her from falling to the Federals; on the Gulf Coast, the *Tennessee* failed against Farragut's swarming warships. But if the invincible warship failed, one of the secret weapons worked—the torpedo, known today as the mine. The idea had been current for centuries, but it had never been used with any notable success until the Confederates developed it into a potent weapon of naval warfare.

Indeed, so many people worked on variations of the theme throughout the Confederacy that its development stands as an illustration of the hypothesis of concurrent invention. It was the quest of the Confederate Navy Department for a practical torpedo that touched off the multiple search. One of the several people who arrived at solutions to the problem at approximately the same time was Lieutenant Beverly Kennon, a Confederate naval officer in New Orleans, who considered torpedoes too good an idea to overlook. He became a claimant for developing the first electrically activated torpedo when he conducted experiments on Lake Pontchartrain in August, 1861. He was unable to produce them on a practical scale, and none were used in the defense of New Orleans. Yet his efforts were by no means wasted, because he appeared at Vicksburg in the autumn of 1862 and imparted his knowledge to Acting Masters Zedekiah Mc-Daniel and Francis M. Ewing. These two men were placed in charge of preparing the torpedoes that were placed in the Yazoo River, and they fulfilled their duty well.

McDaniel and Ewing obtained a number of five-gallon glass demijohns from the Vicksburg and Yazoo City merchants, filled them with black powder borrowed from the artillery, and inserted primers into the necks. Next, waterproofed copper wires were secured to the primers, with one end of the wire connected with a galvanic cell to provide a spark. Attached to wooden floats to provide buoyancy, the torpedoes were submerged several feet below the muddy surface, and anchored in the channel of the Yazoo. The copper wires led to camouflaged "torpedo pits" behind Colonel Benson Blake's recently constructed levee, which paralleled the east bank of the river for several miles. Volunteers posted behind the levee would have the task of detonating the mines.[32]

Captain Walke consulted the captains of his ironclads (Selfridge, Hoel, and Walker) on what course to follow. They determined to send the *Cairo* (lightest and fastest of the Eads ironclads), *Pittsburg,* and the ram *Queen of the West* to protect the tinclads while they cleared the Yazoo of torpedoes. The captains were cautioned by Walke "to be very careful not to run their vessels in among the torpedoes, but to avoid the channel where they were set; to scour the shore with small boats and haul the torpedoes on shore, and destroy them before proceeding farther up the river; that this duty would be performed by the *Marmora* and *Signal.*" [33]

Walke was recovering from a recent bout with malaria, so he placed Commander Selfridge in charge of the projected expedition. He repeated his instructions to Selfridge, cautioning him that if he ran into any difficulty in removing the torpedoes, the expedition was to be abandoned until better means for dealing with them could be devised.[34]

The morning of the twelfth was cool and cloudy. At 7:30 A.M. the five vessels got under way and entered the Yazoo, the *Marmora* leading, followed in order by the *Signal, Queen of the West, Cairo,* and *Pittsburg.*[35] At 10 A.M. the ironclads hammered the woods near Old River from which Confederate sharpshooters had fired on the two tinclads the previous afternoon.[36] By eleven the flotilla had reached a point near where Chickasaw Bayou enters the Yazoo. Here the *Marmora* caught up with a skiff containing two men, a white and a Negro. The former was Jonathan Williams, an overseer on Colonel Blake's plantation. When questioned, Williams admitted, with some reluctance, full knowledge of the whereabouts of the torpedoes. Lieutenant Getty had the overseer thrown into irons, since the Negro had told the naval officers that Williams "was paid $500 for services in pulling off the torpedoes." [37]

The little flotilla was cautiously running upstream when suddenly the rattle of small arms reached Selfridge aboard the *Cairo.* The sound came from the direction of the *Marmora,* up ahead with her bows hidden by a sharp bend in the Yazoo. But Selfridge could see her stern, and observed with alarm that the tinclad had reversed her wheel and was beginning to back water. Selfridge, satisfied that the *Marmora* had been fired on by Confederate snipers, hastened to her support with the *Cairo.* As the ironclad headed upstream, she opened fire on the woods on the south bank of the river with her starboard battery. As the grim, black ironclad drew abreast of the stern-wheeler, Selfridge hailed Getty, demanding to know why his boat had stopped.

Getty replied, "Here is where the torpedoes are."

Selfridge now realized that the musket fire had come from the sailors aboard the *Marmora,* and that the object at which they were shooting was a block of wood floating in the water.[38] Selfridge shouted for the sailors aboard the *Marmora* to cease fire, lower the cutter, and investigate the suspicious object. Some difficulty was experienced in launching the small boat, and Selfridge, growing more impatient by the moment, ordered one of the *Cairo's* four small boats lowered. By the time the *Cairo's* crew had lowered and manned the boat, the *Marmora* had solved her difficulties and her cutter, commanded by Ensign Walter E. J. Fentress, was in the water, pulling toward the shore to reconnoiter and cut the lines and cords which held the torpedoes.

Spying a line, Fentress severed it with his sword, and a large object popped to the surface in mid-channel. Pulling to it by the line, Fentress found that it was a mine. Upon closer inspection, he discovered a copper wire connecting the torpedo with the shore, and was ordered by Selfridge to cut it.[39] Concurrent with Fentress' discovery, the *Cairo's* small boat had fished up the flotsam at which the *Marmora's* sailors had been shooting. It proved to be part of a torpedo exploded the previous day.[40]

In the confusion caused by launching the small boats, the bow of the *Cairo* had drifted into dangerous proximity to the shore, and Selfridge rang for the engineers to reverse the engines. As the big ironclad backed out into the channel, she prepared to head upstream. At the same time, Selfridge shouted for the *Marmora* to get under way. For a moment Getty hesitated, fearing to take his boat into unreconnoitered waters, but Selfridge impatiently reiterated his order, and the *Marmora's* wheel started to turn slowly. Irritated by the delay, Selfridge ordered the *Cairo* forward.

Suddenly Confederate big guns on Drumgould's Bluff opened a long-range fire. With their glasses, the naval officers could see puffs of white smoke as the Rebel guns were discharged. The captain of the *Cairo's* bow battery called for his gun captains to place their two rifled 42-pounders in action.

The *Cairo's* powerful wheel had made only a dozen revolutions when two explosions in quick succession shook the vessel. Her port anchor was hurled several feet in the air. One torpedo had detonated close to her port quarter flooding the forward shellroom, and the other had exploded under her starboard bow. The shock from the former was so great that it lifted the No. 1 port gun with such force that one of the cap squares snapped as if it were pewter, injuring three men. The tube was dismounted from the carriage, and the muzzle of the 32-pounder pointed upward at a rakish angle.[41]

First Class Boy Yost, who had taken his station at the starboard bow rifled 42-pounder, later wrote that "just as we were training on the battery, (2½ miles distant) we were struck by a torpedo, which exploded under our starboard bow, a few feet from the center and some 35 or 40 feet from the bow proper just under our provision store room, which crushed in the bottom of the boat so that the water rushed in like the roar of Niagara. In 5 minutes the forward part of the Hold was full of water and the forward part of the gundeck was flooded." [42]

Initially, sailors on the other vessels of the flotilla did not realize how badly the *Cairo* was damaged. Within several minutes the water was over her fo'c'sle, and Selfridge, who resolved to beach his ironclad if possible, shouted for the pilots to run her aground. The captain of the *Signal* was ordered to bring his tinclad to the aid of the sinking boat. As the bow of the *Cairo* touched the bank, blue-jackets leaped ashore and secured a hawser to a cottonwood, hoping to keep the vessel from slipping off into deep water. Hand and steam pumps were manned in the struggle to keep the ironclad afloat.[43] Selfridge soon realized that his boat was doomed and sadly ordered preparations to abandon her.

By the time the *Queen of the West* came alongside, "the water was waist deep on the forward part of the gundeck." The *Queen* removed part of the crew, while the rest took to the ironclad's three remaining boats. The *Cairo* began to slip backward; the hawser securing her to the cottonwood tautened, held for a moment, and then parted. Slowly and majestically, the *Cairo* slid back into deep water.[44]

Yost recorded the scene as follows:

We were ordered to leave our quarters at the guns and take all the small arms we could and to go on board the Ram, which was done quickly but without confusion. I secured two Revolvers and a few of my personal belongings, including my private journal. . . . Almost everyone saved something; but unfortunately, the "Logbook," the Signal book (which however was bound with leaden covers) and the ship's official papers were all lost. Executive Officer Hiram K. Hazlett, and the writer were the last two persons to leave the sinking vessel which we did by jumping into the "Dingey" which was manned by two sailors, and awaiting us at the stern; we moved off just in time to escape being swallowed up in the seething caldron of foaming water.[45]

Within twelve minutes after the explosion, the *Cairo* had vanished, except for the tops of her chimneys and jackstaffs, from one of which the Stars and Stripes still floated.

Even this catastrophe was not allowed to interrupt the mission of the flotilla. After the *Pittsburg* and *Marmora* had hammered the under-brush-covered banks with shell, canister, and grape, small boats were put out by the surviving vessels. While the crews were taking up and destroying torpedoes, one of the *Cairo's* small boats took down the flag, and the *Queen of the West* pulled down the chimneys and jack-staffs of the ironclad to hide her grave from the Confederates who might try to remove the big guns. Before many moments had passed, the waters of the Yazoo flowed smoothly over the hidden remains of the ironclad.

Besides dragging from the river and dismantling twelve torpedoes, the bluejackets from the *Pittsburg* advanced up the steep east bank as far as Blake's levee. The levee, the Yanks discovered, had been used by the Rebels to shelter the men charged with exploding the mines. After destroying the powder magazine and other materials used to manufacture the torpedoes, and also bashing in about twenty small boats and skiffs found in the area, the flotilla returned to the mouth of the Yazoo.

After reporting to Walke at 4:30 P.M. the sad news that his ironclad had been sunk by the enemy's "infernal machines," Selfridge mustered his crew. The division commanders reported that no lives had been lost in the sinking; about a half dozen men had been injured, but none seriously.[46]

The loss of the *Cairo* earned her captain criticism from many quarters. A fellow officer recalled, "On December 12 Lieutenant-Commander Selfridge of the *Cairo* found two torpedoes and removed them by placing his vessel over them." [47] Selfridge many years later recalled, "As a young officer in command of a large ironclad, the *Cairo,* I had been so unfortunate, by pushing perhaps a little farther to the front than prudence dictated to lose my ship by the explosion of a torpedo in the Yazoo River." [48]

Admiral Porter, upon learning of the loss of the ironclad, notified Secretary Welles that the *Cairo* "incautiously proceeded too far ahead . . . when the torpedo exploded under her, knocking out her bottom." [49] Later in the day, after Porter had studied the reports of the officers involved, he wrote Welles: "My own opinion is that due caution was not observed and that the vessels went ahead too fast." [50] He added, "These torpedoes have proved so harmless heretofore (not one exploding out of the many hundreds that have been planted by the rebels) that officers have not felt that respect for them to which they are entitled. The torpedo which blew up the *Cairo* was evidently fired by a galvanic battery." [51] After a more thorough investigation, Porter advised Welles, "I can see in it nothing more than one of the accidents of war arising from a zealous disposition on the part of the commanding officer to perform his duty." The admiral continued, "Captain Walke sent up and made a reconnaissance and afterwards sent up an expedition agreeable to my orders, but he did not calculate how smart the rebels would be, who in the meantime, put down some hundreds of torpedoes." [52] Selfridge therefore could not be singled out as solely responsible for the loss.

Commander Selfridge and the survivors boarded the *Marmora* on the morning of December 13. Instructions had been issued by Walke for the tinclad to take them to the Cairo Naval Station.[53] The additional personnel—180 officers and men—severely taxed facilities aboard the tinclad. Rations ran short before the *Marmora* reached Cairo, but the crew shared their food with the survivors, and, although for several days all subsisted "principally on water and 'hard tack' no complaints were made." A shortage of blankets caused considerable suffering on the run up the Mississippi. At night the survivors "had to lie down upon the decks in . . . ordinary clothing—having saved neither overcoats nor blankets." [54]

Admiral Porter had left Cairo for the Vicksburg area aboard his flag steamer *Black Hawk* on December 14. On the first night out, the vessel grounded at Island No. 23, and remained there for the next three days. While the flag steamer was still stuck on the bar on the morning of the seventeenth, the lookouts hailed the *Marmora* as she came alongside. The *Marmora* lowered a small boat, and Commander Selfridge boarded the *Black Hawk,* and greeted his superior with the news that his ironclad had been sunk.[55]

This was the first news Porter had received concerning the mining of the Yazoo by the Rebels. Selfridge, seeing that Porter was agitated, remarked, "I suppose you will want to hold a court."

"Courts! I have no time to order courts!" Porter exploded. "I can't blame any officer who seeks to put his ship close to the enemy. Is there any other vessel you would like to have?"

Selfridge answered that he knew of only one at the time without a commander.

"Very well," Porter retorted, "you shall have her." Turning to the captain of the *Black Hawk,* Porter ordered, "Breese, make out Selfridge's orders to the *Conestoga."* [56]

Following this conversation, Porter notified Welles, "I have put . . . [Selfridge] in command of the *Conestoga* . . . , trusting that he may be more fortunate hereafter, this being the second time during the war his vessel has gone down under him." [57] Porter was referring to the fact that Selfridge had been in charge of the *Cumberland's* forward guns when, on March 8 of that year, she was sunk by the *Virginia* in Hampton Roads.

As soon as the survivors from the *Cairo* had landed at the Cairo Naval Station on the afternoon of the eighteenth, they were besieged by newspapermen. The next day the readers of the St. Louis *Daily Democrat* learned from an article datelined Cairo:

> The gunboat *Marmora* arrived to-day from Yazoo River. She brings the crew of the *Cairo*, which gunboat was destroyed by a torpedo, twenty-one miles up, the Yazoo, Friday last, at noon.
> An expedition, consisting of the *Cairo, Pittsburg, Marmora, Signal,* and the ram *Queen of the West* went up to clean . . . out the torpedoes. They had already raised two of the monsters, and were proceeding cautiously . . . , when a torpedo discharged under the port bow of the *Cairo*, tearing a hole in her twelve feet square.
> The concussion knocked down every one on board, but no one was seriously hurt. The *Queen* came along and took the crew off in nine minutes. The *Cairo* sunk in six fathoms water, nothing but the signal mast and chimneys being visible.
> She had just been refitted and clad with railroad iron in front, and was considered the lightest and fastest of iron-clads. Master H. K. Haslett [*sic*] thinks the torpedoe [*sic*] was exploded by a galvanic battery.[58]

As the Cairo paper was a weekly, it was Thursday, December 23, before it informed its subscribers of the sad fate that had overtaken the ironclad named for their city. Using information given him by the survivors, the editor wrote: ". . . she sank out of sight in seven minutes. Nothing was saved but the life on board and that by only the almost super-human exertions of the crews of the other boats in the vicinity. The *Cairo* carried thirteen guns and a splendid magazine. She is a total loss. She proved herself a serviceable craft, having taken active part in nearly every naval engagement on the Western & Southern waters." [59]

The mining of the *Cairo* on December 12, 1862, at 11:55 A.M., was a momentous event in military history for on that day electrically activated torpedoes had sunk an armored warship, thus inaugurating a new era in the history of naval warfare. True, the idea of mines was ancient. Leonardo da Vinci had propounded the notion centuries before, but it was the Confederacy that gave the first practical demonstration of the efficiency of the device in combat: the enormous offensive power represented by the ironclad had been balanced by the defensive power of the submarine torpedo.

8

"OPERATION CAIRO"
BEGINS

THE evidence accumulated in the carefully recorded probes that Don Jacks, Warren Grabau, and I had made during 1956 told us that we really had found the *Cairo*. The hulk's construction and dimensions were right, and it was in exactly the right place. Yet, doubts kept me wondering if by some unhappy fluke we had discovered an old steamboat or a barge. I was hesitant about encouraging further activities, but further investigation was needed. Three years passed before another expedition was organized. Meanwhile, we had discussed the situation with Jackson, Mississippi, scuba divers Ken Parks and James "Skeeter" Hart. They felt they would be able to answer a number of questions I had formulated regarding the sunken ironclad, for the plans of the city-class gunboats on file in the National Archives were very general, and many details of construction were missing. "Diving with tank and regulator," the men explained, "gives the diver freedom of movement not found in other forms of diving." Preparations were made for underwater explorations.

Since the lower reaches of the Yazoo, where the *Cairo* sank, are affected by the stage of the Mississippi, we decided to begin work in the fall; at that time of year the river could be expected to be very low. But before operations could commence, a cold wave invaded the Deep South. The explorers would be operating without coldwater diving suits.

On October 1, 1959, Don Jacks and I probed the depths with long reinforcing rods to locate the pilothouse, the part of the vessel nearest the surface. By the time the scuba divers had put on their gear, Jacks shouted, "Here she is!" A reinforcing rod had stabbed into one of

104

the pilothouse's eight sloping sides. Without further delay, Parks and Hart slipped into the water, swam to the probe, and followed it beneath the water. This was necessary because the Yazoo is one of the muddiest rivers in the world. Below its surface the divers would operate in total darkness.

Hart touched the pilothouse first. Slipping past the top, the two worked their way slowly and cautiously down its sides to the deck. The silt-covered decking appeared to be in good condition, not rotted as we had feared after having been submerged for ninety-seven years. Within five minutes, however, the cold began to affect the men. They were breathing rapidly—their bodies trying to replace heat lost to the icy river—and had to surface to avoid going into shock. Before leaving the deck, they picked up several loose 8-inch spikes, the only artifacts recovered by this expedition. Nothing more could be done without coldwater diving suits. A week later the divers went down again, this time well insulated by coldwater suits purchased with funds advanced by two Jackson businessmen. Parks and Hart felt their way around the pilothouse. On each of its eight sides they found rectangular ports covered by ½-inch iron flaps. The men brought these flaps to the surface one at a time. Each piece had in its center a small circular hole the size of a dollar. When the ironclad was fired on, the flaps could be pulled down, and the pilots would squint through these small apertures. Plans, drawings, and photographs of the city-class gunboats failed to show these flaps. Already underwater archaeology was providing evidence which a study of documents had failed to produce.

The men also determined by feel that the pilothouse was sheeted with 1½-inch iron plates backed by many inches of wood—giant timbers which seemed to be in a good state of preservation, except at the very top. When the divers sought to enter the pilothouse through the top, they found the interior filled to the level of the ports with packed sand. Hundreds of freshwater shrimp, finding their home invaded, swam frantically about. Since visibility was zero, the divers at first were perplexed as to what strange creatures they had encountered. After digging awhile and making little headway, they returned to the spar deck.

In feeling their way aft, they encountered the lower sections of the chimneys—four feet in diameter and made of ¼-inch plating—which remained after the Federals had pulled down the Cairo's chimneys and jackstaffs.

Near the place where the stern should be, a large mound of silt was found which, I theorized, covered the wheelhouse. In an effort to enter the casemate, the divers felt for the gunports, but encountered huge log rafts. These seemingly impenetrable jams of waterlogged trees had over the years found a resting place—lodged against the *Cairo*.

In another dive several hours later, Hart and Parks brought up a number of spikes and loose pieces of decking which were to be exposed to air to see if they would deteriorate. Finally, when the air reserves were exhausted, work was suspended. All had been done that could be accomplished without a high-pressure water jet to force the hard-packed sand from the pilothouse. If one could be used, it might be possible to find an entrance to the casemate.

During the winter of 1959–60, a nonprofit organization, "Operation *Cairo,* Inc.," was chartered with the object of raising and preserving the sunken ironclad as a naval museum. In addition, contact had been established with the Mississippi Commission on the War Between the States, whose chairman was John Holland, mayor of Vicksburg. Since no money was available, all work and equipment would have to be donated. At the mayor's request, the Anderson-Tully Lumber Company of Memphis and Vicksburg agreed to make available to Operation *Cairo,* Inc. for two days without charge a five-ton floating crane and the powerful tug *Porterfield.* By the beginning of September, 1960, preparations for another expedition had been completed.

Before calling for the heavy equipment, the scuba divers, their assistants, and I spent a week at the site getting ready to resume work. A barge with a World War II-vintage pumping unit was towed up the Yazoo and moored to the left bank near the wreck. Scuba divers Parks and Hart and their topside man Jacks attached buoys, made of empty plastic containers, to various known points on the gunboat—the pilothouse, the chimneys, and the paddle-wheel spiders. As soon as the pump was ready and primed, the divers went below and used powerful jets of water to clear the sand from the upper portion of the pilothouse. Since they were working inside an enclosure, the sediment settled almost as rapidly as it was jetted loose. Despite this difficulty the divers were able to clean out the structure to a point several feet below the ports.

We determined to attempt removal of the pilothouse from the spar deck, using the crane which Anderson-Tully had made available. Since records indicated that it was secured by spikes to the deck, whose wood had been softened by the long submersion, we believed that the structure could be removed without damaging the craft. Moreover, we hoped that with the pilothouse out of the way, divers could enter the casemate and assess the damage to the hull caused by the explosion of the torpedoes.

September 14, 1960, was the day scheduled for lifting the pilothouse. Operations commenced long before the *Porterfield* arrived on the scene. Diver Hart reported he had found a large cylindrical object which felt as if it might be a gun tube, or it could be one of the ubiquitous tree trunks. After he discussed its location and position with me, we decided that the object might be one of the ironclad's guns. Hart buoyed the object so it could be investigated further.

By this time the tug *Porterfield* and the floating crane had arrived. Since the divers had to work by touch, it was decided to assign Parks the task of passing the heavy 1½-inch cables through the pilothouse ports so the structure could be slinged. Hart was to take a hose down and jet away the mud from the tubular object.

Within a short time he had cleared away enough mud to confirm that it was indeed a gun. A cable was taken down and secured to the gunport cover so that it could be removed. The cover was found to be of 2-inch oak, in an excellent state of preservation. Shortly thereafter Hart reported that he had cleared away enough mud to get a cable around the muzzle of the tube, and assisted by Parks, he secured a 1-inch cable to the gun. The giant crane took up the slack, then stopped. The strain had been too great and a fuel injector on the engine had blown.

Laboriously the two divers unhooked the cable and held it with lines while a gigantic A-frame, designed to lift fifty tons was jockeyed into position and its massive hook was lowered. As the winch took up the slack, the bow of the barge to which the A-frame was attached dipped lower and lower into the water. Suddenly the 1-inch cable snapped.

Since dusk was falling, the divers reluctantly decided to concentrate on bringing up the pilothouse. As soon as the barge could be maneuvered into position, the hook from the A-frame was attached to the ends of the two cables which scuba diver Parks had passed through the pilothouse ports. Once again the bow of the huge barge began to sink into the river as the cable strained. Something gave, and the barge righted. At the same instant, a line of bubbles shot to the surface, roughly outlining the craft. Subsequently we speculated that the entire hulk had moved a thousandth of an inch before the pilothouse pulled loose. Moments later the top of the pilothouse emerged from the churning, muddy water. Not since the Eads city-class iron-clads had been scrapped after the Civil War had such an object been seen. As this relic from another age emerged from the river in the twilight, shivers ran down my spine. At no moment of my life have I felt a greater awe.

As soon as the pilothouse had been secured, we decided to make one final attempt to recover the gun. By this time it was dark, but the crew of the *Porterfield* switched on the working lights, and within a few minutes, the tug had shifted the barge into position near the buoy marking the location of the gun.

Hart disappeared into the river, taking a 2-inch cable with him. When he surfaced, he called to the A-frame operator to lower the hook. As soon as the cable had been secured to the hook, a steady but powerful pull was exerted. For a few moments, which seemed to the onlookers like hours, it appeared that nothing would give. This time the cable held, and the gun, along with its wooden naval carriage, was pulled from the *Cairo* and deposited on the barge. Historians, scuba divers, and Civil War buffs examined the prize with flashlights. Under its coating of mud, the cannon seemed in perfect condition.

The next morning the gun and carriage were cleaned. On examination the tube was found to be an 8-inch gun. The cap was still on the nipple; the piece was charged with canister. The sight was set at 350 yards, and the brass slide was deeply grooved at this point—a certain indication that most of the firing had been done at minimum ranges. The white oak carriage was in as good condition as it had been on that cold December day ninety-eight years before. Even more remarkable, impressions in the mud on the cascabel and carriage indicated that the hemp lines used to take up recoil had been intact up to the moment the gun was pulled from the casemate.

The gun, carriage, and pilothouse were removed to Vicksburg on the Anderson-Tully barge on September 15. Funds raised by Operation *Cairo,* Inc. were used to defray expenses and to purchase a trailer to house the gun and carriage. As soon as they were landed, a haphazard treatment of the carriage and wooden portions of the pilothouse was started with polyethylene gycol. Photographs and measurements of the objects were taken. Through the cooperation of Senator John Stennis of Mississippi, the assistance of an army demolition team from Fort Benning, Georgia, was obtained and the 8-inch naval gun was disarmed.

Before closing down operations for the year, the area where the pilothouse had formerly rested was examined. Although the structure was gone, a pyramid of packed sand remained. After this was jetted away, the divers recovered artillery short swords, a soap dish, a Colt's Army revolver, pitcher, washbowl, mirror, can of shoe polish, several bottles of medicine, folding chair, tub, communications gear (the signal board and speaking tubes), parts of the wheel, and a saddle. On the signal board was nailed a horseshoe—some sailor had thought it would bring the vessel good luck. A close study of the artifacts which had been recovered reinforced us in our belief that the ironclad could and should be raised.

On February 6, 1962, the Mississippi Commission on the War Between the States authorized the engineering firm of Michael Baker, Jr., Inc. to conduct a survey of the feasibility of raising the *Cairo*. This project was completed and submitted to the commission on March 29. Since the survey was undertaken during a period of high water, no scuba diving operations were attempted at this time. The project engineer relied on information garnered by the scuba divers in the period 1959–61.

The Michael Baker engineers reported:

1. The best method of raising the Gunboat *Cairo* was apparently to use barges positioned on each side of the boat and attached by cables to beams placed underneath the boat. It could then be raised by a combination of a buoyant force and lifting force of the cables.

2. There was no way to predetermine the condition of the boat or repairs necessary until after the actual raising had been accomplished.

3. The boat should be displayed on a permanent barge rather than moved to an inland site.

4. Approximately two months would be required to raise the boat and the operation should be timed with the most favorable river stage.

5. The estimated cost to raise the *Cairo* and place it on display was $300,000. This figure included an allowance of $40,000 for cleaning and renovating the boat after she had been raised. The estimate also included the cost of erecting a one-story building 20 by 50 feet on the permanent barge to provide space for a meeting room, rest rooms, and quarters for the custodian. Ventilating and heating systems should be provided to make the facility comfortable for the viewing public.

In October, 1962, a team of scuba divers from the New England Naval and Maritime Museum at Newport, Rhode Island, which was working on sunken chlorine barges at Natchez, Mississippi, became interested in the *Cairo*.[1] At the request of Operation *Cairo,* Inc. the New England group agreed to make a survey of the craft. Jackson Jenks, the director of the Naval and Maritime Museum, believed his men could determine the condition of the *Cairo's* structural timbers, a critical factor if the ironclad were to be raised. After one day, the team reported they would like to explore the craft further.

Mayor Holland took the New Englanders to Jackson for a meeting with Governor Ross Barnett. The governor listened with interest to what the group had to say and called in the director of the Mississippi Agricultural and Industrial Board, Joe Bullock, and other A & I Board staff members. In a series of meetings, it was decided that future explorations should be conducted with the plan in mind that, if the craft was intact, funds should be collected and the *Cairo* raised and restored as a museum. The board agreed to underwrite a survey of the *Cairo* by the New Englanders. Also at this time the Mississippi Commission on the War Between the States promised additional financial assistance.

In November the diving team returned to Mississippi. Assisted by Parks, Hart, and personnel from the Vicksburg National Military Park led by Al Banton, a thirty-day survey of the sunken ironclad was undertaken. Dr. Walter Johnston of Vicksburg had become the project's most enthusiastic backer, and gave unselfishly of his time and equipment. Johnston's floating drydock had been fitted out as a work barge with an airlift pump, and towed up the Yazoo to the site.

A grid was plotted on a plan of the craft prepared by William E. Geoghegan of the Smithsonian Institution, who is an authority on Civil War naval vessels. The divers buoyed the hulk and, working from known points, explored many parts of the craft. The results of each dive were carefully plotted.

Since the object of the expedition was to establish the condition of the *Cairo,* the men tested all timbers encountered. All structural timbers and beams were pronounced sound. Only the 2½-inch deck planking was pulpy. Using powerful jets of water, the divers cleared away the sand and for the first time entered the forward casemate through a skylight. There they encountered the breech of a large gun. Walt Hendrick, a master diver with the New England team, recalled that placing his hand on the gun as he slowly jetted away the mud was as "thrilling as finding a chest full of gold in clear water." I concluded, after checking the records, the gun was a giant 42-pounder rifle. To avoid damaging the craft, we decided not to remove the gun at this time.

About ten feet abaft the chimneys, an area of the decking where the blacksmith shop was located was pumped clear. Many tools—anvils, vises, hammers, bits, chisels, etc.—were recovered. Also brought up was a piece of sheet metal from which the blacksmith had been cutting patterns when the first explosion occurred. Nearby a carriage for a 12-pounder boat howitzer and an anchor for a cutter were discovered. Records revealed that the howitzer tube had been removed several days before the *Cairo* made her fatal run up the Yazoo.

Fulton Mills, a Jackson engineer, ran a profile check and drew a chart depicting the *Cairo's* position in the stream. In addition, the amount of siltation had been determined. When work was suspended in 1962, it had been conclusively demonstrated that the gunboat's structural timbers were in position. Fears voiced by a number of interested parties that the *Cairo's* back might be broken were alleviated.

Once again—in November, 1962—Operation *Cairo*, Inc. called on Senator Stennis for help. Through the Senator's intervention the Navy Department agreed to transfer title to the vessel to the Treasury Department. Secretary of the Treasury Douglas Dillon, as authorized by 40, U.S.S. Cairo Section 310, vested title to the ironclad in the Mississippi Commission on the War Between the States. Certain conditions were attached to the transfer: the craft would either have to be raised or salvage operations in progress at the end of two years, or the vessel would revert to the United States government. If any gold were found on the wreck, it would have to be turned over to the Treasury. Since the Mississippi Commission on the War Between the States was not a perpetuating state agency, it, in turn, on December 8, 1962, transferred and assigned all rights, title, and interest in the craft to the Mississippi A & I Board.

After the completion of the A & I Board's survey, questions arose as to the possibility of whether the ammunition (black powder and fulminate of mercury fuses) on board the *Cairo* was dangerous. Jackson Jenks of the New England Naval and Maritime Museum argued that it was. The United States Corps of Engineers, taking cognizance of Jenks's statements, declared the *Cairo* "a quasi navigation hazard" and placed buoys around the ironclad to indicate her position and to warn passing tows of the possible danger.

Jenks felt that the ammunition should be removed only by a naval demolition team. Others suggested that the copper containers in which the black powder was supposedly stored had deteriorated and the propellant had gone into solution. A check with the Smithsonian Institution indicated that the copper containers were watertight. Correspondence with United States ordnance personnel and E. I. DuPont explosive experts cast valuable light on the nature of black powder and fulminate of mercury. Several authorities had written that black powder and fulminate of mercury became more unstable with age. Not so, the people at DuPont and United States ordnance countered. A clear-cut opinion from any agency or company on this issue was impossible to obtain. Authorities championing the instability of the powder were convinced that the craft should be declared a hazard to navigation.

Mississippi Governor Ross Barnett met with the A & I Board in early 1963, and was presented with the result of the survey undertaken by Jenks. The governor, who was strongly interested in the project, determined that a plan should be initiated to raise funds for the *Cairo*. It was recommended that a committee be organized to include as representative a group as possible—bankers, engineers, mayors, army officers, lawyers, state and national historians, writers, industrialists, public relations and news media personnel. This committee would handle various functions, such as finance, engineering, legal, equipment, preservation, historical research, liaison, and publicity. These people would form a nucleus to raise funds and attempt to secure "many services at a nominal or no-cost rate." [2]

Governor Barnett on April 3, 1963, named a steering committee to organize the raising of the *Cairo* from the Yazoo. Joe Bullock, executive director of the A & I Board, was appointed director of the committee. [3] After months of behind-the-scenes activity by several members of the steering committee (especially Joe Schmitt and Ken Parks), the group assembled at the Governor's Mansion on August 8 for a briefing session. Members of the committee were given copies of a survey, made by William W. Sykes of Engineering Service of Jackson, which evaluated existing conditions at the *Cairo* site and which charted the position of the hulk in the river bed. Sykes, in explaining the difficulties of the undertaking, remarked that lifting the vessel would be equal to moving a seventeen-story building. Commander T. F. Bachelor, chief of the Damage Control Section of the Navy Department's Branch of Ships Salvage and Personnel Protection, promised that a naval demolition team of divers would be on hand

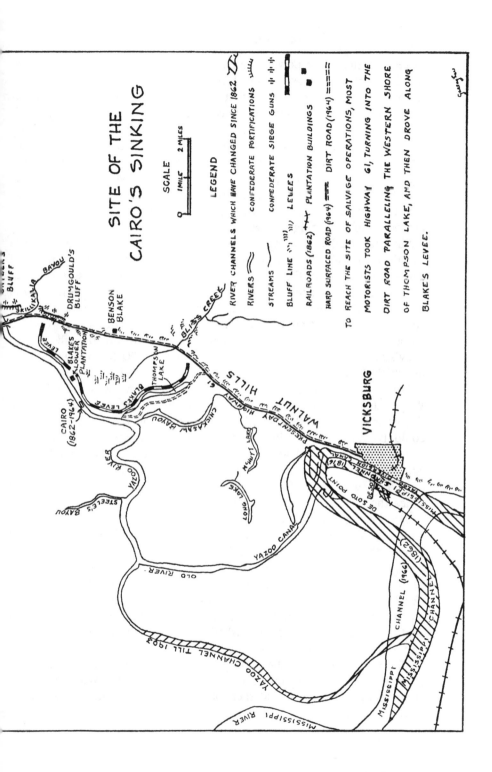

SITE OF THE
CAIRO'S SINKING

SCALE

0   1 MILE   2 MILES

LEGEND

RIVER CHANNELS WHICH HAVE CHANGED SINCE 1862

RIVERS

STREAMS

BLUFF LINE

RAILROADS (1862)

HARD SURFACED ROAD (1964)   DIRT ROAD (1964)

CONFEDERATE FORTIFICATIONS

CONFEDERATE SIEGE GUNS

LEVEES

PLANTATION BUILDINGS

TO REACH THE SITE OF SALVAGE OPERATIONS, MOST
MOTORISTS TOOK HIGHWAY 61, TURNING INTO THE
DIRT ROAD PARALLELING THE WESTERN SHORE
OF THOMPSON LAKE, AND THEN DROVE ALONG
BLAKE'S LEVEE.

to remove the black powder and the fulminate of mercury detonators which might constitute a safety hazard. And the interest of the Union Carbide Company in preservation of the *Cairo* was expressed by its representative, R. H. Aldrich. The financial committee, led by J. C. Williams of the Corr-Williams Tobacco Company, was advised by Williams that his company was pledging $20,000 to begin the salvage work. This company also provided for ten thousand money collection containers which were placed in the fifty-two Mississippi counties and two Louisiana parishes in which the firm operated.[4] At this juncture, members of the steering committee were optimistic at the prospects of salvaging the vessel.

Simultaneously, a campaign was launched in Vicksburg to raise $10,000 to assist in the salvage operation. And to spark national and state interest in the project, the State A & I Board issued attractive certificates signed by Governor Barnett making persons who made contributions to "Operation *Cairo*" members of the "Mississippi Navy" in appreciation of their assistance. The undertaking received an additional financial boost, when I appeared on the short-lived television program "100 Grand" and won $10,000 for a civic project in which I was interested—the raising of the *Cairo*.

Some of the money pledged by J. C. Williams was used by Dr. Walter Johnston and Ken Parks to negotiate for a dredge. Before the debris and silt that filled the casemate of the sunken ironclad could be removed, the blue clay which all but enveloped the wreck would have to be cut away. Johnston and Parks found an interested contractor, Charles L. King of Lake Providence, Louisiana. King agreed to undertake, for a very reasonable sum, the task of cutting away the silt which encased the craft.

On Friday, September 6, the tug *Betty Kay* reached Vicksburg with the dredge *Mary Ann,* a World War II LCI which King had converted into a gravel dredge. The next day the tug pushed the dredge up the Yazoo and into position over the *Cairo,* which had been previously delineated with targets. Meanwhile, Dr. Johnston, assisted by Al Banton and Don Jacks, had constructed a sluice, similar to those used in the gold fields of the West in the nineteenth century, to deposit the spoil gushed up by the dredge near the bank and thus out of the channel.

Plans were made to dig a deep, wide trench around the stern and sides of the craft beginning on the upstream side. When this was completed, the *Cairo* would then be left on a pedestal, so that divers could begin removing debris and silt from inside the casemate. When the barges supporting the sluice were in place, dredge operator James Simpson began working the head of the suction pipe down into position. A stream of muddy water began to gush from the discharge pipe into the sluice. Engineers who were on the spot estimated that the dredge *Mary Ann* was capable of removing eight thousand cubic yards of silt every twelve hours. They had made their calculations, however, without realizing what a tenacious obstacle the buckshot mud of the Yazoo would be. At times, the suction pipe became choked with mud, and the head had to be lifted from the bottom and cleaned out.

To check progress and to see that the suction pipe head was in the desired position, the dredge was stopped at intervals. Scuba diver Parks or his standby "Skeeter" Hart, would descend into the muddy water to ascertain by feel what had been accomplished and report what adjustments were necessary. As the suction pipe worked its way closer to the hull, it was feared that valuable artifacts might be lost as the spoil was carried off. Dr. Johnston and his team solved this problem by constructing a screen which was placed at the end of the sluice. Among artifacts caught in the screen were hard-rubber buttons from the peajackets worn by the *Cairo's* crew.

Before dredging was commenced, it was estimated that the trenches around the craft would be completed in five to seven days. Progress, however, was slowed by the thick layer of clay that had accumulated around the ironclad. And log jams, especially on the downstream side, posed a serious problem. The dredge had to shut down, while Parks felt his way along the bottom and secured cables to the logs. The tug *Betty Kay,* piloted by Captain Malcolm Carr, made a number of runs downriver towing out of the way cypress trees, some of which measured six feet in diameter.

By the end of the first week, the divers reported that the port side of the *Cairo* was clear of mud down to the hull, and the four gunports could be felt. Another seven days saw the dredging nearly completed. An underwater reconnaissance disclosed that a trench from ten to twenty feet deep and many feet across had been opened around the *Cairo's* stern, port and starboard sides. The bow, however, was still covered by the 4,500 cubic yards of bank which had sloughed during the years, but it was determined that this area could be cleared by dragline.

Dredging operations were secured on Wednesday, September 25, and the tug *Betty Kay* and the dredge *Mary Ann* left the area. Initial estimates had called for the removal of 27,000 cubic yards of spoil, but before dredging was stopped, 40,000 cubic yards of mud had been sucked to the surface and deposited several hundred yards downstream.[5]

The United States Coast Guard was cooperative. Before dredging operations began, the cutter *Dogwood* ascended the Yazoo. Personnel from the vessel were detailed to patrol the river and to control and supervise the hundreds of people who came, mostly in small boats, to watch the undertaking. It was soon apparent that the salvage would be time consuming, and that it would be impractical to tie up the cutter for many weeks; consequently, Eighth Coast Guard District headquarters at New Orleans detached three men to the area. Two of them would control river traffic. The third would assist whenever black powder, fuses, and projectiles were brought to the surface and landed. He was to clear the area when the navy men destroyed ammunition that was considered dangerous.

With the mud that had encased the vessel out of the way, the task of removing four hundred cubic yards of silt from the casemate and holds could begin. This had to be done to lighten the vessel, so that she could be lifted from the bottom without snapping her structural timbers.

A contract had been signed by the A & I Board with Gene Collins Marine Divers of Crowley, Louisiana. Collins agreed to raise the *Cairo* for $7,500. Russell Light, a master diver, and his tender Frank Anderson were dispatched to the area by Collins on September 25. Engaged on another project, Collins had contacted Light and Anderson and had asked them to begin operations.

Meanwhile, Commander Bachelor had made good on his promise that the navy would cooperate in removing and rendering harmless the ammunition stored in the *Cairo's* magazines and shellrooms. Explosive Ordnance Disposal, Unit No. 2, stationed at the Charleston, South Carolina, Naval Base, was assigned this task by the Sixth Naval District. Lieutenant Frank Talerico and Chief Boatswain's Mate Wesley Collins had reached Vicksburg on September 13. After visiting the site and making several reconnaissance dives to investigate the problems that would be encountered, Talerico and Collins began assembling equipment—air lifts, barges, etc.—which would be required to remove silt from the vessel's interior and enable them to reach the magazines and shellrooms. Equipment came from many sources: other members of Unit No. 2 brought a truckload of diving gear with them from Charleston; the Corps of Engineers in Vicksburg was called on for help; a number of Mississippi businesses gave generously of their equipment and personnel; some other pieces had to be rented. Vicksburg city officials provided workmen to assist the divers. Especially valuable in the weeks ahead were the services of Bill Ryals and his hard-working team of city employees, who were called on to do all sorts of tasks to assist the divers.[6]

By September 25 the rest of Lieutenant Talerico's team had arrived in Vicksburg. With the dredge *Mary Ann* out of the way, the barges from which the divers—naval and civilian—would work were moored near the hulk. While Light made exploratory dives, the naval personnel buoyed the craft with plastic jugs, pinpointing gunports, skylights, and hatches leading into the casemate.[7]

Making use of two air lifts, one an 8- and the other a 6-inch, the divers began the arduous task of removing some four hundred cubic yards of mud from the casemate. The problem was accentuated by the masses of twigs and leaves which during the years had become intermixed with the silt. Generally, the navy men worked in their deep sea or "hard hat" gear, while Light preferred to use the Hookah.[8]

Since the men worked by touch in total darkness, they tied cords to known points in the craft so that they could locate their position. Reaching the air-lift pump, a diver would use his two-way radio to notify his tender to turn on the air pressure. Moments later, a stream of muddy water would spew from the end of the air lift that protruded above the water. To guard against loss of valuable small articles, the water was screened as it cascaded downward. As the area over the bunkers was cleared, pieces of coal shot out of the discharge end of the pipe with cannon-like force.

The divers who guided the air lifts faced several sources of danger. They had to be careful to avoid getting arms and legs in front of the mouths of the powerful lifts, as the suction was capable of tearing their suits or breaking a limb. Inside the casemate there were hundreds of sharp pieces of metal and glass, which tore at their hands, suits, and air hoses.

After clearing the silt which choked the hatches, the divers entered the casemate. Beginning near the pilothouse hatch, the men used their air lifts as a fastidious housewife uses her vacuum cleaner, working their way aft, and, slowly but surely, removed the mud and debris from the barn-like gun deck.

The divers were amazed at the state of the gun deck. Chief Collins reported timbers and knees in excellent condition. Opening a hatch leading into one of the holds, near No. 3 starboard gun, the chief found little siltation in a storeroom containing barrels and cans and boxes of shoes. Collins replaced and battened down the hatch to keep out silt. He continued his search for the magazines.

Equally surprising was the discovery, when the mud was lifted away from the two huge engines, that the valves and wheels, which were made of copper or brass, could be turned with ease. Rubber hoses were in as good condition as they were 101 years before.

Chief Collins found the first projectile—a solid shot from one of the 32-pounders—which he picked up in the corner of the gun deck. During the next two days, the chief counted about sixty similar balls. Evidently, these projectiles had been knocked from the shot racks by the force of the exploding torpedoes. Several days were required to pinpoint and bring these projectiles to the surface.

An element of mystery was introduced when Russell Light, on the final weekend in September, discovered near No. 3 port gun and brought to the surface a human bone. The bone was identified by Dr. Johnston as a right humerus. As the head of the humerus was missing, it was speculated that it must have been torn from its socket by external violence. Since Commander Selfridge had reported no loss of life or serious injuries in the sinking, the finding of the bone caused all sorts of speculation. Had Selfridge falsified his report? Was there an unaccounted-for Confederate prisoner aboard the boat? Had some nameless contraband, signed on to help with the heavy work, been lost? [9]

The bone was mailed to the Smithsonian Institution for study. Dr. Lawrence Angel, curator of physical anthropology, examined the humerus and concluded that it came from "a slender, muscular and rather long male arm, not necessarily white, perhaps Indian, possibly Negro," and was of greater antiquity than other objects found in the wreck. Dr. Angel believed that the bone measurements and other features resembled the formations found in Mississippi Indians in the institution's humeri collection.[10] Since many Indian mounds are located in the Yazoo-Mississippi Delta, I guessed that the bone could have been carried aboard the ironclad by one of the bluejackets as a memento to show his friends back home.

On Monday, September 30, diver Light located a treasure. While reconnoitering a recently cleared area in front of the wheelhouse, he encountered the boat's bell, which was pulled to the surface by ten husky men. The bell, which still could clang loudly, weighed over four hundred pounds. It was about thirty inches high and at least two feet in diameter at the "flare" or bottom edge. Engraved on the bronze surface was "G. W. Coffin and Co., Buckeye Bell Foundry, Cincinnati, 1860." [11] As the bell was brought up, there burst forth from it a bubble of air which had been trapped there since the vessel's sinking.

Aft of the engine room on the *Cairo's* port beam was located a hatch leading down into a hold. Russell Light, after jetting away the mud, moved through a narrow passage (which subsequently proved to be the passing room) and entered a leadlined room—one of the shellrooms had been found. Because of cramped quarters in the passageway, the shellroom could be explored only in Hookah. When he surfaced, Light brought up a wooden box. Opened on the barge, the box (32″ x 24″ x 24″), whose brass hinges still worked, was found to contain nine fused explosive projectiles (with sabots attached) for a 12-pounder boat howitzer. The howitzer tube had been removed at Memphis prior to the ironclad's final run down the Mississippi; but, I theorized, in the hurry to cast off, the gunner's mates had neglected to send the boxes of howitzer ammunition ashore.

Zero visibility in the inky water made it impossible for divers to count the boxes of ammunition stacked in the shellroom. Lieutenant Talerico, however, was able to feel at least four boxes similar to the one Light had removed. The next day, October 8, the projectiles were taken out to a bunker that had been previously prepared and were detonated—five in the first explosion and four in the second. There was a cloud of black smoke and a roar which could be heard for several miles.[12] In the days which followed, a dozen additional boxes of fused howitzer shells were pulled from the shellroom. All these rounds, except the contents of one box, were detonated; the nine shells in this box were disarmed.

Ten wooden boxes filled with black powder were also found in the shellroom. This proved embarrassing to me, because with my eyes glued to *Naval Regulations for 1861* I had assured the divers that powder and projectiles could not be found in the same room. According to regulations, powder was to be stored in the magazines and projectiles in shellrooms. It appeared that personnel of the Mississippi Squadron were not too impressed by rules and regulations.

A determined effort was then made to pinpoint the forward magazines and shellrooms. Because there was danger of the east bank caving in on the craft and trapping the divers, it was decided to use a dragline and bulldozer to clear the area. The Vicksburg Bridge Commission responded to the emergency by sending a bulldozer and operator, while State Highway Commissioner Felder Dearman made a dragline and operator available. After the bulldozer had cleared the trees and dense undergrowth from the steep bank, a roadway was cut down to the river's edge. Dragline operator Leo Buford drove his machine down the bank and out onto a barge. Skillfully maneuvering the dragline bucket, Buford cleared the bow of thousands of yards of earth which during the years had slid down and buried the area forward of the casemate.

Work was slow, because huge sections of the bank kept breaking off and falling into the river; divers operating in the stern section of the *Cairo* reported they could feel shock waves whenever a large piece dropped near the bow. As soon as the dirt and mud were removed by dragline, the divers worked their way forward from the pilothouse hatch to the shield through which the muzzles of the three bow guns protruded.[13]

While navy divers explored the forward section of the gundeck in a fruitless search for hatches leading to the forward shellrooms, Light, after removing a number of small logs, entered No. 4 starboard gunport. Enough silt and clay had now been cleared to enable the divers to inspect portions of the gunboat's bottom. Although the surface of the planks felt spongy from the century under water, beams when tested were found strong enough to withstand the stress and strain of salvage.

A news team from the Columbia Broadcasting System visited the site on October 19. By this time the gun deck, except for the area near the bow guns, was about 80 percent clear of silt. After discussing the situation with members of the steering committee who were watching operations, diver Light said that it would be possible to remove one of the two stern guns for the benefit of the visiting newsmen. The lift was scheduled for the next morning.

Long before the CBS crew reached Blake's Levee with their equipment, Light and his tender Anderson were on the job. While the newsmen set up their gear and Ordnance Disposal Unit No. 2 stood by, Light descended into the dark waters and secured a cable to the cascabel of one of the stern guns. The surface crew and spectators could hear raps as Light employed a hammer to knock loose the cap square keys, so he could remove the cap squares which secured the gun to its carriage. Being careful to avoid damaging the casemate, Buford maneuvered his dragline so as to winch the tube through the gunport. While television cameras recorded what was happening, a nationwide audience saw the gun, a 30-pounder naval Parrott, lifted onto the barge.

Talerico and his team now took over. When they examined the piece they discovered that its tompion was in position. Since tompions, according to regulations, were to be used only when the piece was unloaded, it was presumed that the big rifle was harmless. But when the tompion was pulled, and a light flashed up the tube, it was apparent that the sailors aboard the *Cairo* had not followed regulations, because the ugly, fused nose of an explosive shell could be seen. Working under the supervision of Lieutenant Talerico and Chief Collins, the men of Unit No. 2 removed the projectile.

Later in the day, a second piece—No. 3 starboard gun—was lifted. There was a large skylight in the area, through which it was possible to hoist the tube and its wooden naval carriage at the same time. When checked by Unit No. 2, this gun, a 32-pounder, was found to be unloaded. An examination showed that the wooden carriage was in better condition, if possible, than the one raised three years before.

During the next seventeen days the ten remaining big guns—two 8-inch navies, five 32-pounders, and three huge, rifled 42-pounders—and their carriages were removed from the gun deck. All pieces were loaded—a number with explosive shell, some with grape, several with canister, and one with solid shot. One of the 32-pounders, No. 1 port gun, was found to have been dismounted by the force of the exploding torpedoes which had snapped one of the iron cap squares.

Commander Selfridge's placement of the *Cairo's* guns was enlightening, because it was different from what historians had assumed from a study of the ordnance tables for the city class ironclads. Instead of mounting his three rifled 42-pounders in the bow, Selfridge had employed two of the 42-pounders and one 8-inch naval gun in the bow battery. The other 42-pounder was the No. 1 starboard gun, while the No. 2 port and starboard guns were 8-inch navies.

Governor Barnett, who was one of Operation *Cairo's* strongest boosters, paid a visit on November 3. Prior to the governor's arrival, preparations had been made to raise No. 3 port gun. A cable was taken down by Russell Light and attached to the cascabel, and with the governor and his staff looking on, the dragline's winch started taking up slack. But although Buford, Light, Bill Ryals and his crew worked for an hour, the tube wedged in the port and refused to budge. So as not to disappoint the governor and his party, Light went down into the casemate and soon popped to the surface with a musket, lantern, and boarding pike. Before he returned to Jackson, Governor Barnett pushed the plunger to detonate a 32-pounder shell the navy people had placed in the bunker.

While the heavy ordnance was being brought to the surface, a vain search for the bow magazines and shellrooms was pressed. Another after shellroom was pinpointed, but was not entered, because of weakened timbers in the area. A number of 87-pound shells for the rifled 42-pounders, and stands of grape and canister for the 8-inch navies and 32-pounders were found on the deck near the bow battery. These projectiles were brought to the surface; although some of the shells were detonated, several were disarmed by Unit No. 2.

Light explored the cabins which were aft of the gun deck, and to the port, starboard, and aft of the wheel. Artifacts were recovered from the cabins which indicated that four had served as quarters for the junior officers—one as the dispensary, another as the mail room, one as the officers' head, another as the officers' mess, and the large after cabin as Commander Selfridge's quarters.

As the middle of November approached, Lieutenant Talerico and his group prepared to return to the Charleston Naval Station. Twice before, the men of Unit No. 2 had been placed on standby to return to their base, but each time their tour of duty was extended as Operation Cairo, Inc. had agreed to reimburse the Navy Department for the men's subsistence. Before leaving Vicksburg, the demolition team prepared to disarm the guns.

The naval demolition experts believed that the only way to unload the cannon without cutting into them with torches was to blow the projectiles free with a specially shaped explosive charge. To do this, an explosive (K-4) was tamped into the barrel and around the edges of the projectile until it formed sort of a gasket or rope. The K-4 was electrically fired, with the hope that the explosion would either shatter the projectile and make it easier to remove, or loosen it sufficiently so that it could be worked free.

After checking with William Geoghegan of the Smithsonian Institution, I protested that this operation could burst the tube, and urged that a powerful rust solvent be pumped into the bore and the tube left with its muzzle elevated for several months. The projectile could then be pulled. But because time was all important, the men of Unit No. 2 decided to use the quicker process. Shaped charges were used to disarm two of the 8-inch navies, four of the 32-pounders, and one 42-pounder rifle. As all these pieces, except the 42-pounder, were charged with either grape or canister, no trouble was encountered. But when the navy men sought to disarm the 32-pounder charged with solid shot they ran into trouble. Too much K-4 was used, sundering the solid iron ball and cracking the tube in a number of places.[14]

After securing their gear, Unit No. 2 left for Charleston. At this time the city of Vicksburg found it necessary to recall Bill Ryals and his crew, who had been supporting operations topside for the previous six weeks. As no more ammunition would be brought to the surface for some time, the Coast Guard personnel headed back to New Orleans. Thus, by the end of the second week in November, the second phase of the salvage operation had been successfully concluded. In Phase I 40,000 cubic yards of mud which enveloped the hulk had been removed and the craft left on a pedestal. Phase II saw silt accumulated during 101 years air lifted from the gun deck and cabins, the fo'c'sle freed from the bank, and twelve guns and eleven carriages brought to the surface. Hundreds of interesting artifacts, many of which cast new light on life aboard the Union ironclad, had been recovered. Phase III, the placing of cables under the Cairo preparatory to raising her, now began.

The contract with Gene Collins Marine Divers for lifting the Cairo had been terminated by mutual agreement, and a five-man executive committee to the Cairo steering committee, which Governor Barnett had named on October 7, was confronted with the vexing problem of locating a new contractor who would undertake the task for the limited funds available.[15] Russell Light agreed to lift the Cairo, but instead of being given a contract, he would be paid a stipulated salary and would be responsible to the executive committee.

The committee in its meetings with Light had matured plans to be followed in getting the craft to the surface. The scheme hit upon as the most feasible way to get the Cairo off the bottom was to slip cables under her keels. These cables then would be secured to two large barges, moored on either side of the hulk, so as to let the gradual rise of the river bring the craft up over a period of several months. Divers using high-pressure hoses could help cut the suction created by the clay. Then the *Cairo* could be moved downstream for placement on a barge to await the restoration work.

To carry out this operation, Joe Schmitt of the executive committee made arrangements with the Corps of Engineers for the lease of two barges (40 feet wide and 235 feet long) on favorable terms. These barges had been designed for transporting fuel and were divided into compartments. As it developed, the compartments would be of considerable importance, because the salvage team could fill them with water and sink the barges, then pump them out and refloat the vessels.

Several weeks before the city of Vicksburg was compelled to recall Ryals' crew, Jim Sherman, civil defense director at the Parchman State Penal Farm, had arrived with three trusties, a dragline, a bulldozer, and several mud pumps. The trusties included a skilled heavy equipment operator, a mechanic, and a welder. Sherman's crew was reinforced soon after the departure of Ryals' men by two more trusties. Like the others, these men had skills that proved indispensable in the difficult and tedious work that lay ahead. Without this help, the project would have had to shut down because of insufficient funds.

After the departure of the dredge *Mary Ann,* the trenches which had been cut around the *Cairo* had partially silted in. Moreover, it had been ascertained that the trench around the stern had not been deep enough in the first place to slip a wire under the two huge rudders. Lack of money precluded rehiring the *Mary Ann;* consequently, Dr. Johnston and Light undertook to build an 8-inch dredge. Two companies were prevailed upon to give assistance: Traxler Construction Company donated a powerful diesel engine, and Girod Construction Company came forward with a mud pump. Assisted by professional mechanics who volunteered their services, the Parchman trusties, together with Sid Champion, Dr. Johnston and Light within a short time assembled a workable dredge, mounted on the floating drydock, which the versatile doctor had devised for docking and lifting boats out of the water. While the dredge cleaned out and deepened the trenches upstream and downstream from the *Cairo,* Buford employed his dragline to enlarge the trench around the bow.

Until the middle of the second week in December, the Yazoo continued to fall—dropping to about minus 5 feet. After a beautiful, dry autumn, the weather turned cold. Unexpected problems arose. Because of the abnormally low stage of the Yazoo and the removal of thousands of cubic yards of mud which had covered the bow, the bank began to slip. To prevent the steep bank from tumbling into the river and undoing the many weeks of hard work, it was necessary to resort to terracing. Simultaneously, difficulties were encountered around the stern. The dredge began to spout sand instead of mud. A reconnaissance by Light disclosed that the sucker head had cut through the blue clay and was in water sand. Almost as fast as the sand was pumped to the surface, additional grains seeped back into the trench; for almost a week the battle with the water sand continued. Persistence finally carried the day; the dredge, with the help of air lifts and jet hoses, gained the upper hand.

By December 15 the salvage crew was ready to slip lead wires under the *Cairo*. One of the huge 235-foot lifting barges was towed into position a short distance upstream and anchored parallel to the sunken craft's port beam. Since the river at its current stage was only one hundred yards wide, the lifting barge all but blocked the channel. One end of the pilot wire was secured to the lifting barge, and the slack end was placed by Light near the *Cairo's* bow. The dragline, which was mounted on a work barge downstream from the hulk, employed its winch to tighten the wire. Although it was not discovered for months, this wire snagged on giant cypress logs embedded in the mud and did not slip under the vessel.

When Light descended into the cold, muddy water to place the pilot wire under the stern, he encountered serious difficulties. The huge rudders were a serious obstacle. And two giant logs, one of which was more than six feet wide across the butt, were in the way. Both logs had to be lifted to the surface with winches before Light could place the cable. As he did this, Light was able to feel his way beneath the vessel through the large excavation dredged in this area.

Heavy rains which pelted the area in mid-December slowed operations. There was a rapid 6-foot rise on the Yazoo, without a corresponding increase in the Mississippi's stage. This caused the current on the lower reaches of the Yazoo to race wildly toward the Mississippi. In addition, an extensive area on the watershed of one of the Yazoo tributaries was being cleared. Large amounts of drift began to build up against the upstream side of the lifting barge moored athwart the river. Within hours the raft covered several acres. Cold and wet, the salvage personnel battled this threat. Utilizing small boats and the dragline, they broke up the raft which for a time threatened operations, but not before the debris tore away one of the pilot wires.

Tragedy now claimed the life of the most enthusiastic supporter of the project, a man who had given hundreds of hours of his time and liberal donations of equipment and money. Late on a bitter cold day, Sunday, January 12, Dr. Walter Johnston and his Negro watchman James Barnes were attempting to wrestle into position on the Yazoo shore, with the aid of two small boats, a houseboat which was to shelter the guard as he stayed with the doctor's boats and equipment berthed below Johnston's camp. During the operation Barnes leaped off the houseboat and attempted to tie a line around a tree to give some control over the big vessel as they fought it through the boiling currents. Dr. Johnston had remained in the one small boat (the engine of the other had failed) they were using to push the houseboat. Moments after Barnes jumped off, he heard the doctor shout through the cold darkness "James, I'm in the river. Where are you?" At this point Barnes lost his grip on the rope to the houseboat. As the river carried the craft downstream, he could hear the doctor calling for help.

Search parties worked through the night. Flurries of snow added to their difficulties in the darkness. The *Sophia J.,* one of the small boats, and the houseboat were found in the river just above the government fleet. The runabout in which Johnston was last seen standing was found in a small eddy between the point of his disappearance and the government fleet, with the paddle still in it.[16] Searchers doubted he would have survived the incident, because his physical condition was weakened by heart trouble and diabetes. Unless he had reached shore and stumbled onto a shelter, there was little hope for his safety. After more than a week's intensive hunting with airplanes and helicopters, the search was abandoned. Up to this time, no trace of Dr. Johnston has been found.

After the search, the salvage team resumed work, grimly determined to raise the *Cairo* as a memorial to Dr. Johnston. Weather conditions improved; for the next several weeks the days were mild and dry. The Yazoo dropped rapidly and the current subsided. Five additional pilot wires were jetted under the hulk and tightened by the dragline. On the third weekend in January, Light and his workers attached a lifting wire (a heavy 1½-inch hemp-core wire rope) to one of the pilot cables which passed under the stern. Dragline operator Buford then pulled the lifting cable into place.[17]

By January 28 eight lifting wires had been placed beneath the craft. Several of the wires were pulled under the craft with ease, but, all too frequently, turnbuckles used to secure the small guide wires to the bigger ones caught on one of the *Cairo's* three keels. Hours of hard work were required to free the turnbuckles.

Discussions between Light and the executive committee resulted in a minor change in plans. It was decided not to wait for the Mississippi to begin its winter rise; instead, the lifting barges would be placed in position and partially sunk. After the wires had been secured and tightened, the barges would be pumped out and their buoyancy used to break the *Cairo* loose from the bottom.

George Rogers (who had taken Dr. Johnston's place on the executive committee), after meeting with Light on January 28, announced that actual lifting operations were expected to get under way within the next two weeks. Light had cautioned Rogers and committee members that the raising process would be gradual. The first lift was expected to bring the *Cairo* up about four or five feet. A check would then be made of the wires and additional cables would be added to points where stress was developing.[18]

As soon as four more lifting wires had been placed under the craft, the second barge, which had been moored near the site for the past several months, was pushed into position parallel to and just below the sunken vessel by the *Kanawha*. The first days of February were devoted to attaching the wires beneath the *Cairo* to the second barge.[19] Making an underwater examination, diver Light encountered and, with the aid of the dragline, brought to the surface an interesting object—one of the ironclad's hand-operated bilge pumps.

The barges positioned on each side of the *Cairo* were compartmented, and pains were taken to sink them at the same angle (about 14 degrees) as that at which the ironclad was believed to rest in her hole. Since there were no seacocks on the barges, a number of gasoline pumps were started and water began tumbling in. By the time the pumps were stopped, the after-ends of the barges had been sunk about nine feet and only two feet of their hulls protruded above the Yazoo, while the bows were submerged about six feet. The winch on the dragline was utilized to draw taut the twelve lifting wires.

Sunday, February 9, was the day selected for the first lift. At an early hour the pumps used to fill the barges were reversed, and the relatively slow process of dewatering the barges commenced. About 2,500 gallons of water per minute gushed from the salvage barges. While the barges were being raised at the rate of about one foot per hour, Light kept close check on the wires, so as to insure an even load distribution along the entire length of the 175-foot vessel.

No disturbance was seen on the surface of the water other than small eddies over the area of the ironclad's stern. Then onlookers scampered as there was a loud crack, when one of the lifting wires suddenly snapped. A second wire popped a few minutes later.

Some observers argued that the vessel had been raised a few inches; others swore that it hadn't moved. These people based their opinion in the fact that Light was using relatively light wires (most of them being 1/2 and 3/4 of an inch) and instead of picking up the ironclad these wires were merely stretching. Subsequently the doubters were proved correct, since the successful lift required an excess of eight hundred tons of pressure exerted on 2½- and 3-inch wires.

The next afternoon Light dove to make an inspection. He examined the hull and reported that the craft had been moved about two feet.[20] Before surfacing, he located a heavy anchor chain. When pulled onto one of the barges, the chain was measured and found to be 750 feet long.

Meanwhile, the Yazoo continued to fall rapidly. Pumps were again pressed into service, and the barges were again flooded to the same depth as before. After the wires were tightened, a second lift was attempted on the thirteenth. Upon checking the results, Light stated that the stern of the ironclad had been moved about one and one-half feet closer to the surface, while the bow came up about six inches.[21] Even so, the Cairo's keels at the stern were still about fourteen feet below the surrounding river bottom while at the bow they were about eight feet. The continuing fall of the Yazoo had both advantages and disadvantages. "We gain less on each lift, but have the advantage of less current and more shallow water in which to work. A rise in the river a little later will be a big help," Light explained.

A third lift was made on February 18. Once again, Light asserted that the vessel was raised several feet. During the preceding days, rain had fallen over the watershed of the Yazoo, and a slow rise was forecast. He explained this time that instead of reflooding the barges, he was leaving the vessel suspended in her cradle of wires. As long as the river was rising, the Cairo would remain in a suspended position, he said. According to him, the lift on the wires from the buoyancy of the barges and the force of the rising river would cause the gunboat to break surface within two to three weeks.[22]

By the middle of the fourth week of February, the Yazoo had

crested and started to drop. The eight- to ten-hour operation of flooding the barges was repeated. After the wires had been tautened, the pumps were reversed, and on the twenty-fifth, the fourth pickup was started. Before the barges had risen two feet, the wires under the *Cairo's* bow went slack. The pumps were shut down.[23] Then the engine on the dredge refused to start. Valuable time was lost while spare parts were begged or borrowed.

A low pressure cell moved into the area, bringing several days of torrential rains. The Yazoo rose rapidly, 12 feet in the first five days of March. Moreover, the Mississippi was at a record low, for this season of the year. (Usually in March there are at least 21 feet of water on the Vicksburg gauge, but on March 5, 1964, the gauge showed only 8.6.) Since the Mississippi was extremely low, the current in the Yazoo was unusually powerful. If the Mississippi had been at its normal stage for this season, the Yazoo at the *Cairo* site would have pooled.

As the Yazoo rushed toward the Mississippi, it carried a vast accumulation of debris,[24] and, as it had in mid-December, the drift began to build up rapidly above the upper lifting barge. By dusk on March 5 the debris covered several acres. Pressure became so great during the night that the huge cottonwood tree to which the cables mooring the upper barge were anchored was uprooted, and the barge flung downstream by the current. Simultaneously, the drift smashed into the lower barge, snapping mooring lines as if they were thread. The few lifting wires that remained beneath the *Cairo* were dislodged. As soon as the last of the wires were stripped away, the two barges rushed downstream. One grounded off De Soto Point, near the government fleet, while the other came to rest against the small craft pier north of the *Sprague*.[25]

There were several days of reflection over what had happened to the ironclad. Some people argued that she might have been carried some distance down the Yazoo before slipping out of the wires. The Corps of Engineers rushed a boat equipped with a fathometer up the Yazoo. A profile of the area showed that the *Cairo* was just where she was before the barges were dislodged. Because of the current, it was almost forty-eight hours before Light could go down, but when he did, he found that the gunboat had suffered no perceptible damage from the accident.[26]

9

SALVAGING
A CIVIL WAR IRONCLAD

THE breaking loose of the barges strengthened the resolution of many backers of the salvage project, especially those living in Vicksburg and in Warren County. Former State Senator H. V. Cooper was named by the board of directors of the Vicksburg Chamber of Commerce to head a committee to coordinate efforts and to make specific recommendations about what could be done to help raise the *Cairo*. To rally support, Cooper scheduled meetings with Vicksburg city officials and the county board of supervisors; both groups assured the senator and his committee of their cooperation and support.

Next, Cooper invited Joe Bullock of the A & I Board to come to Vicksburg and explain what his agency planned to do about the *Cairo*. I pointed out that, according to the terms of the contract entered into between the A & I Board and the United States Treasury Department, the state would lose title to the craft on November 15, 1964, if she were not up by that date or if salvage operations had been abandoned. Ray Sauer, who before retiring had been technical consultant for the president and commissioners of the Mississippi River Commission, told the group that if nothing were done during the summer and fall, the vessel would again silt in and work already done would be lost.

Senator Cooper asked Bullock if the A & I Board would object if a bill were introduced in the legislature authorizing Vicksburg and Warren County to raise the boat. Bullock said that although he was agreeable, such a question would have to be submitted to his executive board. Within the next two weeks the board sanctioned legislation

130

which George Rogers had drawn up, and on May 5 Senator Ellis Bodron of Warren County introduced an act

to authorize and empower counties, municipalities or agencies thereof to engage in the raising, restoration and operation of sunken Civil War gunboats, to authorize the expenditure of funds therefore, to authorize the issuance of bonds and other evidences of indebtedness for such purposes, to authorize the disposition of the operation, control or title to such vessel, to authorize the cooperation of agencies of the State of Mississippi in such project and for related purposes.

This enabling act passed the Mississippi senate on May 12, 1964, and the house nine days later, and on July 1 was approved by Governor Paul B. Johnson.

The legislature did more, however. On March 5 (the day before the lifting barges broke loose) Lieutenant Governor Carroll Gartin and members of the legislature, on their biennial trip to Vicksburg, had been shown the *Cairo* artifacts. In May Senator Cooper visited Jackson and explained to the legislators the problems confronting those interested in raising the *Cairo*. The trip to Jackson quickly bore fruit, for a rider was introduced in the house and senate to the appropriation for the A & I Board, earmarking $50,000 for Operation *Cairo*. During the first week of June, the Mississippi legislature passed the appropriation bill, and it was signed by the governor.[1]

Senator Cooper during the last week of March had established contact with Captain W. A. Bisso, Jr. Bisso, the most experienced salvage man on the Lower Mississippi, had come to Vicksburg and had expressed interest in raising the *Cairo* on a "no cure, no pay" basis. Now that funds were presumed to be available, Cooper and his group opened negotiations. The captain, who was working on a project at Old River, in Louisiana, for the U. S. Corps of Engineers, explained that if an agreement were reached, he would undertake the *Cairo* salvage for a reasonable sum as soon as he finished that task. Bisso on June 30 told Cooper that his price for lifting the *Cairo* off the bottom and placing her on a barge would be $40,000.

Meanwhile, J. C. "Mickey" Lever, as a representative of the U. S. Corps of Engineers, was asked to check to see if one of the 235-foot barges used in the previous salvage attempt could be rented from the government on a long term basis. He would also initiate studies to ascertain if such a barge could support the *Cairo*. Lever was able to report that a barge of the desired dimensions was available and would serve the purpose for which it was wanted.[2]

The problem of whether the city or county should take title to the *Cairo* in accordance with the recently enacted legislation was discussed by Senator Cooper's group. The Board of Supervisors (the governing agency of Warren County) seemed to be the logical group. When approached by the committee, the board expressed interest, and asked Cooper's team to make the necessary arrangements with the A & I Board for transferring title.[3] But the A & I executive board was reluctant to do so without certain assurances. After several weeks of maneuvering, the executive board agreed to release to the Warren County Board of Supervisors $12,500 of the money appropriated for the *Cairo* project by the 1964 session of the legislature. The remainder of the $50,000 would be turned over to the supervisors as soon as Captain Bisso had raised the craft and delivered her to the Vicksburg waterfront.[4]

Bisso, his crew, and equipment—the tug *Rip Tide,* and the powerful floating steam derrick cranes *Boaz, Atlas,* and *Ajax*—had reached the *Cairo* site on Saturday morning, July 25. Details of the plan Bisso proposed to follow in raising the ironclad were released on the last day of July. Employing his three derrick cranes, Bisso would first lift the hulk from the bottom of the Yazoo. Next, the giant barge scheduled to be leased from the Corps of Engineers would be fitted out with waylogs, and pipes and pumps for flooding. The barge would then be sunk in a deep hole in the Yazoo, about a third of a mile below the *Cairo's* resting place. Bisso, after lifting the craft clear of the hole in which she rested, would move her downstream and place her on the sunken barge, which would then be refloated, thus bringing the ironclad to the surface.[5]

The Board of Supervisors hired Ken Parks, who had been associated with the project since 1959, to be its technical liaison man at the site. Parks was to assist Captain Bisso in all possible ways.

On Monday, August 3, preparations were made to move to the site a dragline, which would be manned by Robert Moore, a skilled operator from Warren County, and by Tuesday night the dragline was in position. The next day diver Sam Bongiovanni of New Orleans, who had been recommended by Bisso, arrived and made several exploratory dives. He found that all the hulk, except the forward one-third of the casemate, was again covered with silt. Before any wires could be placed beneath the vessel, a great amount of work with dredge and dragline would have to be done.

While negotiations for a dredge were taking place, the barge with its dragline was moored over the bow of the sunken ironclad. Operator Moore was given the job of removing mud and silt from around the bow. This was the first time he had used a dragline in water, and to make his task more difficult, he had to maneuver the unseen bucket as close as possible to the hulk without tearing off any timbers. Several days were required to develop the proper technique.

Friday evening found a dredge operated by Girod Construction Company of Delta, Louisiana, in position. Like the *Mary Ann,* this vessel was a World War II LCI that had been converted into a gravel dredge. Round-the-clock dredging operations were planned. Bad luck continued to plague the project. By nine o'clock the next morning, the dredge had broken down, and it was necessary to return it to Delta for repairs: during the wait for the dredge, dragline operations were pushed. The dredge was back at the site and in operation on Tuesday, the eleventh. From then until Saturday afternoon, the dredge gushed up blue clay and sand that had accumulated in the trenches cut the previous September by the *Mary Ann.*

About the same hour that the Girod dredge and tugs were leaving the Yazoo, the *Rip Tide* was chugging upriver pushing the *Indiana,* Captain Bisso's dredge. The captain, learning from Bongiovanni that the *Cairo's* casemate had refilled with silt, had sent to New Orleans for the dredge. Sunday, August 16, was spent getting the *Indiana* and the derrick cranes rigged for operation. The next morning Bisso determined to gamble that he could thread a 2½-inch lifting wire under the bow of the hulk. First, the *Rip Tide* pushed the giant working crane *Boaz* into position on the upstream side of the *Cairo,* where she was anchored. The *Boaz'* 80-foot boom was used to pick up and lower a lifting wire into the muddy water between the bank and the vessel. While diver Bongiovanni worked the wire into position, one end was attached to a powerful steam-driven winch aboard the *Boaz* and the other to a timber-head on the *Rip Tide,* which had taken station downstream from the wreck.

As soon as the wire had been slipped below the nose of the bow and the diver was out of the way, spring lines were used to pull the derrick to the opposite side of the river. With the *Boaz* upstream from the hulk, Captain Lucus Sauerwin began maneuvering the *Rip Tide* backward and forward, while the winch on the *Boaz* alternately took up and let out slack, as Bisso and his men sought to work the wire in a see-saw fashion under the *Cairo's* bow. The wire, however, tripped against an obstruction and instead of slipping under the wreck was thrown across the fo'c'sle and against the casemate shield. After this had happened twice, Captain Bisso knew that his gamble had failed—more dredging with dragline was required.[6]

An underwater reconnaissance by Bongiovanni revealed that several logs were embedded in the bank in front of the bow, and it was these that had tripped the wire. After three days of dredging and the removal of two small logs, Bongiovanni was able to pinpoint a huge log, parallel to the bank and in contact with the bow. It was lifted to the surface by the *Boaz's* boom. Before being deposited on the bank, the log broke. The half of the log which did not drift down the Yazoo was found to be twenty-five feet long and two and a half feet across the butt. Near where the log had broken was found the imprint of the *Cairo's* bow: this cypress had been embedded in the mud before the ironclad went to the bottom. Now the mystery of why Light's forward wires had slipped was solved—they had never been farther under the craft than the tip of the bow. Late the next day, another cypress more than thirty feet in length was pulled from beneath the bow. With this obstruction out of the way, the first lifting wire, when work stopped for the night, was within twelve inches of slipping under the hulk.[7]

The next morning Bongiovanni employed a jet hose to blast away enough ooze to enable him to slip the 2½-inch wire into position. The *Boaz* and *Rip Tide* took over, and before the day was over the wire had been see-sawed under the *Cairo's* bow for a distance of eighteen to twenty feet.

When the see-sawing was resumed on the twenty-fourth, the wire encountered another snag. Bongiovanni again descended into the muddy river to see if he could discover the trouble and found large mounds of silt rising as high as the gunports on both sides of the wreck. Rubbish made these mounds formidable obstacles to the passage of the wire. If the *Cairo* had been a steel vessel there would have been no problem, but Captain Bisso was afraid to use too much power on her wooden hull, because of the danger of sawing the craft in two. Therefore he attacked the mounds with the 6-inch jet built by Johnston and Light, and a smaller hose manned by Bongiovanni. After three days, Bisso tried once more to move the wire farther back under the hulk. To break the wire loose, he utilized the *Boaz's* powerful lifting boom, which allowed him to apply pressure from a different angle. Before the day was over, the wire had been moved five feet.

The salvage team now prepared to thread a second wire under the *Cairo*. Mud tumbling into the river from the crumbling east bank had lodged against the bow in the days since the first wire was placed; the greater part of two days (August 29 and 30) was required to remove this accumulation with jet hoses and dragline. Bongiovanni found a hole two planks wide and fourteen feet in length in the *Cairo's* port bow, well below the waterline. Since this was in the area where Commander Selfridge reported one of the torpedoes had detonated, I felt that the diver had located the hole which had eluded us in other salvage operations.[8]

Later on the thirtieth, the second lifting wire was guided by Bongiovanni into position beneath the ironclad's middle keel. When the crew returned to work the next morning, it was found that pressure from the sloughing bank had pushed the wire under the bow. As soon as the wire was positioned, the tug moved the stiff-legged crane *Ajax* upstream, and the ends of the two lifting wires were secured to her huge block.

Before any force could be applied to the bow of the *Cairo* to break the suction holding her to the bottom, silt which had accumulated in the casement since operations were suspended in March would have to be removed. Captain Bisso planned to employ a system he had used successfully many times for cleaning the interiors of barges and tugs. The dredgeboat *Indiana* was moored just below the hulk, her 16-inch pipe was lowered into the casemate, and her giant pump started by Engineer Charles Merwin. A powerful column of water was discharged into the interior of the ironclad, and within a relatively short time the casemate from the forward shield back to the engines had been flushed. Ken Parks and Mike Dillon stood by and picked up artifacts which drifted to the surface during the flushing operation. These were mostly planks from the spar deck, broken during the removal of the guns, but a number of interesting items were rescued —a sewing kit, several canisters, a canteen, and parts of a table.

Captain Bisso on Friday, September 4, decided that the interior of the vessel was clean enough to allow him to try a lift. As soon as the *Atlas* could be stationed below the hulk and opposite the *Ajax,* a lifting wire was secured to each of their booms, and a pressure of eighty tons put on one of the wires and ninety on the other. Red marks had been previously painted on the wires at the water's surface. There were cheers from the onlookers as they saw the marks on the wires move upwards and the barges on which the derrick cranes were mounted dip downward. Sam Bongiovanni made a reconnaissance on the afternoon of the fifth, and he was able to stand beneath the bow. Returning to the surface, Bongiovanni told Bisso that the bow had been lifted about six feet, and that the wires were not cutting into the wood.[9]

Tension was now released and the task of threading a third and fourth wire under the hulk was begun. The first of these went under easily and slipped into place some sixty feet behind the blunt nose of the bow. Much difficulty was experienced in getting the fourth wire positioned. No. 1 wire was secured to a block and hook lowered by the *Ajax,* while Nos. 3 and 4 were suspended from the *Atlas'* boom. For the time being, No. 2 wire, which was nearest the bow, was tied off. When work ceased on Labor Day, 210 tons of stress had been placed on the wires holding the *Cairo's* bow some six feet off the bottom.[10]

The next morning when the diver made an inspection, he reported the wires in position. Better still, the cables were not cutting into the timbers of the hull to any appreciable degree. When Bongiovanni entered the casemate, he was disappointed to discover that during the past four days at least eighteen inches of silt had been deposited on the gun deck. Once again the *Indiana* was moored below the hulk, the pipe lowered, and the pump started.

Two working days were required to clean the boat's interior back to the engine room. On September 10, as soon as a head of steam was raised aboard the *Ajax* and *Atlas,* Captain Bisso put his skilled operators to work and the *Cairo's* bow was raised another twenty inches. Bisso, after discussing the situation with Bongiovanni, concluded that if the lift continued there was danger of breaking the *Cairo's* back, because of the accumulation of silt which clung to the sides of the casemate aft of No. 4 wire. In addition, the ironclad, except for the bow, still rested in a deep depression whose sides were composed of sand overlaying a matting of leaves, bark, and twigs. Until these obstructions were removed, Bisso and Bongiovanni were skeptical of lifting the sunken craft's stern. Arrangements were accordingly made to get a cutterhead dredge.[11]

While awaiting the arrival of the dredge, the task of clearing out the inside of the craft was pushed. By the afternoon of the twelfth, Bisso decided the *Cairo* had been lightened enough to attempt another lift. This time the *Atlas* was shifted to a position directly over the hulk, while the *Boaz* was maneuvered into the anchorage formerly occupied by the *Atlas,* and No. 2 wire was attached to her boom. Employing the three powerful cranes, Bisso and his men lifted the ironclad's bow five feet. Ken Parks was able to walk on top of the casemate shield, and the water reached only to his knees. This was the first time in almost 102 years that anyone, except a person using diving gear, had walked the *Cairo's* deck.

Early the next morning, Bisso decided to increase the tension on the wires, and "test-lifted" the bow of the *Cairo* far enough to expose several inches of the armor-plated casemate shield. The craft was held in this position for several minutes, before the *Cairo's* bow was lowered back into the muddy river, just inches below the surface.

As soon as the *Boaz* could be disengaged from No. 2 wire, a fifth cable was guided beneath the bow by Bongiovanni. Employing the established procedure this wire was passed beneath the ones already in position, and the see-sawing by the *Rip Tide* and *Boaz* commenced. A short distance aft of No. 4 wire, giant logs were encountered, and Captain Bisso on the fourteenth suspended operations pending the arrival of the dredge *Benalu;* by 10:30 P.M. on the twentieth, it was in position above the wreck, lines had been laid, and sightings taken by Ken Parks to insure that the 16-inch cutterhead on its sweeps would get as close to the *Cairo's* hull as possible without damaging the craft.[12]

According to the operation plan worked out in cooperation with Captain Milton Johnson of the *Benalu,* the dredge was to cut giant trenches 150 feet wide, as deep as the ironclad's keels, and extending out into the channel on both sides of the hulk's fantails. Working around the clock, the *Benalu's* crew by 4:30 A.M. on September 23 had completed their task. During this period about thirty thousand yards of sand and mud had been removed from around the *Cairo.* Bongiovanni found that on the upstream side of the gunboat, the trench cut by the *Benalu* extended to within one foot of the port keel. Aft of the craft, water sand had poured back into the ditch as rapidly as removed, and rudders and stern remained partially buried; on the starboard beam, a mound of mud was found just behind No. 5 wire. Because of lack of funds it had been impossible to keep the dredge on standby while the diver was completing his inspection.[13]

Although probing indicated the presence of a number of mud-covered logs, Captain Bisso felt he could pull No. 5 wire into its desired position. It soon became apparent, however, that the *Boaz* and *Rip Tide* could not move this wire until the obstructions were removed. The next day, after the mud had been jetted away, Bongio-vanni located a raft of logs lodged against the vessel's starboard beam about seventy feet aft of the bow. Bisso's operators pulled four giant logs to the surface; the largest was about three feet in diameter and the others one and a half to two feet. An inspection of the logs and the finding of handwrought spikes indicated to me that they had been part of a logging raft, which seemingly had broken up while en route downstream to a sawmill soon after the *Cairo* had been torpedoed.[14]

Now the see-sawing operation could be resumed. At first, No. 5 wire was moved toward the stern of the craft with relative ease. Near the eighty-foot mark additional trouble was encountered—the wire lodged against an immovable object on the upstream side of the hulk. Fears were voiced that the wire was cutting into the craft. An exploratory dive by Ken Parks disclosed that a section of the heavily armored casemate protecting the port side of the craft had toppled backwards and was obstructing the wire. Bongiovanni secured a line to the wreckage. When pulled to the surface and examined, it was found that the wreckage was the section of the casemate between Nos. 3 and 4 gunports, and was plated with iron two and a half inches thick. Of special interest was the discovery that the iron plates were slotted like weatherboarding. Reviewing what had transpired, Captain Bisso and his team guessed that in the muddy water, slack from the cable being used to pull No. 5 wire under the craft had become entangled inside the casemate, and when either the *Boaz* or *Rip Tide* had exerted a strain on it, the thirteen by ten-foot section had been pulled loose. Except for breaking a twelve by twenty-four-inch beam and bending a number of giant spikes, no material damage to the ironclad had been done by this accident.[15]

By the afternoon of September 26, No. 5 wire had reached its optimum point 105 feet back from the bow and beneath the boiler room. Early the next morning, No. 2 wire was removed from the bow, and steps taken to place it under the stern. First, the dredgeboat *Indiana* was moored in position and a powerful column of water used to push away the water sand which enveloped this section of the craft. Diver Bongiovanni spent most of the next two days on the bottom, guiding the wire past the giant rudders and under the vessel, and getting the cable in its desired position eight feet forward of the rudder posts.

Work was also hindered by forty-eight hours of rain which began on the evening of September 27 and dumped from three to five inches of precipitation over the Yazoo watershed. This caused the river to rise five feet at the site. As the current picked up speed, it swept tons of silt and debris downstream. Captain Bisso and his crew now had to battle the drift which built up against his derricks and wires. The *Indiana* was again called into service to use her giant centrifugal pump to keep silt from accumulating inside the sunken craft.

The rising water, however, proved to be a blessing to the project. When Bisso had inspected the iron plating on the casemate he realized that it would be impossible to raise the *Cairo* with the three derricks brought to the site in July. When calculating the weight of the craft, engineers previously associated with the project had used the figure 75 tons of armor on the vessel, as this was the amount stipulated in the Eads contract; they had failed to take cognizance of a change order that had increased the iron plate to be placed on each of the city-class gunboats from 75 to 122 tons. In May, while at the National Archives, I had located this order.

Captain Bisso now approached the Warren County Board of Supervisors and explained that he would have to use his giant floating derrick *Cairo,* which had a lifting capacity of more than 320 tons, to get the ironclad off the bottom. With the river rising he could now get the huge crane (which drew nine feet of water) up the Yazoo. There would be no charge for the use of the *Cairo,* but the county would have to pay towage from New Orleans. The Board of Supervisors approved; Bisso was given the green light.

The derrick reached Vicksburg early on the afternoon of the fourth, just as the rains and high winds from Hurricane Hilda were abating. By 10:30 P.M. it was at the *Cairo* site.

Meanwhile, Captain Bisso's men had pushed ahead. On the last day of September, a messenger cable was pulled under the sunken ironclad, aft of No. 5 wire. This cable was utilized to pull a 3-inch wire into position, so that when the giant derrick arrived, the six lifting wires with which Bisso proposed to lift the ironclad out of her hole had been placed.[16]

Two days, October 5 and 6, were required to get the derricks positioned and the wires secured to the blocks. The *Ajax,* which was moored upstream from the wreck, would handle the two wires supporting the ironclad's bow; the derrick *Cairo,* anchored alongside the *Ajax's* starboard beam, held the wires passing under the hulk amidships; the *Atlas,* which was anchored downstream from the wreck, would handle the two stern wires. Late on the afternoon of the sixth the stern was raised an estimated two feet.[17]

Early on the seventh Captain Bisso secured a smaller cable to wire No. 6, because he felt that more power would be required to level the wreck. This cable was handled by the *Boaz,* anchored alongside the derrick *Cairo.* At a signal from Bisso, the operators and firemen took their stations. Spectators watched the red marks painted on the wires at the point where they emerged from the water, as the *Boaz's* winch was started. No. 6 wire began slowly to creep up; the barge sank lower and lower into the water. Captain Bisso signaled for the operator to stop the winch. In succession, the procedure was repeated aboard the *Atlas, Cairo,* and *Ajax.* After each derrick had exerted a tremendous pull, a break would be taken to allow the ironclad to pull loose from the mud.

A second and third lift were made. The hulk was slowly being lifted out of the hole, when No. 6 wire suddenly jumped. The gap between the exposed ends of the cable narrowed. Bisso shouted for his operators to take some of the strain off the ironclad, while Bongiovanni went down to ascertain what had happened. Feeling his way down the upstream side of the ironclad, the diver found that the wire was in good position. Investigating the starboard fantail, Bongiovanni discovered that the wire had cut deeply into the hull. Bisso, after listening to the diver's report, ordered tension released on the stern wires. The ironclad was simply too heavy. Before she could be successfully lifted out of the hole, additional mud would have to removed from the craft.[18]

Several days were spent jetting mud and sand from the *Cairo.* By Saturday morning, the tenth, Captain Bisso's cranes again began putting pressure on the hulk. As they did, the red markers on the wires crept upwards. No. 6 wire, however, continued to cut deeper into the craft, and, fearing that he was about to cut ten feet off the stern, Bisso ordered operations suspended. Bongiovanni sought to learn what had happened, but the wire had pinched so deeply into the craft that he was unable to pinpoint it. Bisso now realized that he would have to place a seventh wire under the vessel.

It took Bongiovanni three days to work the seventh wire under the stern and into a desired location ten feet in front of wire No. 6. To accomplish this tedious and dangerous task, it was necessary to remove debris sliced from the vessel by wire No. 6. When the wreckage was brought to the surface, it was found to be the starboard rudder and about eight feet of the starboard fantail forward of the rudder post.

Meanwhile, the vessel had continued to accumulate sand and silt. Before another lift could be attempted, the interior of the ironclad's gun deck would have to be given another bath. Four working days were devoted to this operation. This time, Bongiovanni entered and inspected several holds that had heretofore been sealed. We were encouraged to learn that these compartments were only partially filled with silt.

Sunday, October 18, was the day slated for the big lift. By dawn the firemen had stoked the fires and the boilers on each of the derrick barges soon had a head of steam. Rumors of what was about to occur spread, and by 6:15 A.M. the first spectators had started to arrive on the banks. It took Captain Bisso until ten-thirty to redeploy his floating derricks. Captain Sauerwin maneuvered the *Rip Tide* up- and downstream, as the derricks were placed and the deckhands secured the wires to the huge blocks. When the shifting was completed, the *Ajax,* which continued to be responsible for the two wires passing under the bow, was anchored downstream from the wreck; the floating derrick *Cairo,* whose two wires passed under the amidships, remained on the upriver side; the *Atlas,* supporting No. 5 and 6 wires, was moored alongside the *Ajax's* port beam; the *Boaz,* to whose boom wire No. 7 had been secured, was pushed into position next to the *Cairo* derrick.

By the time Captain Bisso sent his operators and observers to their posts, more than a thousand onlookers had gathered on the banks of the Yazoo.

The lift started about 11 A.M. Commencing with the *Boaz,* Bisso placed a strain on the sunken vessel. Excitement mounted as onlookers saw the giant blocks creep upward, a certain indication that the *Cairo* was being moved. After about an hour, Captain Bisso stopped to give his men a break. Hardly had he done so before one of his operators shouted that the strain on his derrick was less than it had been. The captain sent his men scrambling back to their stations; the lifting was resumed. Within a few minutes, the water began to boil and churn, and the tip of the starboard casemate shield poked through the murky surface. Cheers echoed and reechoed from the bank. Before suspending the lift, the *Cairo* had been raised far enough to expose about half of the starboard bow gunport.

Probes and soundings indicated that the *Cairo* was clear of the hole in which she had rested for over a century. Captain Bisso employed the anchor lines to ease the giant derricks holding the ironclad in her cradle of seven slings upstream about seventy-five feet. As soon as soundings demonstrated that the ironclad was above the trough, the derricks were secured and some of the tension on the vessel released.[19]

A call for the lifting barge went out. The 235-foot barge which had been rented from the Corps of Engineers was brought up the Yazoo by Ken Parks on October 19, and within five days it was ready for its mission. Eight by twelve-inch waylogs were laid and fastened to the deck of the barge. Connections for air hoses and pipes to be used in flushing water out of the barge, after it had been submerged, had to be welded into each compartment. Timber-heads to control the position of the barge as she was sent to the bottom were secured to her bow and stern.

On Sunday, the twenty-fifth, the barge was tested and towed downstream to the area adjacent to where she was to be sunk. Operations were slowed by the thousands of people who thronged this isolated spot to watch. Before the barge could be positioned, two of the derricks had to be moved. While the *Cairo* and *Boaz* held the ironclad in their slings, Bisso's men detached the wires from the blocks of the *Atlas* and *Ajax*. After tying off the wires, the two downstream derricks were towed out of the way.

It was the next afternoon before the barge was maneuvered into a desired anchorage downstream from and parallel to the wreck. Pumps were cranked, and the task of flooding the barge began. To keep the craft from being swept out of position by the powerful current, anchor wires leading from the timber-heads were secured to bulldozers on either bank. It was long after dark before the stern, last to be flooded, disappeared beneath the water, and the barge settled into the hole out of which the *Cairo* had been pulled eight days before. Soundings showed that there were nineteen feet of water over the stern of the barge and eleven feet over her bow. We would have liked more water, but it might be months before the winter rise.

October 27 and 28 were spent jetting out sand and silt that had accumulated in the craft since the last lift. When diver Bongiovanni made an inspection late on the twenty-eighth, he reported that he was able to penetrate parts of the *Cairo* never previously explored. The next morning, the twenty-ninth, Bisso's crew returned the *Ajax* and *Atlas* to their positions downstream from the hulk and reattached the four wires that had been tied off while the barge was being scuttled. As soon as anchor lines had been secured, Bisso began the lift which it was hoped would enable the salvage team to slip the ironclad onto the sunken barge was started. Rumors of what was impending spread, and a large crowd again collected on the banks. Each derrick in turn exerted pressure on the *Cairo*. There was excitement as the ironclad was lifted inch by inch toward the surface. Out toward mid-channel, a section of the port fantail with its giant rudder (damaged several weeks before in the first lift attempt) and the four paddle-wheel spiders crept into view. Closer to the bank, the casemate shield again emerged as the water boiled. One of Bisso's men, posted on the *Boaz,* looked inside one of the officers' quarters and spotted a beautiful, white ironstone pitcher and other objects. He was able to thrust his arm through a port and retrieve the pitcher.

Soundings indicated that the ironclad would have to be raised higher if she were to be slipped onto the barge. Bisso calculated that he was already utilizing 850 tons lifting capacity. As more and more of the bow, sheeted with two and a half inches of armor, emerged from the river, the strain on the wires became much greater. Soon the three bow ports were in view. Now the fo'c'sle could be seen. Soundings showed that the midships section of the wreck was within inches of sliding over onto the barge. As inch after inch of the ironclad emerged the crowd grew quiet. While the giant derrick *Cairo* increased its pressure on the hulk, Parks and Bongiovanni shouted for Captain Bisso to let off his anchor lines. Suddenly a warning crackle sounded as one of the derrick *Cairo's* wires twitched—the paddle-wheel spiders sank from sight. Two of the lifting derricks, the *Cairo* and *Atlas,* rushed toward each other as if to crush the ironclad between them. They stopped short with a jolt, and the stunned onlookers saw that a wire had cut deeply into the ironclad's port beam in the boiler room area. Captain Bisso slacked off on the forward derricks while he made an inspection. It was after dark when Bisso prepared to release pressure on the two rear derricks. As he was doing so, the *Atlas's* wire slashed into the starboard beam abreast of the engine room. Bisso was deeply concerned about the slash made by the *Atlas'* wire. He decided that he would have to replace the wire, as the *Cairo* was too fragile and too heavy to risk further lifting with the wires then in use.

On Friday, the thirtieth, while hundreds watched from the banks, a new 3-inch wire was pulled under the ironclad's stern. A check by Bongiovanni revealed that the wire, No. 8, was in good position and resting against solid timbers several feet behind the slash made by the *Atlas'* cable. The next morning the *Atlas'* block was lowered, and the old wire was replaced. A strain was put on the new wire and it tested satisfactorily.

A pump was used to jet clay and sand out of the forward hold, whose hatches had been bared when the fo'c'sle thrust above the yellowish water. Once again, calamity struck. Just as the salvage workers were getting ready to shut down for the night, the derrick *Cairo's* wire, which had slashed into the port beam forty-eight hours before, cut deeply again, this time into the starboard quarter. Captain Bisso feared that continued efforts to bring the ironclad up in one piece would result in extensive damage amidships and that there was grave danger of losing the vessel. He asked for permission to cut the ironclad in half to insure its safe recovery.

We held a dawn meeting with Bisso at the site. It was agreed that the captain would replace the *Cairo's* wire that had cut deeply into the craft and then make a test lift. If this test were unsatisfactory he could raise the craft in two sections. The first day of November was spent slipping the new wire, No. 9, under the bow and into its desired position in front of the one that had cut so deeply into the sides of the ironclad. As soon as the wire was positioned, tension was released on the derricks, and the bow of the ironclad again disappeared.

Plans were made on the second to hook the new wire to the derrick *Cairo's* block. But before this could be done, it was discovered that there had been a major breakdown in the huge derrick's machinery. Salvage operations were shut down for one week, while repairs were made. When work was resumed on the eighth, a strain was put on the wire that had slashed so deeply into the craft. There was no resistance—the vessel had already been cut in two. Indeed, when the wire which had done the damage was winched to the surface, most of us were not aware of what had occurred. Measurements were taken and it was calculated that the ironclad had been severed between the boiler and engine rooms.

The next morning Captain Bisso's team dropped a 3-inch wire in front of the *Cairo's* bow. After Bongiovanni made a descent and reported the wire had slipped under the middle keel, the winch operators took their posts. Progress was slowed as the wire became entangled in debris. Each time this occurred, Bongiovanni went down into the black water and cleared away the obstructions. On the tenth he made dive after dive checking progress and guiding the lifting cable under the forward section of the hulk. Two days passed before the wire was pulled into its desired position, about thirty feet in front of the point where the ironclad had been severed.[20]

The time-consuming task of rigging preparatory to lifting the forward section of the *Cairo* onto the barge was completed by dark on the twelfth. The air was chilly and mist was rising off the Yazoo the next morning as Bisso's crew prepared to lift the bow. Everything seemed to go wrong. A section of the starboard casemate, forward of No. 1 gunport, pulled loose at the knuckle and collapsed inboard. The aft *Cairo* wire bit deeply into the ironclad. It was apparent to me that the old hulk would have to be severed again.

Employing a back and forth motion with the wire that had cut into the hulk, Captain Bisso carried out his unpleasant task. Soon the ironclad was in three sections. The bow, consisting of the seventy feet of craft forward of the fireroom, was cradled by three wires (two attached to the *Ajax's* block and one to the *Cairo's*). A single 3-inch wire from the *Atlas* held the gunboat's heavily armored midships— thirty feet long and containing five boilers—a short distance off the bottom. Two cables, tied off and secured to floats, had been positioned under the gunboat's stern before it had been allowed to settle back into the mud.

Bisso's crew spent the rest of the morning slipping another wire into place under the after part of the forward section of the craft and hooking it up. As soon as this operation had been completed, the derricks *Ajax* and *Cairo* eased the bow toward the surface. Once again, the heavily armored casemate shield with its gunports came into view, along with portions of the fo'c'sle never seen before. We were encouraged, because this time the wires appeared not to bite into the sides of the craft.

Soundings revealed that the bow had been lifted high enough to clear the top of the submerged barge. Slack was let off on the spring lines, and the derricks, with the *Cairo's* forward section cradled in their slings, dropped slowly downstream. All eyes focused on markers placed ashore and on the barge. The task of positioning the bow on the barge was ticklish, as it was only a foot wider than the bottom of the *Cairo*. Bisso and his team were compelled to stop work before the bow had been placed on the barge, because of darkness. The next morning, after several hours of tedious maneuvering, Bisso was satisfied that he had the bow suspended over a desired spot on the barge. A signal was given, and the ironclad's bow was lowered.

While the bow was elevated, members of the artifact committee scrambled aboard. Inspecting a small area of the gun deck, they recovered a number of interesting objects—gunners' tools, including wrenches, a straight razor, pair of scissors, and a metal box containing tallow.[21]

Moving promptly to secure this section of the ironclad, Bisso's men detached the derrick *Cairo's* block from her slings. The big derrick took position upstream from and opposite the *Atlas*. To facilitate the placing of a second wire under the boiler section, a strain of over a hundred tons was exerted on the *Atlas'* sling. A full day was needed to position the new cable, as it was constantly fouled by wreckage. Whenever this happened, Bongiovanni had to go below and cut away the debris.

Early on the sixteenth, the derrick *Cairo* was hooked to the new wire. Captain Bisso now gave a signal, and the marks painted on the wires crept upward. Slowly but surely, the derricks lifted the midships. When the boiler section eased into view, we were shocked to see the starboard knuckle first—the section had turned ninety degrees in the slings. As more and more of the craft was exposed, I saw that the 2½-inch armor extended fifty-five inches below the knuckle. No one had suspected that the city-class boats had any plate iron below the waterline. Enough of the vessel's bottom was seen to confirm that the *Cairo* was flatbottomed. This was contrary to what Captain Bisso and the divers had believed.

Since the midships had tilted, it would be impossible to place this section on the lifting barge, so other alternatives were discussed—one was to place the piece on the bank, the other was to position it on a smaller barge. While bulldozers cleared and sloped the bank, Bisso's people rigged to enable the derrick *Cairo* to handle the midships unaided.[22]

An attempt to place this portion of the ironclad on the bank was frustrated by darkness. During the night Bisso decided to adopt the second option. On the morning of the seventeenth, his crew hoisted the boiler section, the holds of which were filled with tons of mud, and placed it on a barge. The port knuckle came in contact with the barge first, and as expected was unable to support the great weight to which it was subjected. Considerable difficulty was experienced in stabilizing the wreckage. As great chunks of mud sloughed off and dropped into the river, decking and bulkheads gave way. The starboard casemate parted at the knuckle and fell into the Yazoo, nearly carrying Captain Bisso with it. (Later this section was recovered.)

Much of the *Cairo* looked like this when brought to the Ingalls shipyard in Pascagoula, Mississippi, in 1965.

Crumpled paddle-wheel spiders rest beside modern ships.

Timbers and planking are wet down to prevent checking and cracking.

The *Cairo's* bow is partially assembled.

Sections are marked for correct identification and placement.

The partially assembled stern section with one rudder in place.

The bow and stern of the *Cairo* on the beach at Pascagoula.

A capstan rests on the dock.

Ken Parks looks through one of the *Cairo's* gunports.

A hatch opening into one of the holds.

Model of the city-class ironclads in the Smithsonian Institution.

At one time it looked as if the boilers themselves might slide into the Yazoo, but Bisso, skillfully directing the operators of his giant derricks, gradually lifted and settled the midships into a fairly stable position on the barge. Fears were voiced that the section weighed too much for the barge. While the salvage team struggled to secure this section of the *Cairo,* the ironclad's five boilers, mud header, and steamdrum were visible to the thousands of spectators. Scores of on-lookers moaned every time a part broke loose and fell into the river. A number of boxes slid into the water.

Along with other members of the artifact committee, I boarded the barge and found that the wire which had separated the bow and boiler sections had cut through the port and starboard coal bunkers, as well as the fireroom, while the cable that had severed the stern had knifed through a quartermaster's storeroom on the starboard side and an ordnance storeroom on the port beam. These holds, especially the quartermaster's, yielded a rich harvest of artifacts.[23] Glass lamp chimneys (intact and still coated with soot); sailors' personal belongings including straight razors, keen-edged and usable, hair brushes, tooth brushes, writing pens and pencils, sets of keys, the carved wood name stamp "S. May"; bottles of many sizes and shapes, and boiler room tools were carried ashore.[24] While the wreckage was combed for artifacts, Bisso's crew employed the *Boaz* to dismantle partially the ironclad's mid-section.

Saturday, November 21, found Bisso back at work placing additional wires under the *Cairo's* stern. Tactics similar to those used to place the second cable under the boiler section were employed. As soon as the *Atlas'* block had been hooked to a wire that had been previously buoyed, the aft section of the stern was pulled out of the mud. Lead cables, piloted by Bongiovanni, were slipped beneath the craft. These were used to pull two lifting wires into position. Three 3-inch wires were under the stern by nightfall on the twenty-second.[25]

Most of the following morning was needed to rig for what we hoped would be the final lift. The derricks *Cairo* and *Atlas* were given the mission of raising the stern. It required more than four hundred tons of stress to start the stern toward the surface. As on the twenty-ninth, the paddle-wheel spiders first came into view. To get the stern on the submerged barge, it was necessary to expose all the stern down to the knuckles. This enabled us to see that the sides of the casemate had collapsed inboard. Ken Parks, who was on one of Bisso's derricks, spotted the carriage for the 30-pounder Parrott left aboard the iron-clad the previous year, when the rest of the heavy ordnance had been salvaged. Tension on the spring lines was released, and at 3 P.M. on the twenty-third the stern was positioned on the lifting barge, a short distance behind the bow.[26]

Heavy rains that pelted the area on the twenty-fourth slowed work of securing wires to the timber-heads welded to the barge. The derrick *Cairo* would handle the stern wire; the *Atlas'* block was secured to the cable attached to the bow. Bongiovanni worked several days attaching air hoses to connections leading into the compartments of the barge. On Thanksgiving the pumps were started. Captain Bisso and project engineers advised that pumping the 750,000 gallons of water out of the barge would be both time consuming and hazardous. A rapidly rising river (six feet in thirty hours) added to the difficulties. By Saturday sufficient water had been expelled from the barge to enable Bisso to forecast that the *Cairo* would be surfaced within the next forty-eight hours.

The next morning, as air was being used to force water out of the stern compartments of the barge, Captain W. J. Eaves, in response to an order from Bisso, increased the tension on the derrick *Cairo's* wire. A powerful eddy caught the lifting barge and caused it to list and tilt. The after end of the barge shot into sight, and the stern of the *Cairo,* still in its lifting slings, slid off into the water, amid a cracking and snapping of timbers. This accident, the latest in a long series that had jinxed operations, cast a pall of gloom over us.

With the barge tilted at a rakish angle, the *Cairo's* bow was in danger of following the stern. Captain Bisso's men fought to level the barge, and bring the bow of the ironclad out of the water.[27] Slowly but surely the tilt of the barge lessened, as water was forced from the forward compartments. A swift current and cold weather on the last day of November harassed the workers as they struggled to save the ironclad's bow. When work was stopped for the night, all the casemate shield, as well as the fo'c'sle, was in sight.

The next day the artifact committee and soldiers of the 45th Explosive Ordnance Disposal Unit from Fort Polk, Louisiana, commanded by Lieutenant R. R. McGauhey, were able to board the barge. While Captain Bisso's men stabilized the bow by using jet hoses to clean mud out of a port hold containing soap, lard, tallow, and lye, we explored the bos'n's locker. From the locker we removed barrels of white lead, kegs of nails and spikes, boxes of glass, cables, giant blocks to assist the vessel in freeing herself when aground, marlin spikes, oakum, etc.[28] Scattered about the deck of the barge just in front of where the stern of the *Cairo* had rested, were hand grenades, friction primers, and small-arms ammunition. Before work was suspended on December 1, hundreds of artifacts had been salvaged. The barge had been pumped out, and the ironclad's entire bow was out of the water, for the first time since the day the torpedoes sent the *Cairo* to the bottom of the Yazoo.[29]

December 2 saw the army team and artifact hunters policing the gun deck, as well as cleaning a hold used for storing soap, and a heretofore unexplored compartment in front of the bos'n's locker. As mud was washed out of the latter hold, hundreds of items belonging to the *Cairo's* crew were recovered. The most interesting of these were an old glassbase photograph of a woman and child carried by an unknown Civil War sailor, several seamen's chests, the uniform of a man who had been a member of the Massachusetts Militia before transferring to the Mississippi Squadron, and a sailor's neckerchief, still knotted.

The next day, Thursday, a shellroom was pinpointed on the port side of the bow forward of the soap locker. Again using hoses to force away mud, army personnel, assisted by the artifact committee, entered the shellroom, which contained hundreds of rounds of grape, canister, and solid shot for the 32-pounder smoothbores and 8-inch navies. Scattered among the projectiles and protected by mud were a number of additional personal items, including a watch manufactured by Joseph Johnson of Liverpool, England, which had belonged to Fireman James D. Callihan.

Meanwhile, the salvage crew had succeeded in attaching the three wires encircling the ironclad's stern to hooks lowered by the *Atlas* and *Cairo*. On the fourth the two derricks eased the stern from midchannel toward the east bank of the Yazoo. After the barge with the bow had been pushed out of the way, a bulldozer sloped the bank. Captain Bisso would beach the stern.

Rain was falling the next morning, as the *Atlas* and *Cairo* hoisted the stern out of the water and placed it on the muddy bank. So full of silt was the stern that the two powerful derricks were barely able to handle it. The stern, because of the fall from the lifting barge, had turned 180 degrees—the bottom being first to break the surface. It was apparent that when the stern had slid back into the river, it had been damaged severely. The decking covering the race and separating the fantails had snapped like kindling, the paddle-wheel spiders were crushed; the port casemate was nowhere to be seen. The carriage for the 30-pounder Parrott, along with valuable artifacts from the officers' quarters, had been lost to the river.

Teams from the artifact committee entered the starboard fantail before Captain Bisso's people had finished securing the wreckage. A group led by Don Jacks worked its way through the opening left when the rudder assembly was severed. As Jacks's team washed away mud and entered the aft hold, they recovered hundreds of objects—giant earthen jars, bottles, mess gear, a fife, lamps, kettles, coffee urns, and even a dust pan. My team cleaned the ordnance storeroom. As the wire that had separated the amidships from the stern passed through this area, some of the ordnance stores had been spilled. Even so, this storeroom proved a bonanza. It contained spare parts for the gun carriages, a box of artillery short swords, friction primers, small-arms ammunition, brass covers to protect the firing mechanism of the great guns when they were not in use, brass belt buckles (army issue), and direct sighting devices for the big guns. Harold L. Peterson, an ordnance expert with a worldwide reputation, doubted if any living man had heretofore seen the latter.

After the ordnance storeroom had been cleaned, a bulkhead was removed, allowing entrance to a huge leadlined shellroom. Inside were hundreds of square boxes containing loaded and fused projectiles for the *Cairo's* 32-pounders and 8-inch navies. Sabots were attached to the shells, and on the boxes could be seen stenciled in block letters "To Capt. A. H. Foote, Cairo, Ill." Since these shells could be dangerous, members of the ordnance disposal unit took them in charge. Unlike the naval personnel of the previous year, Lieutenant McGauhey's soldiers knew and understood Civil War ordnance. The shells were removed from their boxes and loaded in a truck to be taken to Fort Polk and disarmed.

On the sixth, to facilitate the removal of projectiles from the shellroom, a hole was cut through the bottom of the starboard fantail. This enabled the ammunition detail to get at a section of the leadlined room in which were stored shells for the 42-pounder rifles and 30-pounder Parrott. The projectiles for the bigger guns, however, weighed eighty-seven pounds each, as the tubes, which originally had been smoothbores, had not been redesignated when they were rifled. Even the enthusiasm of a dedicated Civil War buff, like myself, waned after a few hours hefting these shells out of a dark and muddy hold. Within a short time, the big truck which the Fort Polk soldiers had brought with them was loaded to capacity—over seven tons of ammunition. Lieutenant McGauhey determined to return to Fort Polk and get more men and bigger trucks.

Pending the return of the army, work of removing projectiles from the starboard shellroom was pushed by the artifact committee, reinforced by workers rushed to the site by the Warren County board of supervisors. Whenever they grew tired of lifting shells, the artifact hunters returned to the bow section. The storeroom in front of the bos'n's locker was cleaned, yielding a rich harvest of personal belongings. More tintype photographs were found and copied. Also retrieved were a box containing gear used by the boat's cobbler, silk hatbands with "U. S. S. Cairo" in gold letters, sewing kits, and numerous other articles which cast new light on life aboard a Civil War ironclad.

On the ninth Captain Bisso decided to see if the stern had been lightened sufficiently to place the fantails aboard the big barge. When the operators aboard the *Cairo* and *Atlas* put a strain on the stern, they found less stress was required to hoist this section than had been needed earlier. During the lift, the port fantail, access to which had before been prevented by water, was exposed. Bisso, seeing that holds in this section were jammed with mud, called for men with jet hoses. One group entered the hold alongside the port engine; the other worked its way through the opening left when the port rudder area was slashed. The first group, led by Don Jacks and Ron Meyer, cleared away debris and found themselves in another large shellroom. Washing away mud, the artifact hunters began removing boxes of high explosive projectiles for the 42-pounder rifles. A box of Ketchum hand grenades, with tail assemblies and plungers, was found. Meanwhile, the team which I headed worked in the aft compartment, where we salvaged pots and pans, stoneware for the officers' mess, boxes filled with personal gear, and a giant earthen jug filled with coal oil. Before the day was over, tons of mud had been washed from the port fantail.

The next morning Bisso's crew, having ascertained that the decking and beams covering the race had been crushed, prepared to separate the fantails, and place them on the barge. Two 3-inch wires were threaded through the race to be hooked to the *Cairo's* block, and the giant derrick slowly lifted the starboard fantail. After the fantails had separated, spring lines were used to shift the derrick out into midchannel. The tug *Rip Tide* maneuvered the barge, so that when Bisso gave the word, Captain Eaves, up in the *Cairo's* crow's nest, used his controls to lower the fantail. After the wreckage had been secured to the rear of the barge, the derrick was winched back to the east bank. Wires used to beach the stern were now secured to the *Cairo's* hook. On Saturday, the eleventh, 102 years after the ironclad had been sent to the bottom, the pride of Bisso's salvage fleet picked up the port fantail and deposited it on the barge. Despite weeks of heartbreak and frustration, Captain Bisso's crew had succeeded in the task they had set out to accomplish in August.

Lieutenant McGauhey's reinforced unit returned to Vicksburg at this time. Assisted by the artifact committee, the soldiers removed the last of the live ammunition from the starboard shellroom. When the army headed back to Fort Polk on the fourteenth, they took with them more than twenty tons of projectiles. Next, we moved into the port shellroom. This locker was not so large as the one on the opposite side of the vessel. Even so, over four hundred explosive rounds for the 42-pounders, 32-pounders, and 8-inch navies were retrieved and stacked on the deck of the barge for the army to pick up on their next visit to Vicksburg.

Behind the port shellroom, and separated from it by a thick bulkhead, was the ironclad's magazine. This lead-lined hold was filled with box after box of black powder. Using powerful streams of water, we carefully washed mud and powder overboard, for the powder, if allowed to dry, was highly inflammable.

Captain Bisso now started moving his equipment out of the Yazoo. First to go was the derrick *Cairo*. With a rapidly rising Mississippi, Bisso fretted that his giant derrick might not pass under the Baton Rouge bridge. For once in this operation, the captain was lucky, and the derrick passed under this obstacle with only hours to spare.

On December 22 Bisso complied with the final article in his contract. Taking in tow the two barges on which rested the wreckage of the *Cairo,* the tug *Rip Tide* chugged down the Yazoo. Describing the arrival of the ironclad at the government fleet above the city, a member of the press wrote: "The Union ironclad *Cairo* was in port today at this once conquered Confederate bastion, but it was 102 years too late to aid Gen. William T. Sherman's war effort. The once-proud ship, which fell to a Confederate 'infernal machine' a century ago, lay in ruins atop two barges." [30]

The day after Christmas, the last of Bisso's equipment left the Yazoo and headed down the Mississippi. Before starting for a new job, a serious look on his face, Captain Bisso told me, "Please don't find another Civil War battleship."

10

BITS AND PIECES
FROM THE PAST

Oₙₑ of the most difficult but most rewarding tasks associated with the *Cairo* project was the cleaning, preservation, and cataloguing of thousands of priceless artifacts—ranging in size from the tube of a rifled 42-pounder weighing 8,620 pounds to a fragile box containing pins and threaded needles. When brought up from the hulk by divers in the 1963 operation, the artifacts, except for such objects as the big guns and naval carriages, were locked in storage boxes at the site. Even so, a number of valuable small objects were known to have disappeared between the time they were brought to the surface and when they were delivered at the building where they were to be stored. After the *Cairo* had been raised, objects washed out of the mud as the holds were cleaned were trucked to the museum laboratory behind the Visitor Center at the Vicksburg National Military Park.

Mrs. Al Banton and Mrs. W. R. Sund spent many hours cataloging the artifacts, while my wife Margie classified and photographed the objects. Pictures of artifacts which local historians and antiquarians were unable to identify were forwarded to experts in their fields —W. E. Geoghegan of Smithsonian Institution, Dr. Francis Lord of Rockville, Maryland, and John Weigand of Anniston, Alabama. Dr. James W. Hazlett of Wheeling, West Virginia, furnished valuable information on the *Cairo's* ordnance.

Assisted by Al Banton, Don Jacks, and other volunteers, the ladies cleaned the smaller metal artifacts. This proved to be an interesting task. When the mud and scum were scrubbed from the tin mess gear —names, initials, and marks were found scratched into spoon handles and on the bottoms or the sides of plates and cups. By checking a muster roll of the boat's company for November 8, 1862, obtained

153

from National Archives, the ladies were able to identify men who had used the items before the command "Abandon ship" rang out across the Yazoo.

On the *Cairo,* we discovered, the enlisted men were assigned to and ate by messes. Each mess which consisted of about twenty men was assigned a number and a large wooden chest (5' x 2' x 2') in which to store its gear—tin plates, cups, spoons, bottles of condiments, scrub brushes, wash tub, and an earthen jug of molasses. Since each bluejacket was responsible for his gear, he marked it with his name or initials if he were literate, or his mark if he could not read and write. Some of the sailors etched their mess number on their gear.

Typical of the mess cups found were those marked: "Lewis Diemert," "W. H. Elliott," "P. Anderson," "WAB," "A.W.," and "Thomas E. Brown." Checking the muster roll we found that Lewis Diemert was born in France. At twenty-eight with no occupation, he had entered service on February 7, 1862, in New York City. Coming aboard the *Cairo* from the receiving boat *Maria Denning,* Diemert held the rank of petty officer. William H. Elliott had been born in Springfield, Massachusetts, in 1823, making him one of the older members of the crew. Enlisting for three years' service at New Bedford on March 29, 1862, he was rated a seaman and had been assigned to the ironclad from the *Maria Denning.* Peter Anderson was one of three men aboard the *Cairo* with the same surname, one of whom was his brother, Gart. The Anderson brothers, who came from Norway, had enlisted at Cairo, May 31, 1862. Unlike Diemert and Elliott, the Andersons listed occupations—they were farmers. Aboard the ironclad they served as seamen. "WAB" we assumed to be Ward Bassett. Born in New York City in 1835, he had moved to Connecticut, where he worked as a blacksmith. On April 3, 1862, Bassett went to New Bedford and was shipped by a naval recruiter. He was billeted to the *Cairo* from the *Maria Denning,* where Lieutenant Bryant learned of his background and assigned him to be the boat's blacksmith. "A.W." was Albert Webster, a thirty-one-year-old seaman with no fixed occupation. A native of New Hampshire, he had enlisted for two years' service. At the time of the sinking, he served as a seaman aboard the ill-fated ironclad. There were three Thomas Browns aboard the *Cairo,* none of whom listed a middle initial, but one of whom was an Oriental. This made it impossible for us to determine which of them had been issued and used the cup more than a century ago.

Some of the inscriptions on the mess plates were: "S. W. Chandler—

Mess No. 5," "ERB," "J. A. Lee," "J.J.," and "J.W." We were able to identify Sam W. Chandler, as a farmer from Pekin, Illinois. The twenty-year-old Chandler had been assigned to the *Cairo* from the *Maria Denning* on February 4, 1862. "ERB" had to be E. R. Bradley, a twenty-two-year-old Chicago school teacher. He had boarded the ironclad at the same time as Chandler, and they had been messmates. Both men held the rating of seamen. James A. Lee, a nineteen-year-old farmer from Erie County, Pennsylvania, had been mustered into the gunboat service at St. Louis on February 14. "J.J." proved to be John V. Jackson of New York City. Before enlisting for three years on June 18, 1862, he had worked as a plumber. Jackson, who held the rank of corporal, had served aboard the experimental submarine *Alligator* with Commander Selfridge, and when the Navy Department decided that the submarine was impractical and dangerous, he accompanied his captain to the West. "J.W." had to be John Williams, a thirty-six-year-old seaman from Baltimore, who had enlisted for three years' service on May 30, 1861. Williams had been a member of the naval battalion which was rushed from Fort Ellsworth to Cairo in November for duty aboard the ironclads.

Among the personalized spoons were those marked: "BAC," "SWC," "CB," and "H.N.W." "BAC" was B. A. Coffin of Nantucket Island, Massachusetts. A man with a seafaring background, he had enlisted in the navy August 5, 1861, for a three-year hitch. Like Williams, Seaman Coffin, prior to coming aboard the *Cairo,* had been assigned to the naval battalion. "SWC" was an old friend, Sam Chandler, while "CB" was presumed to be Charles Brown. Born in Denmark twenty-four years before, Seaman Brown, who listed no occupation, had been shipped by a naval recruiter at Boston on April 2, 1862. "H.N.W." was H. N. Walcott, born in South Carolina in 1839. At the time of the firing on Fort Sumter, he resided in New York City, where he worked as a blacksmith. One of the three six-footers on the *Cairo,* Walcott had enlisted for three years' service at New Bedford, July 30, 1861, and had traveled to the West with the naval battalion. Assigned to the *Cairo* from the *Maria Denning,* he held the rank of armorer.

One of my most rewarding *Cairo* experiences came about because of the mess gear. In January, 1965, I was asked to present a program on the salvage to the Peoria (Illinois) Civil War Roundtable. Knowing that Sam Chandler came from Pekin, which is in the Peoria area, his plate and spoon were among the artifacts I took along to show.

Prior to the meeting, I appeared on television and told of the raising of the ironclad and showed the Chandler gear. Mrs. Carroll W. Haueisen of Peoria was watching the program and was delighted with what she saw, because Chandler was her great-uncle. She wrote me, "Great Uncle Sam had lived with us and passed away at our home." Sam Chandler, she continued, had transferred from Company K, 17th Illinois to the gunboat service, January 31, 1862. Mrs. Haueisen was the first twentieth-century relative to claim one of the crew as a member of the family.[1]

As was to be expected, the officers dined in a separate mess, and they ate from ironstone and used knives, forks, and spoons produced by Rogers and Brothers and Hartford Manufacturing Company. Much of the ironstone was broken in salvage, but fortunately a representative collection was preserved for display. Markings on the stoneware showed that a great deal of it had been manufactured by "J. Wedgwood," and sold to the government by "J. J. Brown, Importer New Albany, Ind."

Food for the messes was prepared in big copper and iron pots on a "Southern Belle" cooking range, manufactured by S. H. Burton and Company, Cincinnati, Ohio. A rolling pin was evidence that at least the officers ate biscuits and pastries. The commissary storeroom yielded hundreds of barrels, most of which collapsed as the mud was hosed away. These contained beef and hog bones, all that remained of the salt meat which constituted a major item in the Civil War servicemen's diet. Since a large number of staves were piled in one corner of the room, near where we found several sets of scales, a chopping block, and a large two-handed meat cleaver, we knew that it was here that the boat's butcher stood, when he cut up and issued the meat ration to each mess. Food on the ironclad must have been very drab, as we found over three hundred government-issue bottles marked "U. S. Navy" on one side, and either "Pepper" or "Mustard" on the opposite. Some of these bottles still held their original contents.

My favorite item from the boat's commissary is a champagne bottle containing vinegar and green and red peppers to be used for seasoning. When the cork shrank, and before we could place a paraffin seal on the bottle, some of the sauce leaked out. It was so potent that it made my eyes smart for hours. A large wooden keg with the words "Chicago Brewery" inscribed on top was recovered from the commissary storeroom. The contents had seeped out, but when the barrel was placed in a vat filled with preservative, we all noticed a strong odor of beer as the liquid forced the air from the barrel.

Out of officers' country we recovered a handsome wooden ice chest. A variety of whiskey, rum, champagne, and wine bottles found nearby demonstrated that although the rum ration had been dispensed with in July, 1862, the boat carried a well-stocked liquor locker, undoubtedly for "snake bite." Several of the wine bottles were unopened, but none of us had the nerve to sample the vintage. One of the bottles was inscribed "M'Lean's Strengthening Cordial"; there were a number of bottles that had contained soft drinks labelled "J. H. Kump, Memphis, Tenn."

Leather objects (boots, shoes, belts, cartridge-boxes, cap-pouches, book covers, and powder buckets) were treated with Texol-n preservative, supplied by Union Carbide. When we took time to study these items we were amazed by what we found. A number of the leather objects were in excellent condition, but the cotton stitching which had held a boot or cartridge-box together had disappeared. Arrangements were made with cobblers to have a number of these restitched.

There were two types of officers' boots recovered—one for dress and the other for work. The dress boots were soft and of excellent workmanship, and after being treated with Texol-n they became as pliable as an expensive pair of kid gloves. One of the boat's officers had bunions, as was evidenced by a pair of heavy work boots which had been cut and patched by the *Cairo's* shoemaker Autin Rogerson. Of considerable interest to the people from the Smithsonian Institution were the enlisted men's shoes. Hobnailed on the bottom, the soles were attached to the uppers with wooden pegs. Other shoes had horseshoes on the heels. Most government-issue shoes of the Civil War period had a common last, but the *Cairo* shoes were rights and lefts. A child's shoe caused considerable speculation (Its mate was lost in salvage operations.) We finally decided that one of the crewmen had either "liberated" the shoes when the small boat carrying contraband was intercepted prior to the run down from Memphis, or he had asked Rogerson to turn them out in his spare time.

Bottles and jars from the dispensary were cleaned and samples taken from them to be analyzed by State Chemist M. P. Ethridge, Dr. Raymond Bennett of the Mississippi University School of Pharmacy, David B. Sabine of U.S. Vitamin and Pharmaceutical Corporation, and Dr. Gilman Cyr of E. R. Squibb & Sons. Doctors Cyr and Bennett became so interested in the bottles and their contents that they presented papers on their findings before the August, 1964, meeting of the American Pharmaceutical Association. The bottle in which Dr. Cyr became interested was of molded, green glass, containing an almost colorless liquid, with "E. R. Squibb" in raised letters. Smelling very faintly of stale brackish water, it was at first suspected that the bottle's contents consisted solely of river water. Exhaustive tests, together with an examination of drugs available on Squibb price lists for the early 1860's, confirmed that the bottle contained potassium chlorate, a drug prescribed at that time for a great variety of diseases. As yet, Dr. Cyr has not studied the contents of several dozen other bottles marked "E. R. Squibb" recovered when the vessel was raised.

Besides the Squibb bottles, there were a number of others with the manufacturer's name in raised letters. Some of these were: "Dr. Forsha, Alterative Balm"; "J. J. Butler, Cin"; "Arnica Liniment, New York, J. R. Burdsall's"; "Dr. H. A. Ingham's Nervine Pain Killer"; and "Norwod's Tinct. V. Virid." There were tin containers of salve, marked "Alliston, All Healing Ointment, World's Salve."

Other medicines identified by the chemists were: quinine, rhubarb, ammonia, sulphur, an antidote for itch, blue mass for syphilis, zinc chloride used as an antiseptic and as an astringent, and ferric chloride prescribed by the *Cairo's* surgeon J. Otis Burt as an iron tonic.

Contents of some bottles with glass stoppers (which had prevented seepage) we could identify without professional assistance, for many of them were such common household remedies as iodine, sulphur, castor oil, camphor, turpentine, and linseed oil. When the stopper to the iodine bottle was pulled, a thick vapor boiled out and burned the nostrils.

Only a few of the instruments used by Surgeon Burt or Surgeon's Steward John W. Gerten (who before answering his country's call, had been a butcher) were found. This led to the conclusion that they had either gone up the powerful air lift and been lost, or that they had been snatched up and carried off the sinking ironclad. Several silver ear syringes, buckles used on tourniquet straps, rubber bands used as arterial sutures while operations were in progress, and a bed pan were found on the deck of the sick bay. The rubber bands were identified by Dr. Alfred R. Henderson of the Medical Science Division of the Smithsonian Institution, who was incredulous that they were still elastic after more than a hundred years.[2]

Artifacts of greatest human interest were the men's personal gear. Even people with no interest in the Civil War had their curiosity aroused by combs, toothbrushes, writing instruments, etc., used by the *Cairo* bluejackets. Three different types of combs were found. The most common was about six inches long and made of hard rubber, with "U. S. Navy" on one side and "IR Goodyear 1851" on the other. The Amerace Corporation which manufactures today's "Ace" combs found that the company had turned out these combs.[3] [From the original mold, it cast a number of facsimiles of the *Cairo* comb, suitably inscribed for stockholders.] Antiquarians familiar with government-issue items of the Civil War period consider the combs one of the more significant *Cairo* discoveries. One of them bore Gunner's Mate Edward Thompson's name cut into the hard rubber. Several small nit combs were recovered. Master-at-Arms John Lang had marked his comb. Lang, an Irishman, and Thompson, a Dane, had been shipped in Atlantic Coast ports in the summer of 1861; had been assigned to garrison Fort Ellsworth; were ordered to Cairo with the naval battalion; and had served aboard the ironclad from the day she was commissioned. A curved tortoise-shell comb given a sailor by a wife or sweetheart as a keepsake was retrieved from the mud.

Toothbrushes used by the servicemen of the 1860's were much like those purchased in today's supermarket, as were the hairbrushes. The sailors who shaved (this had been an era when beards were high fashion), used straightedge razors manufactured by G. Wade & Butcher, who put on the market many of the straightedge razors used by today's barber. We were disappointed by the small number of shaving mugs recovered from the wreck, but delighted by the variety of vanity mirrors. Cans of shoe polish and brushes were cleaned, treated, and catalogued. The owners, such as Seaman John Laverty, a Chicago Irishman, handcarved their names into the wooden brush handles. To repair their uniforms, the sailors had sewing kits or "housewives." Numerous small tin canisters were found containing pins, needles, linen thread, spare buttons, and thimbles. Scissors of all sizes and types were classified.

To write to families and friends literate crewmen used pens or pencils. Most of the pencils found aboard the ironclad had "A. W. Faber No. 2" imprinted on them. The firm of Eberhard Faber, Inc. was surprised to receive a letter written by my wife using one of their pencils salvaged from the *Cairo*.[4] A mechanical pencil marked "Superfine No. 2" was found. There were slates, slate pencils, and erasers. On one of the slates we could make out part of a verse jotted down by one of the *Cairo* sailors, "From London to Liverpool to France we took. . . ." Ink wells, both field and desk, were cleaned. No writing paper or letters survived the years under mud and water, but we did find rolls of linen tracing paper, such as is used for drawing charts and maps in the field.

The Yazoo contains certain elements that destroy cotton, and no clothing made from that staple was recovered. Woolen uniforms had likewise disintegrated to such a degree that only fragments several inches large remained. As mud was cleaned out of the holds, it was noticed that whenever the water suddenly darkened, four large, hard rubber buttons with "U. S. N., Novelty Rubber Co., Goodyear's Patent, New York, 1851," could always be found. These buttons and the dye which colored the water were all that remained of the sailors' peajackets, except for a few pieces of one coat. Surprisingly, these pieces still had the lining clinging to them, and stitches were clearly visible. Hundreds of brass "U. S. Navy" and "U. S. Army" buttons were collected and classified. When we were through we knew that the crew of the *Cairo* must have presented a strange appearance when mustered for inspection. While many of the sailors were dressed in regulation naval uniforms, others were attired as soldiers, wearing the insignia of the branch of service from which they had been drawn— infantry, artillery, and cavalry. Silk, unlike cotton and wool, suffered no ill effects from the long immersion. A large number of folded neckerchiefs and ribbons for flat hats with "U. S. Cairo" in gold lettering were washed in lukewarm water with mild soap and wrapped in many thicknesses of towels to dry very slowly. When allowed to dry in open air, the silk disintegrated.

Human nature does not change, and the Civil War sailor wore goodluck pieces. Of the five coins recovered, three (a Queen Victoria cent, an Irish halfpenny, and a Portuguese LXXX Reis of the reign of Joseph I) fell into this category. The Portuguese and the Irish coins had been drilled to be worn as ear rings. There was a snake bracelet with attached locket, a patriotic stickpin, and pieces of jewelry— pins and hand-carved rings.

Petty theft was as prevalent in 1862 as it is today. But at that time there were no GI stencils or regulations for marking clothes, so some of the bluejackets took scraps of pine from four to six inches long and a half-inch wide and fashioned stencils bearing their names or initials. Among those who marked their gear in this manner were: "S. May," a fireman from Pennsylvania; "T. Brown," one of three crewmen with that surname and first initial; "R. Lymont," a bos'n's mate from New York; and "F. McG.," a Canadian-born coxswain named Francis McGuire. Others who were unable to read and write (about one-third of the crew was illiterate) carved stamps, in the shape of triangles, stars, etc., with which to mark their belongings. Seaman Charles Nelson of Boston went a step further. He secured a strip of tin, cut his name into the light metal, and with a paint brush painted his name on his property. Master-at-Arms Lang did the same, but unlike Nelson he cut only his initials into his stencil.

Several of the bluejackets undertook more ambitious carving projects in their spare time. A sailor, homesick for the ocean, had started carving a sailing ship, but by December 12 he had completed only the hull. Another man had fashioned a handsome patriotic stamp, utilizing the anchor and eagle as found on the insignia of the U. S. Navy. The scrimshaw, at first, presented a serious preservation problem. Polyethylene glycol which was used to control checking in the white oak turned fragile carving into pulp. Acrylic plastic was tried and the scrimshaw was saved.

There were knives for all purposes aboard the *Cairo*. A few of them were daggers to be employed against men, but most of them, ranging in size from "U. S. Navy" knives with 5-inch blades and no point, to one with a blade less than an inch in length, were for such peaceful pursuits as cutting and splicing lines, carving, and cleaning the fingernails. The government issue knives were bone-handled and had rectangular blades with "U. S. Navy" etched into them. There were pocket knives and lanyard knives in large numbers. On the wooden handles of some of the lanyard knives bluejackets had etched their names or initials. Knives belonging to Blacksmith Ward Bassett and Gunner's Mate Edward Thompson were quickly identified.

In the starboard hold forward of the bos'n's locker, a small wooden chest was recovered. It contained three pocket knives, a razor, shaving brush, a can of shoe polish, two glass plate photographs, a small key, eight "U. S. Navy" condiment bottles (four pepper and the others mustard), and a sewing kit, with thread, two needles, six bone buttons, and two large brass buttons with the insignia of the Massachusetts Volunteers. We concluded that one of the men who had stowed his gear in this chest had transferred from the army to the gunboat service. The glass plates were of heavily bearded men, one hoary with age, the other a handsome man in his forties. These men possibly were relatives of the owner or owners of the chest. Two of the knives had been inscribed, one, "T. Power" and the other "H. B." A check of the muster roll showed us that there was an H. R. Brown aboard the *Cairo*. Brown, who held the rank of seaman, had joined the service

in Boston on March 24, 1862. As there was no "T. Power" aboard
the ironclad at the time the crew signed the payroll on November 8,
1862, we decided that Brown had either traded for or found the
knife engraved "T. Power." Also, since each military man is responsible for his own gear, it seemed unlikely that two men would
have stowed personal effects in the same chest, so we concluded that
these articles had belonged to Seaman Brown.

A number of handsome pipes were catalogued. There were chests
of plug tobacco which could be either smoked or chewed. When dried
the tobacco retained its characteristic odor, but no one except my
friend and fellow historian E. B. Long has yet had the courage to
smoke any. He reported that except for a strong taste of Yazoo mud
the tobacco wasn't too bad.

Three fifes and the silver whistle used by Boatswain's Mate Charles
Smith to pipe the crew to their stations aroused much interest. The
fifes could be played, but, understandably they were out of pitch.
As soon as the pea had been replaced, Boatswain Smith, if he had
been still aboard, could have piped and shouted the familiar call, "All
hands man your brooms, there will be a clean sweep down fore and
aft."

Heretofore, we had assumed that officers aboard the ironclads had
used chamber pots, but we were mistaken. The officers' head (lava-
tory) on the *Cairo* was forward of the wheel, and it contained a toilet
and shower. The toilet bowl, made of an iron alloy, was inscribed,
"J. L. Mott, Iron-Works, N.Y." Water for these fixtures was secured
from the paddle wheel. As the wheel turned, water was carried upward by the buckets. As it poured off the buckets some of the water
was caught in a trough and carried to a tank in the ceiling of the
officers' head. Gravity induced the water to the shower and toilet.

For me the most intriguing objects were six dominoes. These were
probably the ones with which Third Engineer Aiken was playing when
he neglected to check the boiler gauge in November, 1862. Here was
an artifact that told a poignant human-interest story and helps to
make history live.

As our work ashore progressed we grew aware that the preservation
of large wooden objects, unlike that of the metal, glass, and leather
artifacts, would present serious problems. So we got in touch with
Raymond M. Seborg, a research chemist with the United States Forest
Products Laboratory at Madison, Wisconsin. Seborg, who is an expert
on chemical protection of waterlogged wood, had first discussed the

Cairo project with me at the conference on underwater archaeology sponsored by the Minnesota Historical Society in April, 1963. Seborg was no stranger to the problems of sunken boats, having previously cooperated with the officials of the Museum of the Adirondacks in the preservation of hulls of Colonial period bateaux found in Lake George, and with Swedish representatives on the treatment of the seventeenth-century warship *Wasa.* Seborg flew to Vicksburg and spent two days inspecting the artifacts.

To preserve the wooden artifacts, Seborg recommended diffusing polyethylene glycol into the cell walls of the wet wood. This wax-like chemical dissolves in water and diffuses into the fine, lattice-like structure of the wood cells. There it remains when the water dries out and acts as a bulking material to prevent the wood from shrinking and cracking.

Seborg expressed the opinion:

Small pieces, such as the small wooden box which contained pins and needle and thread, can be treated in a relatively short length of time. The larger items such as ammunition cases, the big gun carriages and sea chests will take longer. This treatment should be a continuing process over a number of years for some of the pieces. The chemical must be added into the wood again and again as the moisture moved out.[5]

In Madison, Seborg prepared a report on his trip to Vicksburg. He suggested that the wooden artifacts be submerged in a 25 percent solution of polyethylene glycol-1000. To fight wood decay which had appeared in areas around nails and bolts, Seborg suggested that a preservative chemical (preferably sodium salt of pentachlorophenate) be added to the polyethylene glycol solution.[6]

Almost all funds for the project had been obligated, so Al Banton and his preservation crew were confronted by a serious problem, because polyethylene glycol-1000 currently retailed for thirty-three cents a pound. Ten five hundred-pound barrels of polyethylene glycol were obtained from Union Carbide by the A & I Board on deferred billing. Meanwhile, contact had been established with E. R. Squibb & Sons; Olin Mathieson of which Squibb is a subsidiary donated ten barrels of the expensive preservative. Monsanto Chemical Company, when advised by Joe Schmitt of the need for sodium salt of pentachlorophenate, gave twenty-two hundred pounds.

Eighty-seven dollars worth of lumber, nails, and polyethylene sheeting were purchased, and with these materials a huge tank (45' x 7' x 4') was built by personnel from the Vicksburg National Military Park. Al Banton and Don Jacks in the meantime had been keeping the wooden artifacts wet. All large wooden objects (except several held out for control purposes) were placed in the tank. After ten thousand gallons of water had been pumped into the tank, Banton and Jacks began the hot and tedious task of melting the polyethylene glycol and pouring it into the water. Four hours were required to dispose of each barrel. Then, after putting on masks to protect themselves from the deadly fumes, the two men added sodium salt of pentachlorophenate to the solution. A circulating pump was employed to diffuse the fungicide.

James Neeld of Yazoo City lent a hand. Since he was in the musical instrument business, Neeld was familiar with the steps that should be taken to preserve brass objects. Neeld, on his own time and at his own expense, cleaned and polished the sights and firing mechanisms for the big guns, the brass lighting fixtures, the boat's bell, and the flutes. By the time Neeld had finished, these items looked as though they had been tidied up for a visit to the *Cairo* by Flag Officer Foote.

Since there were many iron artifacts on hand, their preservation treatment would take months. Contact was established with the Oakite Company, and one of their chemists visited Vicksburg to make an on-the-spot study. After examining the objects, he recommended that the cannon tubes be immersed for two hours in a solution of one part Oakite 31 to four parts water. This solution would remove the rust that had accumulated on the tubes in the months since they had been brought to the surface. The tubes should then be washed with caustic soda to neutralize the acid. After a rusticide had been applied, the tubes would be painted black, and the white sighting stripes added.

Assisted by Bob Moore and a crew supplied by the Warren County Board of Supervisors, Banton and Jacks constructed a three-by three-by eleven-foot tank of plywood, lined with polyethylene sheeting, in which to bathe the tubes. The plan suggested by the Oakite representative was workable, and after a week's labor the guns were ready to be put back on their carriages.

The smaller iron objects were dipped in a solution of Oakite 33, if there was no danger of etching the metal. After they were taken from the vat, they were handled in the same fashion as the guns.

Small arms (muskets and revolvers), upon being taken from the giant tank containing polyethylene glycol, were turned over to Vincent

Canizaro. A man long interested in the care of small arms, Canizaro carefully disassembled the weapons, cleaned the metal parts, reassembled them, and returned them for exhibit.

The preservation of the *Cairo* artifacts is a continuing operation. It will be a number of years before all the articles are stabilized and their deterioration arrested. So that the public might view these treasures, the Warren County Board of Supervisors in June, 1965, entered into an agreement with the National Park Service. It was stipulated that for the next three years, or until such time as the *Cairo* was restored, the National Park Service would have custody of the artifacts which were placed on display in a wing of the Visitor Center at the Vicksburg National Military Park.

11

PLANS
FOR THE FUTURE

Now that the *Cairo* had been raised and turned over to the Warren County Board of Supervisors, the problem of restoring the vessel had to be faced. When we had thought the ironclad could be brought up intact, we planned to display the craft on the giant lifting barge. After the mud and artifacts had been removed, the armor and metal parts would be sandblasted and painted, and a saline spray (to control checking and warping) used to impregnate the white oak of which the hull and casemate were constructed. A building of light metal would be erected on the barge to protect the *Cairo* and house the artifacts. Such an undertaking would cost about $250,000. Taking advantage of the authority granted by "Senate Bill 2050" the Board of Supervisors announced they would issue bonds for this amount. With the ironclad on a barge, Warren County would be able to comply with the A & I Board's requirement that it be allowed to send the *Cairo,* during the slack tourist season in Vicksburg, to other river cities for exhibition.

But it became apparent, after the *Cairo* started to break up, that this solution was not feasible. The Board of Supervisors then sought the advice of experts on the best means of preserving, restoring, and displaying the ironclad. A request for assistance from the National Park Service was made by Senator Cooper to Jack Anderson, superintendent of the Vicksburg National Military Park. Anderson forwarded Cooper's letter, with a strong endorsement, to his superiors. National Park Service Director George Hartzog ordered a five-man team, composed of experts in the fields of preservation, interpretation, and architecture, to Vicksburg. This group was in Vicksburg

166

during the period in which Captain Bisso placed the *Cairo's* fantails on the barge.[1]

The Park Service group were impressed with what they saw. A study of the situation satisfied them that it was impractical to restore the *Cairo* on a barge. Instead, they recommended a site on the industrial fill, overlooking the Vicksburg harbor project. Preservation and restoration of the vessel would be a three-phase operation. In Phase I the *Cairo* would be match-marked, dismantled, and the wooden and iron parts treated with preservatives. Phase II would see the construction of a large L-shaped building. In the entrance wing would be the restored section of the *Cairo* forward of the boiler room, while the other wing would house boilers, engines, and paddle wheel. Display cases placed against the walls of this room would utilize artifacts to tell of life aboard a Civil War ironclad and, likewise, the salvage story. During Phase III the central wing of the building would be extended and the rest of the gunboat restored. The cost of Phase I and II was estimated at $993,000. This figure, however, did not include the restoration of the bow of the *Cairo,* as the Park Service team lacked experience in this field.[2]

The Board of Supervisors and Cooper's committee were pleased with the report, but the cost was nearly four times what had been budgeted for the project. Another and more immediate problem now confronted the Board of Supervisors. Captain Bisso and diver Bongiovanni had to be paid. According to the Supervisors' interpretation of their agreement with the A & I Board, the state was now to turn over to Warren County the remainder of the $50,000 earmarked by the legislature for the *Cairo* operation and title to the craft. In August the A & I Board had released $12,500 with the understanding that the remainder would become available if and when the ironclad was docked at the Vicksburg waterfront. Officials of the A & I Board disagreed. They argued that in their agreement with Warren County it had been stipulated that the *Cairo* was to be exhibited on a barge. Only when the vessel was ready for display in this fashion would they turn over the $37,500 and title. While the two sides attempted a settlement, the Board of Supervisors paid the salvor and diver with county funds.

After sounding public opinion, it was apparent that a bond issue for the *Cairo* in excess of $250,000 would be defeated if put to a vote. Confronted by an impossible situation, the Board of Supervisors and the *Cairo* committee determined to ask the A & I Board to turn title to the *Cairo* over to the National Park Service for preservation and restoration as a national historic site.

On January 20, 1965, the Board of Supervisors and members of Cooper's committee met in Jackson with the A & I Board's executive committee. The Warren County group told the A & I group that preservation and restoration of the *Cairo* was too expensive for them to undertake; consequently, it was their recommendation that title to the ironclad be transferred to the federal government and that the vessel be kept in Vicksburg. The A & I Board agreed with this suggestion. Executive director Bullock asked Superintendent Anderson to draft a letter to Secretary of the Interior Stewart Udall for Governor Johnson's signature, requesting that the National Park Service take title to and assume responsibility for the restoration of the *Cairo*. This letter would be presented to the governor upon his return from Washington, where he had gone to attend the inauguration of President Lyndon B. Johnson.[3]

Governor Johnson, however, vetoed the plan to return title to the ironclad to the federal government. The A & I Board's sub-committee on ports and harbors was charged by the governor with studying the feasibility of the state undertaking the preservation and restoration of the *Cairo,* preferably on a barge. Members of the ports and harbors committee made several trips to Vicksburg to inspect the *Cairo* and discuss the situation with the Board of Supervisors and Cooper's group. They also met with Gulf Coast shipbuilders.[4]

Meanwhile, it was decided by the Vicksburg *Cairo* committee to secure help from people who had had experience in the preservation and restoration of historic ships and boats—personnel of the Smithsonian Institution. A call to Senator Stennis brought a quick response. Colonel Howard I. Chapelle, an authority with a worldwide reputation in the field of ship restoration, and his assistant W. E. Geoghegan arrived in Vicksburg on February 23 to study the *Cairo*.[5] Before returning to Washington, Chapelle and Geoghegan met with the *Cairo* committee. They told the Vicksburgers that restoration of the ironclad did not constitute a technical problem but would cost between $500,000 and $800,000.

Chapelle, having inspected the vessel, stressed the need to take immediate steps to preserve the hull and casemate. Commenting about the seriousness of delay, he remarked that leaving the *Cairo* on her barge unattended was like having five thousand gallons of ice cream which must be accounted for later. The vessel should be match-marked, dismantled, and the wooden and metal parts treated separately. Taking cognizance of the high cost of polyethylene glycol, Chapelle suggested that the wooden parts could be sprayed with a salt solution. The men from the Smithsonian, like those from the Park Service, did not believe that restoration of the *Cairo* on a barge was feasible. A barge at least three hundred feet long and a hundred feet wide would be required. Construction and maintenance of the barge would constitute a heavy additional expense. Chapelle explained that he knew of several instances of vessels having been placed on barges to be taken from place to place to be exhibited, but these ventures had failed to provide sufficient revenue to pay operating expenses, let alone retire the capital investment.[6]

While awaiting the report of the ports and harbors group, the Board of Supervisors on March 5 voted to cut off funds from organizations directing restoration of the *Cairo*. Board president Paul Pride explained that this action was taken because title to the gunboat remained with the Mississippi A & I Board. He said also that the board felt it would be a waste of taxpayers' money to spend it at random until there were other developments on the *Cairo* project, or as long as the title and fate of the *Cairo* remained uncertain.

The ports and harbors sub-committee made its report to the A & I Board on March 18. Since the urgency for preservation of the wooden and metal sections of the vessel had been repeatedly stressed, Ingalls Shipbuilding Corporation of Pascagoula was willing to help. The barges on which the *Cairo* rested would be towed down the Mississippi and through the intracoastal waterway to the giant shipyard. At the Ingalls yard the sections into which the ironclad had broken would be match-marked and dismantled, as the first step toward preservation and restoration. The metal would be cleaned and sprayed with a protective paint, and the wood saturated with salt water. Estimates of the cost of reassembling the *Cairo* would then be prepared by naval architects at Ingalls. As soon as this figure had been ascertained, Governor Johnson would poll the legislature to see if a majority would vote to appropriate the necessary funds. If the poll were in the affirmative, Ingalls would undertake the project; if not, another solution would have to be found. The $37,500 remaining from the funds voted by the 1964 legislature would partly be employed to pay for towing the *Cairo* barges to the Gulf Coast and to defray the cost of preservation. The sub-committee's report was adopted by the A & I Board executive committee.[7]

Weeks passed and the wreckage of the *Cairo* remained on the barges exposed to the elements. With the approach of summer, the days became hotter and longer. The drying white oak planks and beams began to check and warp; the ironwork rusted. We became fearful that the A & I group through inaction would permit the *Cairo* to become a pile of junk. Finally, on June 1, more than two months after the agreement with Ingalls had been reached, Joe Schmitt of the A & I Board and one of Ingalls' skilled riggers, John Ryals, arrived in Vicksburg. After checking with the Coast Guard, they learned that the smaller barge on which the dismantled amidships of the ironclad rested was unseaworthy. Ryals examined the big barge on which the bow and fantails had been placed and found that there was sufficient room on which to load the parts from the smaller craft. On Saturday (the fifth) the barges were towed to the Port of Vicksburg terminal. It took forty-eight hours to transfer and secure the dismantled amidships and severed rudder sections aboard the larger vessel.[8]

The big 40- x 235-foot barge with the *Cairo's* remains started down the Mississippi on June 14, towed by the *Ole Miss*. Many of us, who had worked long and hard to see the ironclad raised, wondered if we would ever see her again. Indeed, it seemed that the cruel fate which had dogged the *Cairo* from the day she was launched would insure that she never reach Ingalls. The run down to New Orleans was uneventful. There the *Ole Miss* turned the *Cairo* barge over to the tug *Inland Traveler*. On the run through Mississippi Sound on the sixteenth rough weather and high waves developed. The tug captain feared that his historic cargo might slip into the sea, so a run for the port of Gulfport was made. After riding out the storm in Gulfport, where the remains of the ironclad attracted huge crowds, the *Inland Traveler* headed back out into the sound, but she soon experienced trouble with her steering gear. A call for help went out, and a Coast Guard cutter rushed to her assistance, and towed the tug and barge back into Gulfport. As soon as repairs could be made, the often-interrupted trip to Pascagoula was resumed. On June 18 the *Inland Traveler* entered the Pascagoula River, and the *Cairo* barge was turned over to Ingalls.[9]

Clyde M. Leavitt, chief naval architect at Ingalls, was placed in charge of the *Cairo* project. This was a fortunate choice, because, besides being skilled in designing modern ships, Leavitt had a deep interest in ships and boats of the past. Here was the type of man that we had dreamed would supervise the preservation and restoration of the *Cairo*.

The barge with the ironclad was berthed at Ingalls' small boat yard, within sight of where several nuclear submarines, dubbed "hot ones" by the press, were under construction. Hoses were laid, the water turned on, and timbers and planks which had started to check were kept wet down; within a few days, cracks which had opened in the white oak began to close.

The engines and paddle wheel were removed immediately. Personnel at Ingalls were surprised to find what we had already discovered, that the huge nuts could be turned with relative ease; not a single nut was twisted off. The engines were torn down and painted with Rust Veto 342, an effective preservative. When Leavitt inspected the parts, he saw that the pistons' heads and cylinder walls were pitted, but he had seen many ships operating whose engines were in worse shape. Except for damage done in November when the fantails had slipped off the barge, Leavitt was of the opinion that the engines could have driven the gunboat's paddle wheel. Of special interest was the discovery of a brass plate on one of the engine fixtures, inscribed, "J. R. Anderson &. Co., Richmond, Va., Tredegar Ironworks, 1861." We knew that the engines were built from plans drawn and approved in July, 1861, although President Lincoln had embargoed trade with the state of Virginia three months before. Thus in 1861 there was trading with the enemy, just as there is today. Measurements of the few bent parts were taken, so they can be replaced or straightened at the time that the *Cairo* is restored.

Next, the dismantled sections of the midships were landed with the aid of powerful cranes. After the armor had been separated and marked, the wooden parts (ranging in size from whole sections of the casemate to single planks) were sorted, stacked, and placed under sprinklers. Other portions of the hulk which had separated during the salvage were treated in a similar fashion. Within a short time, Leavitt and his workmen had cleared the barge, except for the *Cairo's* bow and fantails. These sections contained a number of holds that we had been unable to reach while the ironclad was at Vicksburg. Employing the same technique (jet hoses and screens) as we had used, the Ingalls personnel removed the mud from these areas and recovered a number of valuable artifacts. Like so many others, they quickly succumbed to *Cairoitis,* a strange malady that gripped all who had come into contact with the project. The gunboat became their chief topic of conversation, so engrossed were they with the *Cairo's* story.

With the mud out of the way, Leavitt called for welders. A study of the bow and fantails had convinced him that a supporting metal framework would have to be placed inside these sections, or they would collapse when lifted from the barge. After this framing was in position, the barge was towed to the main yard, and on September 18 the bow and fantails were put ashore.

Hundreds of photographs and drawings were made by the Ingalls staff as the boat was being dismantled, to ensure that her restoration would be accurate; at the same time Leavitt made estimates as to what the cost would be.

As the next step in the operation, the many parts into which the *Cairo* had broken were laid out and fitted together. This enabled the naval architect to determine what sections of the craft had been lost in the salvage and what parts were too badly damaged to be used in a restoration. It was like assembling the world's largest jigsaw puzzle. For assistance in his work, Leavitt read plans and specifications of the city-class gunboats (which, unfortunately, were very general), the detailed plans of the ironclads prepared by W. E. Geoghegan, and the many photographs made during the dismantling operation.

Because of limited space in the small boat yard, it was necessary to lay out the boat in two roughly equal sections. Derricks were used to position the parts, which were then secured with wires and props.

When I visited Pascagoula on January 8, I was astounded by what had been accomplished. The sections into which the hull had been sliced by the lifting wires had been fitted into place, and, except for the gaping hole in the port quarter caused by the explosion of one of the torpedoes, the *Cairo,* below the knuckle, looked much as she did when she slid down the ways at Mound City in the autumn of 1861. Her casemate had been repositioned, but it appeared that much more of this part of the boat had been lost to the river than had been thought. I was delighted to see that the water treatment of the white oak timbering, recommended by Colonel Chapelle, had been helpful. Planks and beams had swelled and straightened; no longer were they checked and warped. The visit to Pascagoula and conversations with Leavitt and his associates dispelled fears that an authentic restoration might be impossible.

On January 13, 1966, the A & I Board held a meeting in Jackson, at which Maness Bartlett of the ports and harbors sub-committee reported that Ingalls was willing to undertake the reconstruction of the *Cairo* on a huge barge for $1,500,000. Governor Johnson hoped that the state of Mississippi could raise the necessary money for the reconstruction.

However, as a historian, I was concerned about certain portions of the Ingalls proposal. I recalled the recommendation of experts from the National Park Service and Smithsonian Institution, and of naval architects with whom the *Cairo* had been discussed. I also knew of L. F. Hagglund's experience with the Revolutionary War vessel *Philadelphia,* raised in the 1930's from Lake Champlain, and placed on a barge for exhibition. Although the *Philadelphia* was displayed at the 1939 New York World's Fair, Hagglund had not recouped sufficient money from his venture to meet operating expenses, let alone recover his capital investment. In the end his heirs were compelled to turn the vessel over to the Smithsonian Institution for display in the National Museum. People with experience in historic preservation had told me many times that the *Cairo* as a museum, if housed ashore, would draw thousands of tourists.

Moreover, the Ingalls proposition called for scrapping the vessel's hull below her knuckle. And the white oak planks would be cut into blocks, embedded in plastic to be sold as souvenirs. This I found distressing, because that section of the ironclad is almost intact, while at least 30 percent of the casemate, which according to the Ingalls plan would be restored, was lost in the salvage. Such a plan would present to the public a partial reconstruction rather than a total restoration.

The proposal advanced by Ingalls aroused strong feelings not only in Mississippi but in places as far away as the Twin Cities, Chicago, and Toledo. Protests were registered by Civil War Round Tables throughout the nation, as well as by interested individuals. Members of the legislature from Warren County met with the executive board of the Warren County Historical Society to sample local opinion regarding the future of the *Cairo.* Senator Ellis Bodron informed those in attendance that a lawyer with the A & I Board had prepared a draft of a bill to implement the barge plan. But there were many who voiced their opposition to the plan.

Several days later, Senator Cooper called a meeting of the *Cairo* committee, which was attended by representatives of the Warren County Historical Society and the Warren County Board of Supervisors. A course of action was charted to insure that all groups opposed to the barge plan would be in agreement. George Rogers read a draft of a bill he had prepared which would authorize the state to issue full faith and credit bonds to underwrite a "complete and authentic restoration of the *Cairo.*" If, however, after six months no action had been taken to market the bonds, the governor would be directed to request that the National Park Service take title to the ironclad. The groups in attendance agreed to support Rogers' scheme.

The A & I Board's bill was introduced in the Mississippi senate in April, 1966, where it was referred to the finance committee headed by Senator Bodron, and hearings were scheduled. Frank Everett, a distinguished Warren County attorney and a man well versed in history, was selected to present the case for authentic restoration of the boat on land.

One of those invited to appear before the committee was Clyde Leavitt, who told the senators that he considered the barge plan impractical. Taking cognizance of Leavitt's statements and Everett's presentation, the Mississippi senate passed an act authorizing the A & I Board to enter into an agreement with the National Park Service and to spell out terms under which the federal agency would assume responsibility for the repair, restoration, and exhibition of the *Cairo*.

When informed of the senate's action, Governor Johnson and Gene Triggs, who had succeeded Joe Bullock as executive director of the A & I Board, met with Everett and others from Warren County. Johnson, after hearing Everett's explanation, asked Triggs to draft a letter to National Park Service Director Hartzog offering title to the "salvaged elements" of the *Cairo* if the Service would undertake to restore and exhibit the vessel. Hartzog sent a five-man committee to Mississippi in July to study the gunboat and to recommend possible methods for restoring and exhibiting it as a part of the Vicksburg National Military Park."[10]

The group spent a week in Mississippi, and, when they made their report to Hartzog, recommended that the Park Service accept title to the *Cairo* and proceed with restoration of the craft, to be housed in a building adjacent to the National Cemetery within the Vicksburg National Military Park.[11] Meanwhile, to keep the wooden sections of the boat from deteriorating, the Mississippi legislature in June, 1966, appropriated $70,000. Part of this sum went to Ingalls for its services; the rest was used to defray the cost of protection, storage, and spraying while the ironclad remained in Pascagoula.

12

THE CAIRO RETURNS
TO VICKSBURG

THE years between 1966 and 1977 were grim for the *Cairo,* as bureaucrats and preservationists struggled for funds to finance her return to Vicksburg and restoration. Many pitfalls and problems lay ahead. The cost of war in Vietnam caused the federal government to cut back drastically on money for historic preservation. By the time United States participation in the war ended in January, 1973, the Revolutionary War Bicentennial was approaching, and from the summer of 1973 through 1976 it would command the money, time, and energy of the National Park Service. Then there were shifts in key personnel associated with the Hardluck Ironclad caused by changes in administration, deaths, and retirements. Newcomers were called to take their places, and most of these, fortunately, fell victim to *Cairo* fever.

Because of the estimated high cost of the project and the inflationary spiral gripping the nation, National Park Service officials decided that it was incumbent to secure a congressional mandate to proceed before accepting title to the ironclad from the Mississippi A & I Board. While they wrestled with this problem, the Vicksburg Chamber of Commerce, in October, 1967, notified their U.S. representative, John Bell Williams, that a recent inspection of the vessel indicated that the wooden fabric was deteriorating. Writing Secretary of the Interior Stewart Udall, Williams trusted that the department would "find some means to aid in preserving the *Cairo* until its restoration can be accomplished."[1]

Udall replied that, although the boat was a "national treasure and that no other vessel like it has survived to illustrate so dramatically a major phase of the Civil War," severe monetary restrictions made it impossible for the National Park Service to include funds for restora-

175

tion of the *Cairo* in its current budget submission to Congress. A proposal, however, had been made to earmark money to underwrite several important planning projects for the ironclad.[2]

Taking this as a cue, Senator John Stennis and Representative Charles Griffin succeeded in obtaining a $50,000 allotment from Congress to fund advance planning.[3] The National Park Service employed this money to finance a number of important projects.

(a)   Commander J. Delano Brusstar, retired, a naval architect who had built large wooden sailing ships in World War I, was retained. A resident of Mississippi's Gulf Coast, he prepared an engineering feasibility study determining methods and costs for restoring the vessel and returning her to Vicksburg.

(b)   He also made record drawings of the vessel. In the course of his work, Brusstar became a *Cairo* spokesman, traveling extensively at his own expense to lobby for her restoration.

(c)   Margie R. Bearss, who had been associated with care and preservation of the artifacts since 1960, compiled a detailed catalog, numbering the items and preparing descriptive data as to the condition and location of recovery. The catalog listed 7,229 objects or groups of objects, and Ken Parks prepared a photographic record of the artifacts to supplement the catalog.

(d)   Virgil Carrington Jones, author of the popular three-volume *The Civil War at Sea,* wrote a 56-page illustrated, interpretative booklet, *U.S.S. Cairo: The Story of a Civil War Gunboat.* It sold well, and it answered numerous worldwide requests for information about the vessel.

(e)   Because of possible subsoil instability in the area of the Vicksburg National Military Park, which was proposed for exhibition of the *Cairo,* a survey was made by Ware Lind Engineers. Included were borings and soil tests to assess building problems.

(f)   A handsome model of the ironclad was constructed by Arthur Henning of Mt. Vernon, New York. During the next nine years the model logged nearly as many miles as the Civil War ironclad, being transported to the Washington, D.C., area, where it was shown to congressmen and interpretative planners and designers. When not in transit the model was an important component of the small *Cairo* exhibit at the Vicksburg National Military Park.

(g)   Ken Parks Associates of Jackson, Mississippi, produced a 28-minute film detailing the salvage. Parks was an ideal choice, because he had been closely identified with Operation Cairo since 1960, when

Photo of *Cairo* crewman Peter Ole Hill was furnished by a descendant, Orson Hill.

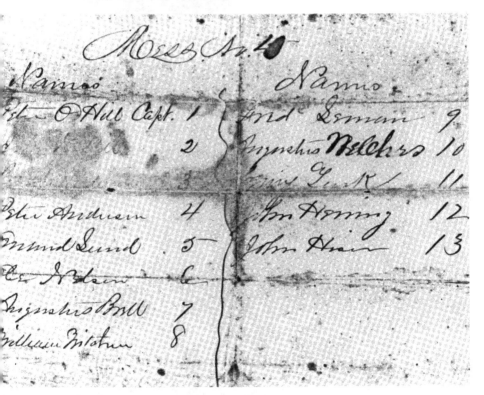

Mess list for Mess No. 4, handwritten by *Cairo* crewman Peter Ole Hill, was found among his possessions. Strangely, the mess chest containing the gear of this mess was found intact.

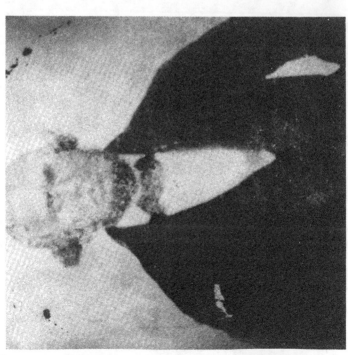

Photo from a glass negative found on the *Cairo*. It was mounted in a copper frame. The image faded from the glass with exposure to air.

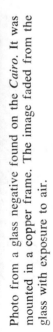

Cairo crewman Sam Chandler carved his name on his mess gear. Photo given by a descendant shows Chandler in his later years.

A view of the model of *Cairo* showing the existing fabric has been built by Douglas Ashley and Tom McGrath. Mr. Ashley, historical architect, is at bow of model, with Gordon Whittington, project supervisor.

Ed Bearss and Al Scheller of the National Park Service show the model to visitors. Courtesy Paul Ashworth.

The paddle wheel shaft was among components returned from Ingalls Shipyard to Vicksburg.

The *Cairo* hull is cradled in a concrete tub and waits further preservation and restoration. The museum which will house the artifacts is the concrete structure in background.

This is a view of *Cairo* from midships looking forward. Note the flooring of the hold and height of gundeck. All three keels show.

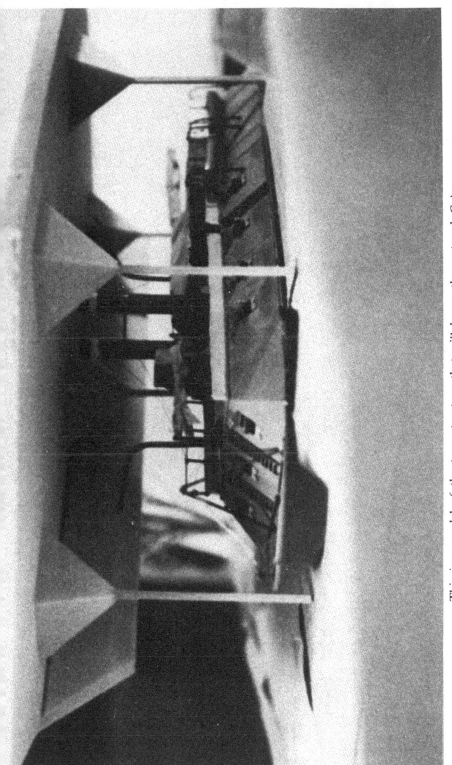

This is a model of the type structure that will house the restored *Cairo*.

The Cairo Project
Vicksburg National Military Park
Vicksburg, Mississippi

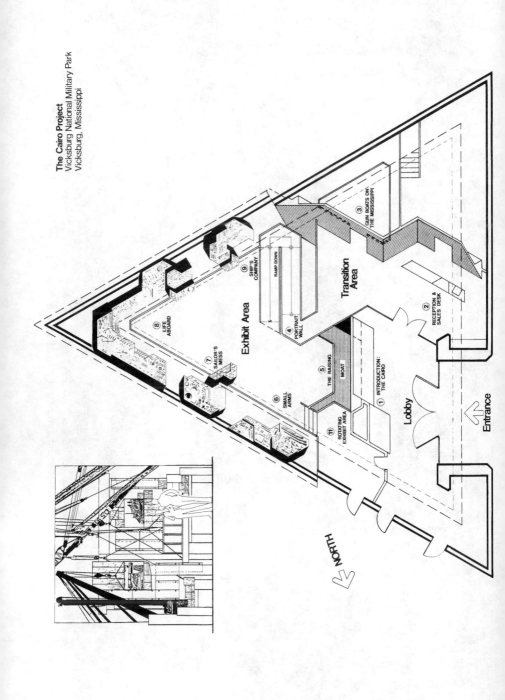

NORTH

Entrance

Lobby

① INTRODUCTION: THE CAIRO

② RECEPTION & SALES DESK

③ GUN BOATS ON THE MISSISSIPPI

Transition Area

④ PORTRAIT WALL

RAMP DOWN

⑤ THE RAISING

MOAT

⑨ SHIP'S COMPANY

Exhibit Area

⑧ LIFE ABOARD

⑦ SAILOR'S MESS

⑥ SMALL ARMS

⑪ ROTATING EXHIBIT AREA

the pilothouse was removed. This documentary, which had its Vicksburg premiere in February, 1970, proved popular with buffs and with the general public.[4]

The Hardluck Ironclad had a brief change of fortune when killer Hurricane Camille savaged the Mississippi and Louisiana gulf coasts on August 17–18, 1969. The eye of the storm passed to the west of Pascagoula, and winds and tides were not as high there as at Biloxi and Gulfport. Friends of the *Cairo,* familiar with her history, feared the worst. They were, however, soon reassured by the report of a newsman, who surveyed the area from the air and reported that the Ingalls Shipyard "bears few physical scars, and even the *Cairo* which couldn't survive a Rebel mine in the Yazoo during the bloody fighting around Vicksburg in the Civil War seems safe—but unreconstructed."[5] Two *Cairo* fans, naval architects Leavitt and Brusstar, separately braved debris, fallen power lines, and high water to visit the site and confirm that she had weathered Camille.[6]

While the *Cairo,* especially during the first several years, was at Ingalls large numbers of people found their way to the isolated Walker Yard. "They came from all parts of the country—from Maine to California—just to look" at the battered hulk.[7]

Some seven months after her escape from disaster, the *Cairo* was subjected to a blistering and humiliating attack by members of the Mississippi legislature. This was sparked by debate concerning a request by the A & I Board for $36,000 to underwrite protection and preservation costs for Fiscal Year 1971. One senator sputtered, "The State of Mississippi pays out $3,000 a month, largely for keeping that pile of rotten splinters damp."

"That's right. The belief is that, after over a century under water, the wood would simply disintegrate if it is not wetted down," was the reply.

Senator Bob Crook, a *Cairo* friend, added that the A & I Board had made a bad decision in 1965, when it had the vessel barged to Pascagoula. If it had been left at Vicksburg, the reconstruction might have been underway, and "we'd have a tourist attraction beyond value."

"It is time for the U.S. Parks System to put up or shut up," interrupted a senator. "This is the last time I will vote this $3,000 a month." In the end the allotment was approved, but the hot words indicated that time was running out for the Hardluck Ironclad.[8]

Then, in March, 1971, the Mississippi congressional delegation, taking cognizance of the situation, introduced companion bills into both houses of the 1st Session, 92nd Congress, "to authorize the secretary of the interior to provide for the restoration, reconstruction, and exhibition of the gunboat 'Cairo,' and for other purposes."

The Vicksburg *Evening Post,* a long-time friend, hailed this news, because it revived "hope the boat might be restored and brought to Vicksburg as one of the great historical naval museums in the nation." Many people, the editorial continued, had "worked long and hard to effect the raising of the *Cairo."* Among those cited was Dr. Walter E. Johnston, who had lost his life in the endeavor. It was hoped that the Congress would look kindly on the project and would appropriate funds necessary to reconstruct the vessel.[9]

On Thursday, June 10, the Mississippi A & I Board voted to send a delegation to meet with Secretary of the Interior Rogers C. B. Morton to seek departmental support for restoration of the ironclad. Upon learning of this action, Ray Sauer, who had been named to head the Vicksburg Cairo Steering Committee following the death of former State Senator H. V. Cooper, told the press, "We feel like it is now or never for the *Cairo.* We want to know specifically whether or not the National Park Service is still interested in the restoration. We know the boat is deteriorating at a rapid rate."[10]

The board moved with alacrity, and on Monday, June 14, a group of politically powerful Mississippians, headed by Governor John Bell Williams, met with Secretary of the Interior Morton, to champion the cause of the Hardluck Ironclad. Attending the conference in the House Rules Committee Room was Director of the National Park Service Hartzog, a suporter of the *Cairo* since the day he had stood on the banks of the Yazoo nearly seven years before and watched as preparations were made to lift the vessel.

State Representative George Rogers, who had been associated with the project almost from the beginning, traced the history of the salvage, reported on the value of the artifacts, and the interest that they and the vessel would generate if she were returned to Vicksburg and placed on display. Secretary Morton's curiosity and interest were fired by Rogers presentation.

Governor Williams spoke next. He coupled his remarks with a plea for swift federal action. "We are at the licklog on the Cairo," he noted, as he told of the amount of money Mississippians had already spent on the vessel.

Senator Stennis, a friend of the *Cairo* since 1960, discussed with Morton the legislation already introduced in both the Senate and House authorizing the Department of the Interior to restore the ironclad. Representatives William H. Colmer and Jamie Whitten, influential members of the House, voiced their support. Colmer remarked that time was of the essence and Whitten discussed the great additional appeal the gunboat would provide for visitors to the Vicksburg National Military Park.

At the close of the 45-minute meeting, Secretary Morton announced that he would support efforts to obtain congressional authorization and that he would have the National Park Service dovetail its *Cairo* restoration plans in preparation for the funding. He said he recognized the historical value of the *Cairo* and that he would come to Mississippi to see the craft's remains at Pascagoula.[11]

Secretary Morton's decision had immediate repercussions. On June 25 the department notified Senator Henry M. Jackson, chairman of the Committee on Interior and Insular Affairs, that it recommended enactment of Senate Bill 1475. Cost of the project was placed by the department at $4,490,000 (June, 1971, prices), which broke down:

Roads and Trails:
    Entrance drive, parking for 100 cars and walks ....$ 200,000
    Gravel pad for ship, grade and repair existing road 11,000
Buildings, utilities, and miscellaneous:
    Water, sewer, power, and telephone 81,000
    Structure with visitor facilities for enclosing ship 2,475,000
    Restoration of Ship 1,500,000
    Interpretive exhibits 120,000
    Security fencing 8,000
    Planting and grounds improvements 95,000

Grand Total ....$4,490,000[12]

Although Governor Williams was present to lend prestige, the August hearings on Senate Bill 1457 before the subcommittee chaired by Senator Alan Bible were difficult. The absence of Director Hartzog, the department's most articulate and persuasive spokesman, hurt. Senator Bible questioned the need to spend the sum stipulated on the undertaking. When Bible's subcommittee submitted its report, it slashed the sum recommended by more than $2 million.

Director Hartzog, in view of what had occurred, made it a point to be present at the early November hearings before the House Committee on Interior and Insular Affairs. As was the practice, he met with key staff members on Friday preceding the Monday hearings. Dissatisfied with their presentation and backup information, he told them to ready four viable alternatives, ranging from total reconstruction of the ironclad to restoration of the forward one-third of the vessel. Such a comprehensive program dictated a long, hard weekend for several of the people involved, particularly the architects, Don Benson and Dick Kusek. But by Monday morning, they had completed a series of handsomely rendered drawings and plans, illustrating the alternatives, along with the costs thereof. As an added measure to insure a successful presentation before Roy A. Taylor's subcommittee, Hartzog had Superintendent Dan Lee of the Vicksburg National Military Park put the Henning *Cairo* model into his car and drive it to Washington. This was the first of many such trips for the park staff and the model.

With Director Hartzog at the helm and four of the five House members of the Mississippi congressional delegation in attendance, Representative Taylor convened his subcommittte. Hartzog was at his best. Employing the drawings, model, and witnesses, he presented a forceful case for full restoration of the vessel. Committee members were impressed and in executive session recommended that $4,500,000 be authorized for "restoration, reconstruction, and exhibition" of the *Cairo*.

On December 4, 1971, the Senate passed Senate Bill 1475, authorizing expenditure of $2,481,000 for the project as recommended by Senator Bible's subcommittee. The House, on August 14, 1972, acted favorably on the bill, after striking out the Bible figure and substituting the sum suggested by Representative Taylor's group. House Resolution 6618 was then tabled.[13]

The House and Senate now had to agree on the cost. This was done in the first week of October, and Senate Bill 1475 was amended to authorize "to be appropriated not more than $3,200,000 for the restoration of the 'Cairo' and for the development of protective and interpretive facilities associated therewith."[14]

On October 12 President Richard M. Nixon signed the bill into law. *Cairo* fans hailed this anxiously awaited news. Many did not realize that the legislation merely authorized an expenditure of federal funds and expected the hulk to be returned to Vicksburg and the restoration to begin as soon as the Mississippi A & I Board transferred title to the craft to the National Park Service. Many months slipped by before the A & I Board, in the early summer of 1973, signed such an agreement, initiated by the Department of the Interior, returning title to the ironclad to the United States.[15] The National Park Service now found itself saddled with a fixed monthly maintenance charge for as long as the vessel remained at Ingalls.

In October, 1973, personnel from the Park Service's Harpers Ferry and Denver Service centers held a series of on-site meetings with Superintendent Lee and key members of his staff at Vicksburg and Pascagoula. At these meetings guidelines were hammered out for restoration and display of the *Cairo*. Plans had to be molded to fit within the monetary constraints established by Congress. It was decided to place the vessel on a huge bathtublike concrete pad on the site previously selected and tested between the Vicksburg National Cemetery and the Naval Memorial. The vessel, below the knuckle, would be supported in the recess. The forward one-third of the *Cairo*—mounting seven of her thirteen guns, the two chimneys, and pilothouse—would be stabilized and restored. The remainder of the starboard one-half of the vessel, to the centerline, would likewise be restored, while the port one-half of the casemate, much of which had been lost in the salvage, would be left open to serve as a viewing area. A visitor center and parking area were needed.[16]

During the next three years, planning funds became available, and the Park Service contracted with Godfrey, Bassett & Tuminello of Jackson and Vicksburg to prepare plans and specifications for the visitor center complex. Guidelines for this undertaking were prepared by the Denver Service Center. Care was taken by the Mississippi firm to insure that these facilities, both as to materials and scale, would harmonize with and enhance the display of the most valuable artifact—the 175-foot-long ironclad.

Barry Howard & Associates of Scarsdale, New York, was given the task of preparing the interpretive and exhibit plans. This proved a fortunate choice, because Barry and Emelie Howard promptly succumbed to *Cairo* fever. As the Dick Kusek/Barry Howard plan evolved it called for the restored, reconstructed gunboat, set in a river of brick pavers, to dominate the terraced area. A visitor center, occupying "an excavated portion of the site," would function in "dramatic counterpoint to the gunboat itself." The visitor center's interior was to be designed to develop "a harsh foreboding mood dominated by 'battered' interior wall partitions and several building walls."

The public, passing beyond the entrance wall, was to enter a confined area, which would provide a graphic and written overview of why the river ironclads were built, the war on inland waters in which they made a significant contribution to the success of the Union campaign to seize control of the lower Mississippi and divide the Confederacy, and a profile of James B. Eads.

A ramp was to lead downward from the entrance to a triangular museum floor. One side of this area would be "dominated by a sculpture of material and graphics reflective of the discovery and raising of the *Cairo*." A pictorial record of the events associated with rediscovery of the ironclad was to be presented on two video monitors.

Positioned on angular platforms around the museum floor would be arrayed nearly five hundred carefully selected objects from the vessel. These, along with accompanying graphics, would bring to life for the visitor the story of the *Cairo* and her crew.[17]

In the autumn of 1976 Ingalls' management informed the Service that they needed the facilities where the *Cairo* was stored. Placed on short notice, the Service responded with alacrity. Dave Wright, deputy regional director of the Southeast Region, was given the task of coordinating the project. Lieutenant Colonel Robert Calland, a retired Marine officer and transportation specialist, who had been associated with the Smithsonian Institution for a number of years, was placed in charge of moving the gunboat back to the selected Vicksburg site from Pascagoula. His principal assistant was Architect Jim Smeal of the Denver Service Center. Superintendent Dan Lee of the Vicksburg National Military Park, a longtime *Cairo* enthusiast, detailed men from his maintenance staff, as did the superintendent of Gulf Islands National Seashore, to assist Colonel Calland.

Before beginning work on the project in early January, Calland and Smeal spent several days in the Washington area meeting with Smithsonian and Harpers Ferry wood and metal preservationists, reviewing the Bearss *Cairo* archives, and discussing with Earl Geoghegan the revised gunboat plans and drawings he was preparing for Barry Howard & Associates.[18]

Calland and Smeal reached Pascagoula on January 10, 1977. Upon visiting Ingalls, they saw that in the months since October, 1973, the ½-inch wire cables positioned by Clyde Leavitt in 1965 to hold the casemate shield and the port and starboard sections of the casemate forward of the No. 1 gunports had distintegrated. The former sprawled across the deck, while the latter lay crumpled on the ground. Sea grasses had sprouted and thrived wherever any Yazoo mud remained. The 55-gallon drums in which the ironclad's coal had been stored were rusted out.

The maintenance men turned to cleaning up the boat and disposing of the nonhistoric debris; Smeal prepared "as is" drawings of the sections of the vessel below the knuckle and flagged the various pieces to identify cuts, breaks, etc.; Colonel Calland arranged for needed tools and equipment, established liaison with key Ingalls personnel and local contractors, and met with the media. Although more than thirteen years had passed since the raising of the ironclad, the *Cairo* was still popular with the press and television.

In the third week of January an ad hoc advisory committee named by the National Park Service met with Colonel Calland. After inspecting the boat, engines, etc., the committee determined that the "moving process" should consist of cradling the sections as they were, after taking adequate care for their protection; their transportation to Vicksburg; and then positioning them on a concrete pad in their permanent situation, preparatory for restoration. To insure against loss of data, all portions of the craft were to be recorded photogrammetrically by Perry E. and Myra F. Borchers before being moved.[19] The Borcherses accomplished this project in late February, employing a Coast Guard helicopter for a number of their shots.

After departure of the committee, Colonel Calland and his people began sorting through the "lumber pile," those parts of the *Cairo* that had separated from the sections mocked up in 1965. Most pieces were identified by size or nailing pattern. These timbers were in various stages of decay, some crumbling into nothing and others showing only surface damage. Architect Smeal estimated that about 80 percent of the existing fabric could be salvaged and employed in the restoration. They were sorted and stacked according to size—beams, frames, decking, etc. Pieces too far deteriorated for future use were laid aside for destruction.

Iron fastening, ranging from 8-inch nails to 1-inch drift pins, many as much as 30 inches in length, were removed. Hardware was left in place where it would assist in subsequent identification. All salvaged ironwork was placed in boxes for transfer to Vicksburg.

By mid-February the lumber pile had been disposed of, and the men began removing and crating sections of the casement that had been propped in place. First, however, they removed and tagged the railroad iron that had armored the port and starboard quarters forward of the No. 1 gunports. They next began cleaning out with compressed air and water the large sections of the *Cairo* that were to be barged to Vicksburg. On doing so, they recovered several interesting artifacts— an 1857 penny, a wooden caulking mallet, and a bottle.

To secure professional guidance on measures to be taken for preservation of the wooden fabric, samples from various members of the vessel (bottom planking, decking, and beams) were collected and hand carried to the Smithsonian. In late March, Terry L. Amburgey of the U.S. Forest Products Laboratory in Gulfport traveled to the site and examined the *Cairo*. He confirmed what had been long suspected: the pine decking, except about 10 percent, was beyond salvage, but the white oak and other hardwood timbers, except for surface checking and various degrees of shrinkage, were in surprisingly good condition. To preserve these, he recommended that they be given a spray treatment of pentachlorophenol and a waterproofing agent in a petroleum base.

After considerable discussion with authorities, it was agreed to treat the wood with Hydrozo and pentachlorophenol. But, because of the toxic character of pentachlorophenol, care must be exercised. Consequently, a polyethylene sheet and a thin layer of sawdust was first spread between the ground and cribbing, and then section after section of the vessel sprayed with preservatives. After each component was treated, the sheeting was carefully gathered up and the sawdust boxed for disposal.[20]

After being braced, photographed, and diagrammed, the sections of the vessel were carefully cradled. The larger components were handled by Fabricators, Inc. They were then loaded by crane aboard two 195-foot steel barges. The Corps of Engineers' tug *M. V. Lipscomb* took the barges in tow, and on June 19 the *Cairo* returned to Vicksburg. She had been away twelve years, which seemed a lifetime to the battered ironclad's friends.[21]

The engines, armor, paddle wheel, coal, boxes of nails and pins, capstan, and timbers salvaged from the lumber pile had preceded the vessel. After being carefully boxed or crated they had been trucked.

Meanwhile, a contract for construction of the huge tublike concrete pad had been awarded to Lewis Miller Construction Company. Work commenced in March, and, despite heavy spring rains, it was completed by the time the barges arrived. The task of transferring the braced components of the craft from the barges moored at the harbor project to the site began. On arrival in the park, the sections constituting the hull, below the knuckle, were positioned in the tub.

During the autumn of 1977 the Denver Service Center awarded contracts for the *Cairo* visitor center, parking facilities, walkways, and utilities. To insure that the visitor center harmonizes with the scene, much of the structure was to be underground. Plans called for the center to be open to the public by the summer of 1980.[22]

Funds for restoration of the *Cairo* were included in the Service's fiscal year 1978 program. But, before any steps could be taken, an onsite investigation was mandatory to make a final determination of the extent of restoration, reconstruction and stabilization. A large group representing divergent views met at Vicksburg on March 14. After inspecting the vessel, followed by a sometimes heated discussion, the group decided that, although fifty-four months had passed since the 1973 meeting, the goals then outlined were still viable. The vessel from the chimneys forward and below the knuckle would be stabilized and restored; the hurricane and gun decks aft of the chimneys were to be reconstructed; the pilothouse was to be restored and the chimneys, jackstaffs, and wheelhouse were to be reconstructed; the port casemate at No. 4 gunport was to be opened to allow visitors to enter the vessel from the watercourse terrace and walk the gundeck aft of the chimneys; visitor access to the hurricane deck was to be provided by way of a gangway from the rear observation deck; all new materials were to be painted the historic colors, while the original fabric was to retain its natural appearance; wherever needed lexon would be employed in the reconstructed portions of the craft to allow the public to look into the engine room, wheelhouse, shellrooms, magazine, holds, etc.; and a ramp was to provide access to an area from which visitors could view the splintered planking of the port quarter stove in by the force of the exploding torpedoes.

It was agreed that architect Douglas Ashley, son of a naval architect, would construct a large-scale model (½-inch equals 1 foot) to document and differentiate between the historic and the new fabric, and to guide the restoration.[23]

Gordon Whittington was given the task of overseeing the restoration of the ironclad. This was a fortunate choice, because Whittington possessed impressive credentials. During his twenty-two years with the National Park Service, he had been involved in many important and diverse restorations, ranging from Mount Locust on the Natchez Trace to Thomas Edison's New Jersey home. A Mississippian, he was familiar with the *Cairo* and welcomed the challenge. Douglas Ashley would work closely with Whittington and his people.

To familiarize themselves with the vessel, its fabric, and local problems, Whittington and Ashley met with key members of the Vicksburg National Military Park staff (Superintendent Dan Lee, chief of Information and Visitor Services Bowie Lanford, *Cairo* curator Nancy Miller, and chief of maintenance David Lyons), Colonel Robert Calland, and historian Edwin C. Bearss in late March. Colonel Calland inventoried and identified the fabric, and explained how the components had been matchmarked. He and Lyons reviewed the manpower situation and offered suggestions as to where Whittington might find skilled craftsmen for his restoration force and local shops able to handle heavy metal work. The location, dimensions, and capabilities of the *Cairo* workshop were discussed. This was important, because the restoration of the vessel was programmed to extend over a number of years, and it would be accomplished as an interpretative exhibit. Park visitors (sidewalk superintendents), with only limited restraints on access, would be permitted to view the gunboat, as Whittington and his men undertook the reconstruction.

Additional sources of documentary information focusing on the *Cairo* and the "City Series" ironclads were discussed. These were to be made available to Douglas Ashley to facilitate construction of the model and preparation of drawings of the cabins and other sections of the vessel shattered in the salvage. A list of people, recognized authorities in ship restorations and preservation, was compiled. These people were to be asked to constitute a board of consultants to review the plans before restoration began. They would have to move with celerity, because Whittington planned to complete his work in Tennessee at Fort Donelson's Dover Hotel by autumn and move to Vicksburg.[24]

To assist with construction of the model, Ashley secured the services of another architect, Tom McGrath. The two men reached Vicksburg in November and spent the autumn and winter studying and inventorying the shattered remains of the ironclad and building the large-scale model. When completed it provided three-dimensional documentation of how much of the Hardluck Ironclad had survived the terrible years since her salvage. For the first time since the fall of 1965, when Clyde Leavitt and his people had mocked up the craft, technicians could evaluate the condition of the fabric and determine what sections of the vessel remained and could be used in her preservation/restoration. Long-time friends of the *Cairo* were dismayed and disappointed to see that, during the intervening thirteen years, a number of wooden sections of the craft had deteriorated to a degree where they had either been discarded or had disappeared.

Ashley and McGrath, upon studying the wooden remains and sending samples to preservation laboratories, determined that the haphazard watering down of the craft during the Ingalls years, following Hurricane Camille, had been extremely detrimental to the sturdy white oak. The gain and loss of moisture this entailed had led to severe surface decay and warping and checking. The interior of cut samples were found to be very solid. To reduce and curtail this degradation, it was mandatory that the moisture content of the timbers, which was found to be excessive and conducive to the growth of fungus, be radically and promptly reduced and a state of equilibrium obtained.

They also discovered that the heavy Mississippi rainfall was eroding the exposed wooden surfaces. If the now fragile fabric were to survive, the craft must be promptly provided with a shelter to ward off the rains and the sun, and the timbers subjected to a controlled and periodic treatment by wood preservatives. The shelter would also provide protection to visitors during bad weather.

Measures would have to be taken to preserve the ironwork from exfoliation and control the chemical reaction between iron and wood.

The *Cairo* model, as anticipated, enabled National Park Service managers to come to grips with the project's scope and complexities. They were likewise able to evaluate various alternatives outlined by Ashley and McGrath for preservation and restoration of the vessel. Hedged in by financial constraints and reluctant to go to Congress for additional money, it was determined to adopt an alternative providing for retention and use of all existing fabric, where it could be identified. A structural support system like that used in museums to display remains of dinosaurs, besides holding the fabric in place, would link the components. It would aid in unifying these sections, and provide an outline of the ironclad as she would have appeared in 1862. Use of laminated wood beams in the support system would give a visual contrast between old and new fabric, in addition to being subject to less exfoliation.[25]

Some of those associated in the heartbreaking struggle to raise the gunboat were understandably disappointed by this course of action, and agreed with restoration specialist Whittington, "The lawmakers thought in the beginning they were going to get a whole boat, but what they are expecting is one thing and what they are going to get is another."[26]

Despite differences of opinion, it now seems that the Hardluck Ironclad's fortunes have finally changed, and she will become the central feature in a dynamic exhibit interpreting the role of the Mississippi Squadron and its men in the decisive struggle for America's heartland.

Appendix

DATA ON IRONCLAD RIVER GUNBOAT *CAIRO*

August 3, 1965

Courtesy:

THE INGALLS SHIPBUILDING CORPORATION
A DIVISION OF LITTON INDUSTRIES
PASCAGOULA, MISSISSIPPI 39567

TECHNICAL DATA

GENERAL

Type: Ironclad River Gunboat
Class: City Class
Number of Vessels in Class: Seven
Area of Operations: Lower Mississippi River

PRINCIPAL CHARACTERISTICS

Length Overall: 175'-0"
Breadth: 51'-2"
Full Load Keel Draft: 6'-0"
Displacement, Full Load, F. W.: 888 tons
Tonnage: 512
Number of Hull Compartments: 7
Speed: 6 knots
Estimated built weight of wood hull and casemate: 350 tons
Hull Form: Flat bottom, knuckle bilge
Number of Keels: 3

ARMAMENT

3: 7" bore 42-pounder Army rifle
3: 8" bore 64-pounder, 63 cwt Navy smoothbore
6: 32-pounder, 42 cwt Navy smoothbore

189

1:   30-pounder Parrott
Bow ports: 3
Side ports: 4 each side
Stern ports: 2

ARMOR

Thickness of plate armor: 2½ "
Designed weight of plate armor: 75 tons
Weight of plate armor added by changes: 47 tons
Total weight of plate armor: 122 tons
Plate armor material: Charcoal iron
Armor plate sizes: 13" wide by 8½ ft. to 11 ft. long
Wood backing for armor on three front panels of pilot house: 19½ "
Wood backing for armor on five side and back panels of pilot house: 12"
Casemate side inclination: 35°
Casemate end inclination: 45°
Thickness of casemate timbers & sheathing: 26"
Location of plate armor: Casemate front and casemate sides abreast
    machinery
Rail Armor: Railroad iron over heavy timber engine and boiler casings

MACHINERY

Type: Reciprocating steam—non condensing
Number of engines: Two
Cylinder size: 22" diameter x 72" stroke
Cylinder inclination: 15°
Piston rods: 4" diameter x 110" long
Paddle Wheel Diameter: 22'-0"
Paddle Wheel Deck Opening: 60'-0" x 18'-0"
Type: Return flue
Number of boilers: 5
Boiler size: 36" diameter x 24'-0" long
Chimneys: 3-8" dia. twin abreast—28'-0" high
Fuel: Coal
Boiler pressure: 140 lbs./ sq. in.
Fuel consumption per hour: 18 to 20 bushels, 1980 pounds, 0.885 tons

AUXILIARY MACHINERY

Steam driven capstan
Steam driven pumps
Hand pumps

PAINT COLORS

Exterior: Black
Interior: White washed
Chimneys: Colored bands for identification

COMPLEMENT

Officers: 17
Petty Officers: 27
Seamen: 111
Landsmen: 3

Apprentices: 1
Firemen: 12
Coal Heavers: 4
Total Enlisted Men: 158
Total Complement: 175

COST DATA

Contract price for each of seven boats: $89,600
Average cost of changes: $12,208
Total average cost: $101,808
Uniforms and clothing for crew: $6,430.00
Small stores: $1,142.00
Ground tackle, hawsers, hammocks, bags, coal, engineer's and carpenter's stores: $7,150.00
Carpenter's wages: $2.00 per 10 hour day
Carpenter's overtime wages: $0.25 per hour
Hulls built by 600 men using wood from 7 saw mills.

NAMES

Designer: Samuel M. Pook, Naval Constructor, U.S.N.
Engine Designer: A. T. Merritt, Cincinnati, Ohio
Hull Builders: Hambleton, Collier and Company, Mound City, Illinois (3 hulls)
 The Carondelet Marine Railway and Drydock Company, Carondelet, Mo. (4 hulls)
Engine and Boiler Builders: Hartupee and Company, Pittsburgh, Pa. (2 sets of machinery)
 Eagle Foundry, St. Louis, Mo. (5 sets of machinery)
 Fulton Foundry, St. Louis, Mo. (5 sets of machinery)
Armor Plate Manufacturer: Gaylord, Son and Company, Portsmouth, Ohio and Newport, Kentucky
Gun Carriage and Ordnance Implement Manufacturers: Eagle Iron Works, Cincinnati, Ohio
Owner: United States Army, later United States Navy (October 1, 1862)
Owner's Representative: Quartermaster General Montgomery C. Meigs, U.S.A.
Commanders: Lieutenant James M. Pritchett, U.S.N.
 Lieutenant Nathaniel Bryant, U.S.N.
 Lieutenant Commander Thomas O. Selfridge, U.S.N.
Names of seven City Class Ironclad River Gunboats: St. Louis (later Baron De Kalb), Carondelet, Cairo, Cincinnati, Mound City, Louisville, Pittsburg

DATES

Completion of Plans and Specifications: July 6, 1861
Request for Proposals: July 18, 1861
Contract Signing: August 7, 1861
Contract Delivery: October 10, 1861
Actual Delivery: January 15, 1862

Commissioning: January 15, 1862
Transfer from Army to Navy: October 1, 1862
Sinking: 11:55 A.M. December 12, 1862
Contract building time for seven boats: 64 days
Actual building time for seven boats: 161 days
Actual keel laying to launching: 48 days

PLACES

Building Sites: Mound City, Illinois for Cairo, Cincinnati, Mound City
Carondelet, Missouri for St. Louis (later Baron De Kalb), Louisville,
Pittsburg, Carondelet
Cairo's *Namesake:*   Cairo, Illinois
Site of sinking of Cairo: Sixteen miles from mouth of Yazoo River
in six fathoms.

Notes

Chapter 1

1 *Official Records of the Union and Confederate Navies in the War of the Rebellion* (31 vols.; Washington, 1895-1929), Ser. I, Vol. XXIV, 203, hereinafter cited as *O.R.N.* Unless otherwise indicated, all citations are to Series I.
2 *O.R.N.*, XXV, 141, 499.
3 Secretary of Navy to Secretary of Treasury, November 12, 1879 (National Archives—Diplomatic, Legal and Fiscal Branch).
4 Surveyor of Customs to Secretary of Treasury, December 16, 1879 (National Archives—Diplomatic, Legal and Fiscal Branch).
5 Copy of contract between Nash Wrecking Company and the Treasury Department (National Archives—Diplomatic, Legal and Fiscal Branch).
6 Cairo (Ill.) *Bulletin*, April 2, 1880.
7 Vicksburg *Evening Post*, November 26, 1933; Memphis *Commercial Appeal*, November 30, 1952.
8 Joseph Burney, Assistant Engineer, to Mississippi River Commission, June 29, 1874 (files, Mississippi River Commission).

Chapter 2

1 Benjamin J. Lossing, *Pictorial History of the Civil War in the United States of America* (Philadelphia, 1866-68), I, 338.
2 James B. Eads, "Recollections of Foote and the Gun-Boats," in *Battles and Leaders of the Civil War,* ed. Robert V. Johnson and Clarence C. Buel (New York, 1884-87), I, 338.
3 *Ibid.*, 338-39; Florence Dorsey, *Road to the Sea: The Story of James B. Eads and the Mississippi River* (New York, 1947), 53-54; Louis How, *James B. Eads* (Boston, 1900), 26-27; See also *The War of the Rebellion: A Compilation of the Official Records of the Union and Confederate Armies* (73 vols. 128 parts; Washington, 1880-1901), Ser. I, Vol. LIII, 491, hereinafter cited as *O.R.* Unless otherwise indicated, all citations are to Series I.
4 *O.R.*, LIII, 491. Cairo at this time, Eads wrote, had "a broad levee front on the Ohio River, raised about fourteen feet above the natural level of the city and extending for a distance of about three miles immediately along the river."

Along the Mississippi there was a levee of similar height and length, but "removed from the bank of the river from 100 yards to half a mile distant, to be out of danger from the caving in of the bank." North of Cairo, the levees were connected by a third. Besides protecting the town from flood waters these levees would afford admirable defenses upon which to emplace batteries.

The Illinois Central Railroad, in addition to the Ohio and Mississippi rivers, would provide means of throwing large numbers of troops, munitions of war, and provisions into Cairo.

5   *Ibid.*, 491-92.
6   *Ibid.*, 490-91.
7   *O.R.N.*, XXII, 279.
8   *Ibid.*, 280.
9   *Ibid.*, 284-85; How, *James B. Eads*, 27. The three side-wheel river steamers purchased by Rodgers were the timberclads *Lexington, Tyler,* and *Conestoga.*
10   *O.R.N.*, XXII, 286.
11   *O.R.*, LII, Pt. 1, p. 164.
12   John Lenthall to Joseph G. Totten, June 1, 1861 (National Archives—Records of the Office of Quartermaster General, Record Group No. 92, hereinafter cited as QMG Records).
13   *O.R.*, LII, Pt. 1, p. 165.
14   *O.R.N.*, XXII, 285-86.
15   John Rodgers to Montgomery C. Meigs, July 6, 1861; plans drawn by Samuel M. Pook, July 2, 1861 (QMG Records).
16   Meigs to Gideon Welles, July 19, 1861 (QMG Records).
17   B. F. Isherwood to Welles, July 20, 1861 (QMG Records).
18   F. Blair, Rollins & Noell to Meigs, July 15, 1861 (QMG Records).
19   M. Blair to Meigs, July 31, 1861 (QMG Records).
20   James B. Eads to Meigs, August 1, 1861 (QMG Records).
21   *O.R.*, Ser. III, Vol. II, 816-17.
22   *Ibid.*, 818-20.
23   *Ibid.*, 820-32.
24   St. Louis *Daily Democrat,* August 14, 1861.
25   A. F. Temple to H. L. Lane, August 14, 1861 (QMG Records).
26   A. Thomas Merritt to Meigs, July 22, 1861 (QMG Records).
27   Rodgers to John Litherbury, August 8, 1861 (QMG Records).
28   Rodgers to Meigs, August 29, 1861 (QMG Records).
29   *O.R.N.*, XXII, 308.
30   *Ibid.*, 306.
31   *Ibid.*, 336.
32   *Ibid.*, 344.
33   St. Louis *Daily Democrat,* August 20, 1861.
34   Rodgers to John C. Frémont, August 28, 1861 (QMG Records).
35   St. Louis *Daily Democrat,* August 22, 1861. The advertisement inserted by Eads read:

SHIP CARPENTERS WANTED

Good Ship Carpenters can find employment by applying to the undersigned at his office in the Exchange Bldg. on South Main, between Market & Walnut Street.

36   Mound City (Ill.) *Gazette,* August 22, 1861; Evelyn Snyder to Edwin C. Bearss, October 5, 1964.
37   Eads to Meigs, August 30, 1861 (QMG Records).
38   Eads to Meigs, September 14, 1861 (QMG Records).
39   Hartupee and Company to Meigs, September 18, 1861 (QMG Records).

40 Eads to Meigs, September 18, 1861 (QMG Records).
41 Eads to Meigs, October 2, 1861 (QMG Records).
42 St. Louis *Daily Democrat,* September 18, 1861. (QMG Records).
43 Eads to Meigs, January 27, 1862 (QMG Records).
44 George Engelmann diary (Missouri Historical Society), May 16, 1860-February 22, 1864.
45 St. Louis *Daily Democrat,* September 21, 1861.
46 Merritt to Meigs, October 6, 1861 (QMG Records).
47 Merritt to Meigs, October 8, 1861 (QMG Records).
48 St. Louis *Daily Democrat,* October 14, 1861.
49 *Ibid.*

Chapter 3

1   *O.R.N.,* XXII, 388-89, 391, 393-94.
2   Andrew H. Foote to Montgomery C. Meigs, October 26, 1861 (QMG Records).
3   James B. Eads to Meigs, January 27, 1862 (QMG Records).
4   *O.R.N.,* XXII, 432.
5   *Ibid.*
6   *Ibid.*
7   *Ibid.,* 428.
8   *Ibid.,* 432-33.
9   *Ibid.,* 433.
10 Henry H. Walke, *Naval Scenes and Reminiscences of the Civil War in the United States on the Southern and Western Waters, During the Years 1861, 1862 and 1863* (New York, 1877), 31.
11 *O.R.N.,* XXII, 442.
12 *Ibid.,* 435.
13 *Ibid.,* 439.
14 *Ibid.,* 444, 448-49; St. Louis *Daily Democrat,* December 2, 1861; Dorsey, *Road to the Sea,* 63.
15 St. Louis *Daily Democrat,* December 2, 1861.
16 *O.R.N.,* XXII, 446.
17 *Ibid.,* 449-50.
18 *Ibid.,* 453. General McClellan, following the Union defeat at First Manassas, had been placed in command of the Army of the United States.
19 *Ibid.*
20 *Ibid.,* 464.
21 *Ibid.,* 474-75.
22 *Ibid.,* 475.
23 *Ibid.,* 475-76.
24 *Ibid.,* 478.
25 John Litherbury and Foote to Eads, December 21, 1861 (National Archives, Records of the Office of QMG, Record Group No. 92).

COPY

United States to James B. Eads.
Dec. 21. For building and delivering to Cairo, Ill. Seven Gunboats according to contract made by Brig. Gen. M. C. Meigs U. S. A. Quartermaster General.
August 7th, 1861 at $ 89,600 Each
$627,000.00
Credit
Sept. 21, By cash on estimate of

Aug. 27, 1861 $ 43,736.55
Oct. 12, By cash on 2d & 3d Estimates
dated 14th & 30th Sept. $111,150.00
Nov. 3, By cash on 4th estimate
recd. of Assist. Q. M. Wise   223,751.00
By cash on 5th estimate
recd. of Assist. Q. M. Wise   99,637.45
                                            $478,275.00
Amount still owed Eads.
St. Louis Dec. 21, 1861 $148,925.00

26 Dorsey, *Road to the Sea,* 65.
27 Eads to Meigs, December 28, 1861 (QMG Records).
28 *O.R.N.,* XXII, 471.
29 *Ibid.,* 489.
30 *Ibid.,* 491.
31 *Ibid.,* 492-93. The steam drums furnished "a chamber in which the foam and watery particles carried out of the boilers by the current of steam on its way to the engines, may settle and flow back to the boilers instead of passing into the engines, where an accumulation of water might cause the breaking of the cylinder by the sudden checking of the piston, if brought in contact with any considerable quantity of it."

According to Pook's plan the depth of the vessels' holds was sufficient to receive only the boilers. Before they were installed, Merritt had had the steam drums raised half their diameter. This brought them partly above decks. At Eads's suggestion, a porthole on each side of the boats opposite the ends of the steam drum was closed up and plated with iron. Merritt's purpose in raising the drums was to insure the engines against receiving water with the steam. The elevation was not believed to be sufficient by a board of officers appointed by Flag Officer Foote.

At Cairo, the steam drums accordingly were placed on top of the boilers at an expense of $1,200 per boat. St. Louis *Daily Democrat,* June 26 & 28, 1862.

32 *O.R.N.,* XXII, 494.
33 *Ibid.,* 498.
34 *Ibid.,* 502-503; St. Louis *Daily Democrat,* January 17, 1862.
35 *O.R.N.,* XXII, 500.
36 *Ibid.,* 504.
37 *Ibid.*
38 *Ibid.,* 501.
39 *Ibid.,* 507-508.
40 *Ibid.,* 510.
41 "Nathaniel C. Bryant," *National Cyclopaedia of American Biography,* Vol. III (New York, 1893), 167.
42 George R. Yost Diary (Naval History Branch, Department of the Navy), January 25-February 7, 1862; Yost to R. N. Scott (Naval History Branch, Department of the Navy). Yost kept a "journal" during his sixteen months' service, which according to him, was the only one saved when the *Cairo* went to the bottom. In November, 1889, Yost sought to sell his "story" to the War Department, but his offer was rejected. Undaunted, he copied the more important entries, had them certified, and on February 12, 1896, mailed them to the Navy Department. These sections were edited by Yost. He condensed certain periods when there was slight activity. For example, he wrote, "I visited the State House and saw *then* acting governor Andrew Johnson. . . . These two patriotic men seemed to attract the most attention *at that time* of any person in Nashville. . . . occurred *during our stay* in Nashville. . . ." (underlining supplied, in each instance). During periods of action, Yost seemed to have

copied his diary word for word. A check of the *Cairo's* muster roll and Yost's service record confirms that he was aboard the ironclad from January 1862 until she was sent to the bottom. Executive Officer Hiram K. Hazlett of the *Cairo* signed documents attesting to the accuracy of the Yost journal.

The extracts from Yost's journal were filed by the Navy Department, where they remained until May, 1964, when they were discovered by the author. Letters were then addressed by the author to the Yost heirs, in hopes that one of them might have the original "journal." The heirs, however, failed to respond.

43 *O.R.N.,* XXII, 529.
44 *Ibid.*
45 *Ibid.,* 533.
46 Yost diary, February 7-16, 1862.
47 St. Louis *Daily Democrat,* February 15, 1862. On the 14th, Confederate heavy ordnance mounted in the Fort Donelson water batteries had bested the guns of the *St. Louis, Louisville, Pittsburg,* and *Carondelet.* The four city-class ironclads had been compelled to retire, seriously damaged.
48 Eads to Meigs, January 27, 1862 (QMG Records).
49 Dorsey, *Road to the Sea,* 65.
50 Eads to Meigs, February 5, 1862 (QMG Records).
51 O. M. Dorman to Meigs, February 12, 1862 (QMG Records).
52 Meigs to Comptroller, February 15, 1862 (QMG Records).
53 J. M. Cutts to Meigs, February 20, 1862 (QMG Records).
54 *O.R.N.,* XXII, 617-19.
55 Yost diary, February 19, 1862; St. Louis *Daily Democrat,* February 27, 1862.
56 St. Louis *Daily Democrat,* February 27, 1862.
57 *O.R.N.,* XXII, 617. In the Clarksville area the Union sailors captured eight Confederate cannons—three in Fort Defiance, three in Fort Clark, and two in an emplacement a short distance up Red River.
58 *Ibid.,* 619.
59 *Ibid.,* 618.
60 *Ibid.,* 622-23.
61 *Ibid.,* 621.
62 *Ibid.,* 624.
63 *Ibid.,* 626-27.
64 *O.R.,* Ser. I, Vol. VII, 638.
65 *Ibid.,* 424, 649.
66 Yost diary, February 20-23, 1862.
67 *O.R.,* VII, 662; St. Louis *Daily Democrat,* February 26, 1862.
68 E. Hannaford, *Story of a Regiment, A History of the Campaigns and Associations in the Field, of the Sixth Regiment Ohio Volunteer Infantry* (Cincinnati, 1868), 195-201.
69 William Grose, *The Story of the Marches, Battles and Incidents of the 36th Regiment Indiana Volunteer Infantry* (New Castle, Ind., 1891), 95-96; Hannaford, *Story of a Regiment,* 201-202.
70 Hannaford, *Story of a Regiment,* 201-202.
71 *O.R.,* VII, 659; *O.R.N.,* XXII. 676; Hannaford, *Story of a Regiment,* 202.
72 *O.R.N.,* XXII, 640-41; Hannaford, *Story of a Regiment,* 203-204.
73 Yost Diary, February 25, 1862.
74 *O.R.,* VII, 425, 659.
75 *O.R.,* X, Pt. 2, p. 41.
76 *Ibid.,* 44.
77 *Ibid.,* 46.
78 *Ibid.,* 49. General Smith's division had been pulled out of Clarksville during the first week of March.
79 *Ibid.,* 51.

198   NOTES

80   *Ibid.*, 48.
81   *Ibid.*, 49; *O.R.N.*, XXII, 677; Yost Diary, March 25, 1862.
82   *O.R.*, VIII, 122. On March 25 the *Tyler* had engaged and silenced the East-
     port battery. Five days later, the *Lexington* and *Tyler* had made a run up the
     Tennessee River to within two miles of Eastport. When the gunboats failed
     to draw any fire, a landing party was put ashore and found the battery deserted
     and the gun removed. Resuming their run up the river, the *Tyler* fired several
     projectiles in the direction of a second battery below Eastport, but no response
     was elicited. As the timberclads dropped down toward Pittsburg Landing, they
     were fired on by sharpshooters. Rounding to, the *Tyler* shelled the woods and
     landing from whence the shots had come.
83   *Ibid.*; *O.R.N.*, XXII, 785; *O.R.*, X, Pt. 2, pp. 83-84; Yost diary, April 1, 1862.
     Lieutenant Shirk had been assigned to command the *Lexington* on January 1,
     1862. *O.R.N.*, XXII, 481.
84   *O.R.N.*, XXII, 674, 699-700. Foote had commenced operations against Island
     No. 10 on March 12.
85   *O.R.*, VIII, 122; Yost diary, April 3-5, 1862.

Chapter 4

1   Yost diary, April 5-12, 1862; Edwin A. Olmstead to Mrs. Edwin C. Bearss,
    July 12 and 25, 1964. Mr. Olmstead, of Mount Holly Springs, Pennsylvania,
    is an engineer and Civil War buff. By making use of measurements of the
    Cairo's pilothouse obtained by Mrs. Bearss, Olmstead was able to prepare
    accurate drawings which proved that, following the setback at Fort Donelson,
    the Federals made a number of modifications in the pilothouses of the city-
    class ironclads.
2   Yost diary, April 11, 1862; *O.R.N.*, Vol. XXIII, 3.
3   *O.R.N.*, XXIII, 3-4.
4   The Confederate gunboats said to mount six to seven guns each were the
    General Polk, Pontchartrain, Livingston, McRae, Ivy, and Maurepas.
5   *O.R.N.*, XXIII, 3-4. The guns at Fort Pillow were reported as five or six 10-
    inch columbiads, a number of 8-inch columbiads, and the remainder 32-
    pounders.
6   Yost diary, April 12, 1862; *O.R.N.*, XXIII, 3-4.
7   Yost diary, April 12, 1862; *O.R.N.*, XXIII, 4, 675.
8   *O.R.N.*, XXIII, 4, 667; *O.R.*, X, Pt. 2, p. 106; Ben LaBree (ed.), *The Con-
    federate Soldier in the Civil War, 1861-1865* (Louisville, 1895), 400-401. The
    transports with General Pope's troops had left New Madrid at midnight. In
    the engagement, the Confederates fired four rounds; one shell burst over the
    Benton's bow but resulted in no casualties or damage.
         Flag Officer G. N. Hollins commanded a squadron of gunboats charged
    with the defense of the Mississippi River. Following the loss of Island No. 10,
    Hollins had hastened to New Orleans to confer with the officer commanding
    the units of the Confederate navy based on the Lower Mississippi, threatened
    by an oceangoing Union squadron. The Federal warships had entered the
    Mississippi and were preparing to attack the forts guarding the approaches to
    the Crescent City. Before leaving for New Orleans, Hollins had placed Captain
    Huger in charge of the naval units based on Fort Pillow. *O.R.N.*, XXII, 840-42.
9   *O.R.N.*, XXIII, 4, 667; LaBree (ed.), *The Confederate Soldier in the Civil
    War*, 401.
10 Yost diary, April 13, 1862.
11 *O.R.N.*, XXIII, 4-5, 667; *O.R.*, X, Pt. 2, 106-107.

NOTES   199

12 Yost diary, April 14, 1862.
13 *O.R.*, X, Pt. 2, pp. 107-108.
14 *O.R.N.*, XXIII, 5-6.
15 *Ibid.*, 7-8; St. Louis *Daily Democrat*, April 18, 1862.
16 *O.R.N.*, XXIII, 7. On the 16th the transports with Pope's soldiers had crossed the Mississippi River and tied up at Osceola, Arkansas.
17 Yost diary, April 15, 1862.
18 *O.R.N.*, XXIII, 10-11.
19 Yost diary, April 27, 1862.
20 *O.R.N.*, XXIII, 63.
21 *Ibid.*, 62.
22 *Ibid.*, 63.
23 *Ibid.*, 69.
24 *Ibid.*, 70.
25 *Ibid.*, 84.
26 Walke, *Scenes and Reminiscences*, 250; Yost diary, May 8, 1862; *O.R.N.*, XXIII, 669; LaBree (ed.), *The Confederate Soldier in the Civil War*, 401.
27 Yost diary, May 8, 1862; *O.R.N.*, XXIII, 677.
28 *O.R.N.*, XXIII, 669; Junius H. Browne, *Four Years in Secessia* (Hartford, 1865), 164-68.
29 Walke, *Scenes and Reminiscences*, 248.
30 Yost diary, May 9, 1862; Walke, *Scenes and Reminiscences*, 250; *O.R.N.*, XXIII, 677.
31 Jay Monaghan, *Swamp Fox of the Confederacy: The Life and Military Service of M. Jeff Thompson* (Tuscaloosa, 1956), 52; *O.R.N.*, XXIII, 54-56.
32 Walke, *Scenes and Reminiscences*, 249.
33 *Ibid.*
34 *Ibid.*, 249, 250-51; Yost diary, May 10, 1862.
35 Walke, *Scenes and Reminiscences*, 251; *O.R.N.*, XXIII, 15.
36 Henry H. Walke, "The Western Flotilla," *Battles and Leaders of the Civil War*, I, 447; Walke, *Scenes and Reminiscences*, 251.
37 *O.R.N.*, XXIII, 54-56; Eliot Callender, "What a Boy Saw on the Mississippi River," *Military Order of the Loyal Legion of the United States-Illinois*, Vol. I, 60-61 (hereinafter cited as *MOLLUS* [followed by name of state]).
38 *O.R.N.*, XXIII, 15, 677. Up to the time the Confederates were spotted, the mortar scow had fired five shells into Fort Pillow.
39 *Ibid.*, 18, 677; Walke, *Scenes and Reminiscences*, 251-53; Yost diary, May 10, 1862.
40 Walke, "The Western Flotilla," 447; Walke, *Scenes and Reminisences*, 253.
41 Callender, "What a Boy Saw on the Mississippi," *MOLLUS-Illinois*, 61.
42 *O.R.N.*, XXIII, 15, 56; Callender, "What a Boy Saw on the Mississippi," *MOLLUS-Illinois*, I, 61; Walke, *Scenes and Reminiscences*, 253; La Bree (ed.), *The Confederate Soldier in the Civil War*, 401. One of the projectiles fired by the *Cincinnati* struck the *Sterling Price* "between wind and water, cutting off the supply pipes and causing her to leak."
43 St. Louis *Daily Democrat*, May 17, 1862.
44 Callender, "What a Boy Saw on the Mississippi," *MOLLUS-Illinois*, I, 61-62.
45 *O.R.N.*, XXIII, 17.
46 Yost diary, May 10, 1862.
47 *O.R.N.*, XXIII, 19; Walke, *Scenes and Reminiscences*, 255; Walke, "The Western Flotilla," 448.
48 *O.R.N.*, XIII, 56.
49 *Ibid.*, 15, 19, 669; Walke, "The Western Flotilla," 448; St. Louis *Daily Democrat*, May 17, 1862.

200   NOTES

50 *O.R.N.,* XXIII, 19, 20; Walke, *Scenes and Reminiscences,* 256.
51 Walke, *Scenes and Reminiscences,* 256; Callender, "What a Boy Saw on the Mississippi," *MOLLUS-Illinois,* I, 62-63; *O.R.N.,* XXIII, 19.
52 H. Allen Gosnell, *Guns on the Western Waters: The Story of the River Gunboats in the Civil War* (Baton Rouge, 1949), 89-90.
53 *O.R.N.,* XXIII, 19, 55, 56.
54 Gosnell, *Guns on the Western Waters,* 90-91.

Chapter 5

1   *O.R.N.,* XXIII, 24, 26, 108; Walke, *Scenes and Reminiscences,* 270.
2   *O.R.N.,* XXIII, 13, 21, 24, 88.
3   *Ibid.,* 24. This with other letters written by Phelps at this time leads one to suspect that the lieutenant on May 10 had mistaken the *St. Louis* for the *Cairo.* According to Yost's diary, the *Cairo* and not the *St. Louis* had followed the *Mound City* downriver.
4   *Ibid.,* 27, 97.
5   Walke, *Scenes and Reminiscences,* 270-71.
6   *O.R.N.,* XXIII, 669; Yost diary, May 13, 1862. Davis wasn't named flag officer until June 17. *O.R.N.,* XXIII, 213.
7   *O.R.N.,* XXIII, 670, 678; Yost diary, May 21, 1862; New York *Tribune* May 30, 1862.
8   *O.R.N.,* XXIII, 35, 53, 678.
9   *Ibid.,* 17.
10 Theodore H. Parker, *The Federal Gunboat Flotilla on the Western Rivers During its Administration by the War Department to October 1, 1862* (Pittsburgh, 1939), 113-14; *O.R.N.,* XXIII, 29-30.
11 *O.R.N.,* XXIII, 32-36.
12 *Ibid.,* 37-41; Norman E. Clarke, Sr. (ed.), *Warfare Along the Mississippi: The Letters of Lieutenant Colonel George E. Currie* (Mount Pleasant, Mich., 1961), 43.
13 *O.R.N.,* XXIII, 42.
14 Yost diary, June 3, 1862.
15 *O.R.N.,* XXIII, 41; La Bree (ed.), *The Confederate Soldier in the Civil War,* 401.
16 *O.R.N.,* XXIII, 43-44.
17 Yost diary, June 3, 1862.
18 *O.R.,* X, Pt. 1, p. 899; *O.R.N.,* XXIII, 47, 53; *History of the Forty-Sixth Regiment Indiana Volunteer Infantry, September, 1861-September, 1865.* Compiled by Committee (Logansport, Ind., 1888), 28.
19 *O.R.,* X, Pt. 1, p. 899.
20 *Ibid.,* 902-903.
21 *O.R.,* X, Pt. II, 574.
22 *O.R.,* Series I, Vol. LII, Pt. I, 39; La Bree (ed.), *The Confederate Soldier in the Civil War,* 401.
23 Yost diary, June 4, 1862; New York *Tribune,* June 11, 1862.
24 *O.R.,* X, Pt. 1, pp. 899-900.
25 New York *Tribune,* June 10, 1862.
26 *O.R.,* X, Pt. 1, p. 900; Walke, *Scenes and Reminiscences,* 271-72; *O.R.N.,* XXIII, 48-49, 671.
27 *O.R.,* X, Pt. 1, p. 901.
28 *O.R.N.,* XXIII, 50, 51; Walke, *Scenes and Reminiscences,* 272.
29 *O.R.N.,* XXIII, 119, 670, 679, 684.
30 Yost diary, June 5, 1862.

31 St. Louis *Daily Democrat,* June 10, 1862.
32 New York *Tribune,* June 11, 1862.
33 Walke, *Scenes and Reminiscences,* 275; *O.R.N.,* XXIII, 133, 671, 674.
34 St. Louis *Daily Democrat,* June 10, 1862.
35 *O.R.N.,* XXIII, 119, 122, 671, 679, 684; Walke, *Scenes and Reminiscences,* 276; St. Louis *Daily Democrat,* June 18, 1862; La Bree (ed.), *The Confederate Soldier in the Civil War,* 401, 403.
36 *O.R.N.,* XXIII, 139; St. Louis *Daily Democrat,* June 18, 1862.
37 *O.R.N.,* XXIII, 139-40; *O.R.,* LII, Pt. 1, p. 39.
38 *O.R.N.,* XXIII, 119, 122, 671, 679, 684; Walke, *Scenes and Reminiscences,* 276; St. Louis *Daily Democrat,* June 18, 1862.
39 Yost diary, June 6, 1862, New York *Tribune,* June 11, 1862.
40 Yost diary, June 6, 1862, New York *Tribune,* June 11, 1862; St. Louis *Daily Democrat,* June 10, 1862; *O.R.N.,* XXIII, 119, 122, 671, 679, 684; Walke, *Scenes and Reminiscences,* 276.
41 *O.R.N.,* XXIII, 129, 133; Alfred W. Ellet, "Ellet and His Steam-Rams at Memphis," *Battles and Leaders of the Civil War,* I, 456; Clarke (ed.), *Warfare Along the Mississippi,* 47-48.
42 *O.R.N.,* XXIII, 125, 128, 129. First Sergeant E. W. Sutherland of the *Lancaster* reported that before the *Lancaster* ran aground, her captain was leaning over the guards, and although admonished of the danger by the boat's carpenter, failed to respond to the emergency until his vessel was within thirty feet of the shore.
43 Memphis *Argus,* June 6, 1862; St. Louis *Daily Democrat,* June 18, 1862.
44 *Ibid.*
45 Walke, *Scenes and Reminiscences,* 286.
46 *Ibid.,* 286-87; *O.R.N.,* XXIII, 125, 134; *O.R.,* LII, Pt. 1, pp. 39-40; New York *Herald,* June 11, 1862; Memphis *Argus,* June 6, 1862. Flag Officer Montgomery reported that just as Captain J. C. Delancy of the *General Lovell* was directing his boat at the *Queen,* one of her engines failed and she became unmanageable.
47 Walke, *Scenes and Reminiscences,* 279; Memphis *Argus,* June 6, 1862; *O.R.N.,* XXIII, 120, 125, 134, 135, 684.
48 *O.R.N.,* XXIII, 134.
49 Memphis *Argus,* June 6, 1862; *O.R.N.,* XXIII, 120, 125, 135-36, 679, 684; Walke, *Scenes and Reminiscences,* 287. The crew of the *Beauregard* was rescued by the tug *Intrepid.*
50 *O.R.N.,* XXIII, 120, 684; Walke, *Scenes and Reminiscences,* 280-81; *O.R.,* LII, Pt. 1, p. 40.
51 *O.R.N.,* XXIII, 684.
52 Walke, *Scenes and Reminiscences,* 281, 282. When naval officers inspected the *General Bragg* and *Sumter,* they found that the vessels were much more valuable prizes than was first supposed. Their outward appearance, however, "was very shabby, and they were painted all over with a dull ochre, to make them the same color as the Mississippi water, and therefore hard to distinguish at a distance." St. Louis *Daily Democrat,* June 10, 1862; New York *Tribune,* June 11, 1862.
53 *O.R.N.,* XXIII, 120, 121, 125, 136, 684; Walke, *Scenes and Reminiscences,* 281; Yost diary, June 6, 1862.
54 Walke, *Scenes and Reminiscences,* 290, 292; *O.R.N.,* XXIII, 149, 684-85; St. Louis *Daily Democrat,* June 17, 1862.
55 New York *Tribune,* June 11, 1862.
56 Walke, *Scenes and Reminiscences,* 290; Memphis *Argus,* June 6, 1862.
57 *O.R.N.,* XXIII, 218.

Chapter 6

1   St. Louis *Daily Democrat*, June 14, 1862.
2   *O.R.N.*, XXIII, 152.
3   Yost diary, June 12-September 9, 1862.
4   *Ibid.* Captain Davis on June 13 had sent part of his squadron down the Mississippi and up White River. These vessels on June 17 had attacked the Confederate fort at St. Charles. During the engagement, a projectile from one of the Rebels' rifled 32-pounders penetrated the *Mound City's* "port casemate a little above and forward of the gun port" and exploded her steam drum. Casualties aboard the *Mound City* numbered 105 killed and 37 wounded.
5   Yost diary, June 12-September 9, 1862.
6   *O.R.N.*, XXIII, 213, 219. Davis had been "appointed flag-officer in command of the U. S. naval forces employed on the Mississippi and its tributaries" on June 17.
7   *Ibid.*, 228.
8   *Ibid.*, 145, 246. Lieutenant Egbert Thompson of the *Pittsburg* had learned from several Confederate deserters that a small steamer was anchored up the Hatchie. On the morning of June 9, Thompson had dispatched an armed party in a small boat to capture the boat. The bluejackets encountered no difficulty in carrying out their mission. The prize steamer which was 84 feet long and had a beam of 17½ feet was renamed the *General Pillow.*
9   *Ibid.*, 248. Upon being relieved, the *Little Rebel* would report to Lieutenant McGunnegle at Memphis.
10 *Ibid.*, 270, 287, 307.
11 Yost diary, July 13-14, 1862; *O.R.N.*, XXIII, 255-57.
12 *O. R. N.*, XXIII, 255.
13 *Ibid.*, 257.
14 Thomas O. Selfridge, *Memoirs of Thomas O. Selfridge, Jr., Rear Admiral, U.S.N.* (New York, 1924), 71. The sailors who had taken their chances with Selfridge on the *Alligator* continued to serve under him on the ironclad. All these men came from New York City, and most listed themselves as having no profession prior to their enlistment, which leads one to speculate that they may have been derelicts.
15 *O.R.*, Series II, Vol. IV, 266-68.
16 Cairo (Ill.) *City Gazette*, August 28, 1862.
17 *O.R.*, Series II, Vol. IV, 454.
18 *O.R.N.*, XXIII, 325-26, 331, 338, 339. The ram *Queen of the West* had assisted the *Eastport* in escorting the transports on the run down from Cairo.
19 *Ibid.*, 341-42. The convoy reached Young's Point, 12 river miles above Vicksburg, and the point designated by the Confederate authorities for the delivery of the prisoners on the evening of September 10. *O. R.*, Series II, Vol. IV, 152,
20 *O.R.*, Series II, Vol. IV, 458, 459, 470-71, 484, 491.
21 *O.R.N.*, XXIII, 357-58.
22 Yost diary, September 17-21, 1862.
23 *Ibid.*, September 23, 1862.
24 Cairo (Ill.) *City Gazette*, September 25, 1862.
25 Yost diary, October 4, 1862.
26 *O.R.N.*, XXIII, 278.
27 *Ibid.*, 388-89.
28 Thomas O. Selfridge to Charles H. Davis, October 18, 1862 (National Archives—Naval and Military Service Branch, Record Group No. 45).
29 *O.R.N.*, XXIII, 425.
30 *Ibid.*, 425-26, 432.

31 *Ibid.*, 447. The *Carondelet*, having suffered extensive damage in her engagement with the *Arkansas* on July 15, had been sent to the Cairo Navy Yard for repairs. It had taken almost two and one-half months to again get the powerful ironclad ready for combat.

32 *Ibid.*, 455. When the navy took over the Mississippi Squadron, it became necessary to rename the *St. Louis*, because there was already a vessel by that name on the navy's list. The *St. Louis* was accordingly renamed the *Baron De Kalb*. Commander John A. Winslow had been captain of the *De Kalb* since mid-August.

33 Selfridge to David D. Porter, October 29, 1862 (National Archives—Naval and Military Service Branch, Record Group No. 45).

34 Yost diary, October 28, 1862.

35 *Ibid.*, October 30, 1862.

36 *O.R.N.*, XXIII, 467.

37 Yost diary, October 30-November 3, 1862.

38 *Ibid.*, November 5-6, 1862; *O.R.N.*, XXIII, 486.

39 *O.R.N.*, XXIII, 467.

40 *Ibid.*, 471.

41 Yost diary, November 13, 1862.

42 Selfridge to Porter, November 17, 1862 (National Archives—Naval and Military Service Branch, Record Group No. 45).

43 *O.R.N.*, XXIII, 485-86.

44 Yost diary, November 18, 1862.

45 *O.R.N.*, XXIII, 485-86.

46 *Ibid.*, 484, 485.

Chapter 7

1 *O.R.N.*, XXIII, 478.

2 *Ibid*, 479.

3 *Ibid.*, 487-88.

4 *Ibid.*, 495.

5 *Ibid.*, Porter, on taking charge of the Mississippi Squadron, had moved promptly to bring into play an innovation in boats that was to have considerable importance to the Union campaign to exploit the shallower rivers in carrying the war to the Confederacy. He introduced the "tinclads," which were designed especially for the work they had to do. Hastily acquired at Cincinnati and other points and converted from peaceful use, they were light-draft sternwheelers covered with an inch and a quarter of boiler iron to make them bulletproof. But they had virtually no protection against heavier projectiles. They drew on an average only three and one-half feet of water and mounted a number of big guns.

6 *Ibid.*, 501.

7 *Ibid.*, 497, 504, 507. The *Pittsburg*, which drew seven feet of water, had been compelled to anchor five miles below Memphis, when it was found that the bar at that point was covered with six feet of water. In addition, Lieutenant William R. Hoel reported that when "General Quarters" sounded, there were only enough men to man six of the thirteen guns.

8 *Ibid.*, 688. The wounded officer was Ensign Henry H. Walker of the *Marmora*. When the surgeon examined the wound, he found that Walker had been shot in the right hip, and pronounced the injury painful but not dangerous.

9 *Ibid*, 515-17, 688-89.

10 *Ibid.*, 517; Selfridge, *Memoirs*, 72-76.

11   *Carondelet's* Log, November 30 and December 1, 1862 (National Archives—
      Naval and Military Service Branch); *O.R.,* Series II, Vol. V, 774. The *Lex-
      ington, Pittsburg,* and *Metropolitan* had left Helena on November 27. *O.R.N.,*
      XXIII, 510-11. These prisoners had reached Cairo from various Northern
      prison pens during the third and fourth weeks of November. Informing his
      readers of these movements, the editor of the Cairo paper confidently wrote,
      "These prisoners will all arrive in [Vicksburg and be exchanged] in time to be
      added to Pemberton's army and to receive a thrashing from Grant."
          The prisoners were heard to declare that "President Lincoln's Emancipa-
      tion Proclamation could never be enforced." They claimed that it had "banded
      the whole South determinedly together and that as long as there is a man
      to fight against its enforcement, there will be deadly resistance." These, like
      all other prisoners with whom the editor had visited, declared that the South
      could never be conquered—"that its people . . .[were] Americans, and will
      never suffer themselves to be subjugated." *Cairo Evening Standard,* Novem-
      ber 20 and 27, 1862.
12   *O.R.N.,* XXIII, 522-30. When she left the fleet, the *Signal* took in tow the
      empty coal barges. All the contrabands that had turned themselves over to
      Walke's men were placed aboard the *Signal,* prior to her departure. The
      Negroes were landed at Helena, from where they would be sent to Cairo at
      the first opportunity. *Carondelet's* Log, December 4, 1862 (National Archives
      —Naval and Military Service Branch).
13   *O.R.N.,* XXIII, 533; *O.R.,* Series II, Vol. IV, 720. Thirty miles above Mem-
      phis, the *De Kalb* had surprised a small steamer tied up to the bank. When
      the ironclad had hove into view, a number of people, many of whom were
      armed, took to their heels. A landing party from the ironclad found that the
      steamer was the *Lottie,* with papers signed by the Memphis board of trade
      to purchase cotton. One of the passengers claimed to be a Treasury agent,
      but had no papers to prove it. Because the boat had a small cargo of tea,
      liquor, and cotton cards, Walker placed a prize crew aboard and sent her to
      Memphis. One day had been spent at Memphis, securing 10-inch shot for
      the *De Kalb's* guns. Walker had recently relieved Winslow as the *De Kalb's*
      captain.
14   *Carondelet's* Log. December 4 and 5, 1862 (National Archives—Naval and
      Military Service Branch).
15   *O.R.N.,* XXIII, 502.
16   *Ibid.,* 534, 689. Walke's flotilla had returned to the anchorage off the mouth
      of the Yazoo on December 5.
17   *Ibid.,* 498.
18   *Ibid.,* 496.
19   *Ibid.,* 505.
20   *Ibid.,* 505-506. General Sherman's column marched from Memphis on the
      26th, and rendezvoused with Grant's army near Oxford, Mississippi, Decem-
      ber 5.
21   *Ibid.,* 512.
22   Yost diary, November 25, 27 and 28; Selfridge, *Memoirs,* 72-76.
23   Yost diary, December 2, 1862.
24   *Ibid.,* December 4, 1862; *O.R.N.,* XXIII, 536. The *General Bragg* had been
      sent upriver from Helena.
25   Yost diary, December 8, 1862; Thomas O. Selfridge to David D. Porter, De-
      cember 8, 1862 (National Archives—Naval and Military Records Branch).
26   *Carondelet's* Log, December 8 and 9, 1862; Yost diary, December 9, 1862.
      Smith was to be taken to the naval hospital at Mound City, Illinois.
27   Yost diary, December 10, 1862.
28   *O.R.N.,* XXIII, 540. A white man who lived on the Yazoo boarded the *Caron-*

delet on the eighth, and told Walke that the Rebels were building two or three rams at Yazoo City.

29   *Ibid.,* 546. Twenty-five of the *Cairo's* men, armed to the teeth, boarded the *Signal,* and a like number from the *De Kalb* went aboard the *Marmora,* for the run up the Yazoo. *Carondelet's* Log, December 11, 1862 (National Archives—Naval and Military Service Branch).
30   *O.R.N.,* XXIII, 546.
31   *Ibid.*
32   J. Thomas Scharf, *History of the Confederate States Navy* (New York, 1887), 752-53; *O.R.N.,* XXIII, 548-49; H. D. Brown, "The First Successful Torpedo and What it Did," *Confederate Veteran,* XVIII (1910), 169; Benson Blake diary, in possession of D. C. Blake, December 17, 1862.
33   *O.R.N.,* XXIII, 546-47.
34   *Ibid.,* 547.
35   *Ibid.,* 551; *Carondelet's* Log, December 12, 1862 (National Archives—Naval and Military Service Branch).
36   Yost diary, December 12, 1862.
37   *O.R.N.,* XXIII, 547, 553, 689; Yost diary, December 12, 1862.
38   *O.R.N.,* XXIII, 553, 554; Yost diary, December 12, 1862. The crews of the *Signal* and *Queen of the West* had also opened fire at suspicious-looking objects floating in the water. Ensign Fentress commanded a detail of sharpshooters sent aboard the *Marmora* from the *De Kalb.*
39   *O.R.N.,* XXIII, 547-48, 549, 551, 552, 554, 689. After severing the wire, the Federals took the torpedo in tow and started for the *Marmora.*
40   *Ibid.,* 549. When both the Yazoo and Mississippi rivers are rising, but the Mississippi is rising faster, the water in the lower reaches of the smaller river pools and there is no current. This explains why the debris from the torpedoes exploded on the eleventh was still in the area.
41   *Ibid.,* 550- 51.
42   Yost diary, December 12, 1862.
43   *O.R.N.,* XXIII, 550-52, 554, 689. As soon as Lieutenant Hoel of the *Pittsburg* realized what had occurred, he ordered a small boat lowered. The crew of the cutter took with them a tarpaulin which they hoped to draw under the *Cairo's* bottom to stop the leak.
44   *Ibid.,* 541, 550-52, 554, 689.
45   Yost diary, December 12, 1862.
46   *Ibid., O.R.N.,* XXIII, 555, 689.
47   George W. Brown, "Personal Recollections of the War of the Rebellion," MOLLUS-*New York,* I, 302.
48   Thomas O. Selfridge Papers (Manuscript Division, Library of Congress).
49   *O.R.N.,* XXIII, 544.
50   *Ibid.,* 545.
51   *Ibid.*
52   *Ibid.,* 580.
53   *Carondelet's* Log, December 13, 1862 (National Archives—Naval and Military Service Branch).
54   Yost diary, December 13-17, 1862.
55   *O.R.N.,* XXIII, 544-45, 693.
56   Selfridge, *Memoirs,* 116-18; Selfridge Papers; Richard West, *The Second Admiral: A Life of David Dixon Porter* (New York, 1937), 182-83. Lieutenant Commander K. Randolph Breese commanded the *Black Hawk.*
57   *O.R.N.,* XXIII, 545.
58   St. Louis *Daily Democrat,* December 19, 1862.
59   Cairo (Ill.) *City Gazette,* December 23, 1862.

Chapter 8

1 Besides Jenks the New England group included Walter Hendrick, dive master; John Bower, artist and diver; Dick Suschena, diver and rigger; Butch Hendrick, cook and line tender.

2 Mississippi A & I Board to Stennis, March 29, 1963.

3 Members of the Steering Committee named by Governor Barnett on April 3 were: *Finance:* R. D. Gage, III, Port Gibson; Mayor John Nossor, Natchez; George Godwin, Clarence Lott, J. C. Williams, Fred Beard, Zach Hederman, J. W. Roberts, and Calvin W. Wells, III, all of Jackson; George Chaney, Vicksburg; Ben LeTourneau, LeTourneau; Hainon W. Miller, Greenville. *Legal:* Wesley R. Lominick, Vicksburg; Ed Cates, Jackson. *Engineering:* Fulton S. Mills, Ken Parks, W. D. Sturdivant, M. B. Higman, and James "Skeeter" Hart, all of Jackson; Major General Ellsworth I. Davis and Victor E. Kurtz of Vicksburg. *Equipment:* Robert Crook, Jackson; Don Jacks and Bart C. Tulley of Vicksburg. *Preservation:* Jack Anderson and Albert Banton of Vicksburg; Robert S. Neitzel, Jackson. *Liaison:* Dr. Walter E. Johnston and Mayor John Holland of Vicksburg; Joseph B. Mauldin, Washington; Sidney T. Roebuck, Newton. *Historical Research:* Edwin C. Bearss, Vicksburg; Charlotte Capers, Jackson; Claude Gentry, Baldwyn; Mrs. Florence Sillers Ogden, Rosedale. *Publicity:* Joe L. Howell, Hagen Thompson, Frank Wallace, Gary Moore, Bill Keith, and Joe Schmitt, all of Jackson.
Subsequently, other interested parties were added to the Steering Committee. They were: Claire Davis, Dr. Robert Dye, and W. B. McCarty of Jackson; Ed Reed, J. E. Blackburn, E. W. Haining, and Louis Cashman of Vicksburg; W. D. Lum of Port Gibson; Commander T. F. Bachelor, Washington, D.C.; Robert H. Aldrich of New York City.

4 *Cairo Report* 19, Mississippi A & I Board; Jackson *Clarion-Ledger,* August 11, 1963; *Evaluation of Existing Conditions—U.S.S. Cairo,* William W. Sykes Engineering Service (Jackson, 1963); Joseph Schmitt to Edwin C. Bearss, July 29, 1963, and Joseph Bullock to Bearss, July 28, 1963.

5 Jackson *Clarion-Ledger,* September 7 and 11, 1963; Vicksburg *Evening Post,* September 8, 10, 11, 12, and 16, 1963; *Cairo Reports* 25, 26, Mississippi A & I Board; *The Civil War Roundtable of Mississippi Newsletter,* II (October 1963).

6 Vicksburg *Evening Post,* August 11 and September 12 and 26, 1963; Jackson *Clarion-Ledger,* September 7 and 11, 1963; *Cairo Reports* 25, 26, 27 and 28, Mississippi A & I Board. Among the firms which volunteered equipment at this time were: W. J. Runyon Construction Company and Byrd's Truck Stop, both of Vicksburg.

7 The three other men assigned to Explosive Ordnance Disposal Unit No. 2 detailed to the project were: Gunner's Mates Gerald L. Chubb and Cecil H. Dunn, and Mineman David Grampp. Lieutenant Donald R. Lund of the U. S. Naval Explosive Ordnance Disposal Facility at Indianhead, Maryland, was also assigned to the project for four weeks.

8 Hookah consists of a regulator with hose connection for air which is pumped from above with a compressor and a two-way telephone. When diving in Hookah, the diver wears a wet suit.

9 Vicksburg *Evening Post,* September 30, 1963; Jackson *Clarion-Ledger,* October 1, 1963; *Cairo Report* 31, Mississippi A & I Board.

10 Lawrence Angel to Dr. Paul Darien, Dr. Donald T. Imrie, and Walter Johnston, October 22, 1963.

11 Vicksburg *Evening Post,* October 2, 1963.
12 *Ibid.,* October 8, 1963; Chicago *Tribune,* October 9, 1963.
13 *Cairo Report* 31, Mississippi A & I Board.
14 Lieutenant Lund had returned to his station at the end of four weeks, while Chubb and Dunn at the end of October had been replaced by two new men. Personnel from the Army's 45th Explosive Ordnance Disposal Unit from Fort Polk, when shown the gun and shattered projectile, estimated that the navy men had used a charge seven times in excess of what should have been employed.
15 Governor Ross Barnett to Steering Committee, October 7, 1963. Members of the Executive Committee were: Joe Bullock, chairman, Dr. Walter Johnston, Ken Parks, Joe Schmitt, and Bill Sykes.
16 Vicksburg *Evening Post,* January 13, 1964.
17 *Ibid.,* January 21, 1964.
18 *Ibid.,* January 29, 1964.
19 *Ibid.,* January 31, 1964.
20 *Ibid.,* February 11, 1964.
21 Jackson *Clarion-Ledger,* February 14, 1964, Vicksburg *Evening Post,* February 14, 1964.
22 Vicksburg *Evening Post,* February 19, 1964.
23 *Ibid.,* March 1, 1964.
24 *Cairo Report* 38, Mississippi A & I Board.
25 Vicksburg *Evening Post,* March 6, 1964.
26 *Ibid.,* March 7, 1964.

Chapter 9

1 Vicksburg *Evening Post,* June 3, 1964; Heber Ladner to Bearss, September 21, 1964. (Heber Ladner is the Mississippi Secretary of State.)
2 Cooper to members of Cairo Committee, June 25, 1964.
3 Members of the Board of Supervisors were: Paul Pride, chairman, Alvin H. Hall, John L. McCaskill, P. T. Hullum, and Robert P. Dowe.
4 Vicksburg *Evening Post,* July 31, 1964.
5 *Ibid.*
6 *Ibid.,* August 17, 18 and 19, 1964.
7 *Ibid.,* August 23, 1964.
8 *Ibid.,* August 31, 1964.
9 *Ibid.,* September 6, 1964.
10 *Ibid.,* September 8, 1964.
11 *Ibid.,* September 10, 1964.
12 *Ibid.,* September 13-22, 1964.
13 *Ibid.,* September 13, 23, 1964.
14 *Ibid.,* September 23, 24, 1964.
15 *Ibid.,* September 26, 1964.
16 *Ibid.,* October 1, 2, 1964.
17 *Ibid.,* October 6-7, 1964.
18 *Ibid.,* October 8, 1964.
19 Jackson *Clarion-Ledger,* October 19, 1964; Memphis *Commercial Appeal,* October 19, 1964.
20 Vicksburg *Evening Post,* November 9-11, 1964.
21 *Ibid.,* November 13-15, 1964.
22 *Ibid.,* November 16, 1964.

208 NOTES

23 Jackson *Clarion-Ledger,* November 18, 1964; Vicksburg *Evening Post,* November 17, 1964. Members of the artifact committee who helped remove objects from the boat were: Ken Parks, Hank Hanisee, Vincent Canizaro, Jim Gorman, Don Jacks, Ron Meyer, Ed Clark, Al Banton, and Ed Bearss.
24 Vicksburg *Evening Post,* November 18, 1864.
25 Jackson *Clarion-Ledger,* November 23, 1964.
26 Vicksburg *Evening Post,* November 24, 1964.
27 *Ibid.,* November 30, 1964.
28 The plate glass was used to replace lights in the skylights which might have been broken.
29 *Ibid.,* December 1 and 2, 1964. Other members of Lieutenant McGauhey's unit were: SP6 Delbert Randles and Sp4 Oliver J. Pollitt.
30 Natchez *Democrat,* December 24, 1964.

Chapter 10

1 Mrs. Carroll W. Haueisen to Edwin C. Bearss, January 31, 1965.
2 William E. Geoghegan to Mrs. Edwin C. Bearss, January 13, 1965.
3 Robert Laffan to Mrs. Edwin C. Bearss, February 16 and 24, 1965. The American Hard Rubber Division of Amerace has a subsidiary: the Goodyear Hard Rubber Co. Basic patents for making hard rubber such as was used in the comb had gone from Nelson Goodyear, to Charles Goodyear, to Meyer & Poppenheusen of Brooklyn, and the Amerace predecessor company was the owner of trade mark, 58,361 with the "IR Goodyear 1851" label.
4 Faber to Mrs. Bearss, February 3, 1965.
5 R. M. Seborg *Memorandum report on: Trip to Vicksburg About Preservation of Wood Parts in U.S.S. Cairo,* U. S. Dept. of Agriculture (Madison, 1964), 3-5.
6 *Ibid.*

Chapter 11

1 Members of the Park Service team were: Charles E. Shedd, chairman, Regional Chief Division of Interpretation, Southeast Region; Harold L. Peterson, Chief Curator; Donald F. Benson, Architect; Edward Zimmer, Landscape Architect; Russell Hendrickson, Chief, Eastern Museum Laboratory.
2 *Union Gunboat Cairo, Recommendations for Preservation and Display, A Report to the Warren County Board of Supervisors* (Richmond, 1965).
3 Vicksburg *Evening Post,* January 21, 1965.
4 *Ibid.,* February 18, 1965. Members of the ports and harbors sub-committee were: Ben Chase Callon of Natchez, chairman; Mayor Danny Guice of Biloxi, Mississippi, Maness Bartlett of Pascagoula, Mississippi, and Senator Ellis Bodron of Warren County, Mississippi.
5 *Ibid.,* February 23, 1965. Colonel Chapelle is curator of the Division of Transportation, Smithsonian Institution, while Geoghegan is museum specialist in the Division of Transportation.
6 *Ibid.,* February 26, 1965.
7 Mississippi A & I Board, *Cairo* Release No. 41, March 18, 1965.
8 *Ibid.,* No. 43, June 11, 1965. Earlier the five giant boilers and the mud header had been removed and trucked to the Vicksburg National Military Park.
9 New Orleans *Times-Picayune,* June 21, 1965.

10   Members of the *Cairo* Committee sent to Vicksburg by Director Hartzog were: Harold L. Peterson, chairman; Charles E. Shedd, Edwin C. Bearss, Donald F. Benson, and Chester Brooks. At Vicksburg the group was joined by Landscape Architect Edward Zimmer.

11   "Report of the *Cairo* Committee," August, 1966 (files, National Park Service).

Chapter 12

1   Williams to Udall, October 10, 1967, in Bearss Collection.

2   Udall to Williams, October 20, 1967, *ibid.*

3   John Bell Williams had been inaugurated as governor of Mississippi in January, 1968, and Charles Griffin had been elected as his replacement.

4   Vicksburg *Evening Post,* July 14, 1968, February 27, 1970.

5   *Ibid.,* August 21, 1969.

6   Brusstar to Margie Bearss, August 26, 1969, Leavitt to Mrs. Bearss, September 5, 1969, in Bearss Collection.

7   Annie Lee Saunders, "Problem of Museum is Urgent: Gunboat Cairo Preserved," Vicksburg *Evening Post,* June 22, 1969.

8   Vicksburg *Evening Post,* March 18, 1970.

9   *Ibid.* On March 25, 1971, Senate Bill 1475 was introduced by Senator John Stennis, for himself and Senator Jim Eastland. House Bill 6618 was introduced by Representative Charles Griffin and cosponsored by J. L. Whitten, Tom Abernathy, G. V. Montgomery, and W. M. Colmer.

10   *Ibid.* June 11, 1971. Senator Cooper had died in 1968. Rogers Morton had succeeded Walter Hickel as secretary of the interior on January 27, 1971.

11   Jackson *Daily News,* June 14, 1971; Jackson *Clarion-Ledger,* June 16, 1971; Vicksburg *Evening Post,* June 11, 1971. Attending the meeting with Secretary Morton and Director Hartzog were: U.S. Senator Stennis, U.S. Representatives W. H. Colmer, J. L. Whitten, Charles Griffin, and G. V. Montgomery; Bill Simpson representing U.S. Senator Jim Eastland and Mrs. Clair Stevens of U.S. Representative Tom Abernathy's office; Governor Williams; State Representatives George Rogers, C. B. Newman, and George Payne Cossar; Jimmy Ward, editor of the Jackson *Daily News;* Jim Carraway, Frank Barber, and Wiley Carter of the A & I Board.

12   Pecora to Jackson, June 25, 1971, in Report to Accompany Senate Bill 1475, December 2, 1971.

13   *Congressional Record,* 92nd Cong., 2nd Sess., 28071–73; "History Will Live," *Mississippi Educational Advance,* LXIII, (April, 1972), 16–17, 27–28.

14   Public Law 92–483, 92nd Cong., 2nd Sess.

15   The A & I Board signed the agreement in late June, 1973, and on May 7, 1974, Secretary of the Interior Morton approved the documents transferring the vessel to the National Park Service.

16   People attending these meetings were: Superintendent Dan Lee and Bowie Lanford, Vicksburg National Military Park; Dave McLain and Art Allen, Harpers Ferry Center; Don Benson, Warren J. Oliver, Richard J. Kusek, James G. Kiryakakis, L. Clifford Soubier, C. Gordon Cummings, and Edwin C. Bearss of the Denver Service Center; William H. Hendrickson of the Southeast Regional Office; and Commander J. Delano Brusstar.

17   Howard to Bearss, May 4, 1978, in Bearss Collection. Barry Howard is president of Barry Howard & Associates.

18   "Smeal's Log Describing the Return of the *Cairo* to Vicksburg National

Military Parks," 3–7, in files, Vicksburg National Military Park. Superintendent Lee assigned these men to the operation: Kerry King, Jerrell Cooper, Marshall Whatley, Richard Wildee, Overton Randolph, and Garvis Hensley; the Gulf Islands superintendent sent Handy Mallard, Eugene Vincent, and Charles McMillian.

19 *Ibid.*, 19–21. Members of the committee were: Edwin C. Bearss, Denver Service Center; Henry Judd, chief historical architect; John Garner, southeast regional architect; and Ira Mitchell of the southeast regional office.

20 *Ibid.*, 60, 62, 75, 78–80, 82, 84, 109–17.

21 *Ibid.*, 57–58.

22 Anderson Construction Company of Jackson was awarded the contract for visitor center and associated facilities.

23 Kiryakakis to Bright, April 4, 1978, in files, Vicksburg Military National Park. Participants in the March 14–15 meeting were: Ralph Maisel, Bob Bassett, and Skip Tuminello, Architect/Engineer contractors; Henry A. Judd, Washington Office, National Park Service; Gordon Whittington, Walter Bruce, and John C. Garner, Jr., southeast regional office; Dave McLean and Ben Miller, Harpers Ferry Center; Nancy Miller, Dan E. Lee, Bowie Lanford, Jr., and Geri Herrmann, Vicksburg National Military Park; and Douglas S. Ashley, George Thorson, Edwin C. Bearss, Richard Kusek, James G. Kiryakakis, and Ken Hanaki, Denver Service Center.

24 Ashley to Bright, April 17, 1978, in files, Vicksburg National Military Park.

25 *Cairo* Restoration Alternative Reports by Ashley and McGrath, presented to regional director Joe Brown and others at Vicksburg, Mississisppi, April 9, 1979; Ashley to Bearss, April 23, 1979, in Bearss Collection; telephone interview, Thorson with Bearss, May 1, 1979; Vicksburg *Evening Post,* April 10, 15, 1979. Participants in the April 9 meeting were: Ralph Maisel and Bob Bassett, Architect/Engineers, contractors; Gordon Whittington, George Thorson, Douglas Ashley, Tom McGrath, and Harold La Fleur, Denver Service Center; Joe Brown, Walter Bruce, Vince Gannon, John Garner, and Boyd Finch, Southeast Regional Office; Dave McLean and Ben Miller, Harpers Ferry Center; Dan Lee, Nancy Miller, and Geri Herrmann, Vicksburg National Military Park.

26 Vicksburg *Evening Post,* April 15, 1979.

Bibliography

Manuscript Material

Mrs. E. C. Bearss. *Cairo* letters and material, Arlington, Virginia.
Benson Blake Diary. In possession of D. C. Blake, Redwood, Mississippi.
Building of Gunboats on Western Waters, Records of the Office of the Quartermaster General, Record Group No. 92, National Archives.
James B. Eads Papers. Missouri Historical Society, St. Louis.
Charles Ellet, Jr., Papers. Transportation Library, University of Michigan.
George Engelmann Diary. Missouri Historical Society, St. Louis.
Andrew H. Foote Papers. Library of Congress.
Letters Received by the Secretary of the Navy from Commanding Officers of Squadrons: Mississippi, 1861-62. National Archives, Record Group No. 45.
Letters Sent by the Secretary of the Navy to Officers ("Officers, Ships of War"). National Archives, Record Group No. 45.
Log of the *Carondelet*. National Archives.
Muster Rolls of the *U.S.S. Cairo*. National Archives.
S. Ledyard Phelps Papers. Missouri Historical Society, St. Louis.
Thomas O. Selfridge Papers. Library of Congress.
Water Transportation File, Office of the Quartermaster General. National Archives, Record Group No. 92.
George R. Yost Diary. Naval History Branch, Department of the Navy.

Personal Reminiscences and Unit Histories

Brown, George W. "Personal Recollections of the War of the Rebellion." *Military Order of the Loyal Legion of the United States–New York*, Vol. I, New York, 1891.
Browne, Junius H. *Four Years in Secessia*. Hartford, 1865.
Callender, Eliot, "What a Boy Saw on the Mississippi River," *Military Order*

211

of the Loyal Legion of the United States–Illinois. Vol. I. Chicago. 1891.
Grose, William. *The Story of the Marches, Battles and Incidents of the 36th Regiment Indiana Volunteer Infantry.* New Castle, 1891.
Hannaford, E. *Story of a Regiment, A History of the Campaigns and Associations in the Field of the Sixth Regiment Ohio Volunteer Infantry.* Cincinnati, 1868.
History of the Forty-Sixth Regiment Indiana Volunteer Infantry, September, 1861–September, 1865. Compiled by Committee. Logansport, 1888.
Johnson, R. U. and C. C. Buel (eds.). *Battles and Leaders of the Civil War.* 4 vols. New York, 1884–1887.
LaBree, Ben, (ed.). *The Confederate Soldier in the Civil War, 1861–1865.* Louisville, 1895.
Michael, W. A. C., "How the Mississippi Was Opened," *Military Order of the Loyal Legion of the United States–Nebraska,* Vol. I, Omaha. 1902.
Miller, Francis T. (ed.). *The Photographic History of the Civil War.* 10 vols. New York, 1911.
Moore, Frank, (ed.). *The Rebellion Record: A Diary of American Events with Documents, Narratives, Illustrative Incidents, Poetry, etc.* 11 vols. New York, 1864–68.
Selfridge, Thomas O. *Memoirs of Thomas O. Selfridge, Jr., Rear Admiral, U.S.N.* New York, 1924.
Walke, Henry H. *Naval Scenes and Reminiscences of the Civil War in the United States on the Southern and Western Waters, During the Years 1861, 1862 and 1863.* New York, 1877.

Other Primary Sources

Cairo Reports. Mississippi A & I Board, 1962–1966.
William W. Sykes Engineering Service. *Evaluation of Existing Conditions–U. S. Cairo.* Jackson, 1963.
Journal of the Congress of the Confederate States of America 1861–1865. 7 vols. Washington, 1904–1905.
Official Records of the Union and Confederate Navies in the War of the Rebellion. 31 vols. Washington, 1895–1929.
Richardson, James D. (ed.). *A Compilation of the Messages and Papers of the Confederacy Including the Diplomatic Correspondence 1861–1865.* 2 vols. Nashville, 1905.
Southern Historical Society Papers, 1876–1959, 52 vols.
The War of the Rebellion: A Compilation of the Official Records of the Union and Confederate Armies. 73 vols. 128 parts. Washington, 1880–1901.

Secondary Sources

Published Material

Abbott, Willis J. *The Blue Jackets of '61.* New York, 1886.

Anderson, Bern. *By Sea and By River*. New York, 1962.
Boatner, Mark M. *The Civil War Dictionary*. New York, 1959.
Davis, Charles H. *Life of Charles H. Davis*. Boston, 1899.
Dorsey, Florence. *Road to the Sea: The Story of James B. Eads and the Mississippi River*. New York, 1947.
Gosnell, H. Allen. *Guns on the Western Waters: The Story of the River Gunboats in the Civil War*. Baton Rouge, 1949.
Hoppin, James M. *Life of Andrew H. Foote*. New York, 1874.
How, Louis. *James B. Eads*. Boston, 1900.
Jones, Virgil Carrington. *The Civil War at Sea*. 3 vols. New York, 1960–62.
Lansden, John M. *A History of the City of Cairo, Illinois*. Chicago, 1910.
MacBride, Robert. *Civil War Ironclads*. Philadelphia, 1962.
Mahan, Alfred T. *The Gulf and Inland Waters*. New York, 1883.
Monaghan, Jay. *Swamp Fox of the Confederacy: The Life and Military Service of M. Jeff Thompson*. Tuscaloosa, 1956.
National Cyclopaedia of American Biography. 37 vols. New York, 1892–1951.
Perry, Milton F. *Infernal Machines: The Story of Confederate Submarine and Mine Warfare*. Baton Rouge, 1965.
Porter, David D. *The Naval History of the Civil War*. New York, 1886.
Pratt, Fletcher. *Civil War on Western Waters*. New York, 1956.
Scharf, J. Thomas. *The History of the Confederate States Navy From Its Organization to the Surrender of Its Last Vessel*. New York, 1887.
West, Richard C. *Mr. Lincoln's Navy*. New York, 1957.
———— *The Second Admiral: A Life of David D. Porter*, New York, 1937.

Newspapers and Periodicals

Cairo (Ill.) *Bulletin*, 1880.
Cairo (Ill.) *City Gazette*, 1861–62.
Chicago *Tribune*, 1963.
Civil War Roundtable of Mississippi, Newsletter, 1962–66.
Confederate Veteran, 40 vols. 1893–1932.
Harper's Weekly, 1861–62.
Jackson *Clarion-Ledger*, 1960–66.
Memphis *Argus*, 1862.
Memphis *Commercial Appeal*, 1952–64.
Mound City (Ill.) *Gazette*, 1861.
Natchez *Democrat*, 1964.
New York *Herald*, 1862.
New York *Tribune*, 1862–63.
St. Louis *Daily Democrat*, 1861–62.
St. Louis *Missouri Republican*, 1861–62.
Vicksburg *Evening Post*, 1960–66.

Index

215

CPSIA information can be obtained
at www.ICGtesting.com
Printed in the USA
LVHW081319140122
708602LV00011B/187

9 780807 106